Harrods
KNIGHTSBRIDGE

A YEAR'S DINNERS

A YEAR'S
DINNERS

365
SEASONABLE
DINNERS
AND HOW TO COOK
THEM

BY

MAY LITTLE

INTRODUCTION BY
MICHELLE BERRIEDALE-JOHNSON

STUDIO EDITIONS
LONDON

LIST OF PLATES

Jacket: Adriaen van Utrecht, *Still Life – A Pantry*, Prado, Madrid. **17**: David Emil Joseph de Noter, *A Maid in the Kitchen*, Christie's, London. **18**: William van der Miers, *A Woman and a Fish Peddler*, The National Gallery, London. **35**: Anton Weiss, *Still Life of Lemons*, Rafael Valls Gallery, London. **36**: Jan Davidsz de Heem, *Still Life of Dessert*, Louvre, Paris. **53**: Isaac van Duynen, *Still Life of Fish on a Table*, Johnny van Haeften Gallery, London. **54**: Joris van Son, *A Still Life of Fruit on a Draped Ledge*, Johnny van Haeften Gallery, London. **71**: Reynier van Gherwen, *Still Life of Oysters and Lobsters*, Rafael Valls Gallery, London. **72**: Osias Beet, *Still Life*, Prado, Madrid. **89**: Theophile Schuler, *Picnic near Strasbourg*, Musée Historique, Strasbourg. **90**: Lucas van Valkenborch, *An Allegory of Summer*, Johnny van Haeften Gallery, London. **107**: Alexander Coosemans, *Still Life with Fruit*, Johnny van Haeften Gallery, London. **108**: Lucas van Valkenborch, *Vegetable Market*, Kunsthistorisches Museum, Vienna. **125**: Pieter Claesz, *Still Life with Roemer, Pie and Peeled Lemon*, Harold Samuel Collection, Corporation of London. **126**: Alexander van Adriaessen, *Still Life*, Prado, Madrid. **143**: Ferdinand Wagner, *The Vegetable Market*, Christie's, London. **144**: Cornelis de Heem, *A Still Life of Fruit*, Johnny van Haeften Gallery, London.

PHOTOGRAPHIC CREDITS

The Bridgeman Art Library, London: Jacket, 17, 35, 36, 53, 54, 71, 72, 90, 106, 107, 125, 126, 143, 144. The National Gallery, London: 18. E T Archive, London, 89. All line drawings come from the collection at the Hulton Picture Company, London, and from Mary Evans Picture Library, London.

A Year's Dinners was first published
by Harrods in 1910.

This edition published 1990. Produced and
designed for Harrods Limited by Studio Editions
Princess House, 50 Eastcastle Street
London W1N 7AP, England

ISBN 1 85170 606 2

Printed and bound in Portugal.

CONTENTS

INTRODUCTION

When May Little's book of 365 dinners first came out in 1910, England was at the height of her Edwardian glory. Still to come were the grim days of the Great War which despatched the butler to the trenches and the cook to the munitions factory, leaving their mistress to battle with the range, the delivery boy and cleaning the house. In 1910 even the poorest middle-class family aspired to having at least one servant who was expected to include cooking among her many duties. The mistress' task, then, lay more often in planning rather than in actually preparing the meal.

But planned it had to be, and along fairly rigid lines. Mrs Little is quite specific on what is to be included in a 'complete dinner' and how this may be truncated for a 'light dinner' or a luncheon. And you will notice that, although she suggests only (only . . .) nine courses for the 'complete dinner', many of these would usually include two or more dishes.

This profusion of food was nothing new. The Victorians saw lavishness as a demonstration of wealth and success, and although a little restraint in the number of dishes might have produced a more enjoyable meal, such considerations were as nothing compared to the length, and, therefore, impressiveness of your menu. But however many the courses, and despite Mrs Little's adjurations to avoid monotony, the choice of dishes was, inevitably, shaped by the times. Today, we have a profusion of cuisines from around the world at our fork tips; in 1910 the first shipment of frozen beef from Australia had only just arrived and, as strawberries from France were still a rich and rare treat, cooks had to rely on locally grown food.

The sheer quantity of food and its heavy emphasis on high protein, rich and fatty ingredients, combined with, for the upper classes at least, a very sedentary lifestyle, played havoc with the average digestion. Allocating a 'digestion period' to each food was one way the Edwardian dyspeptic attempted to deal with the problem – although one wonders how they computed that boiled turkey would take five minutes less to digest than roast turkey . . .

But if digesting the food proved a problem for the diners, preparing it was no less of one for the cook, be she the mistress of the house or merely of the kitchen. Although by 1910

Harrods was producing catalogues with modern gadgets, such as egg whiskers and boilers, coffee grinders and apple corers, most of the hard grind of beating, mixing and mincing still had to be done by hand. It was not that long since a cake instruction had told one to 'beat hard for four hours'. The nearest that the average kitchen came to a refrigerator for setting jellies (for which Mrs Little gives ten specific recipes, ignoring all her chilled soufflés and mousses) was an outside larder. Although electric cookers, toasters, ovens and hot plates had been available since the 1890s, few were the kitchens that could boast more than a dirty coal range. And even devotees of the modern 'Aga' might have had trouble producing a reliably good meal from their belching, smoking predecessors.

Whether or not one follows Mrs Little right through from January to December, it is fun to be able to dip into her seasons and abstract a couple of meals which will convey the flavour of the times. Her recipes are concise and fairly accurate although it is unlikely, according to the practice of the time, that they had all been tested; her instructions as to 'Methods of Cooking' and 'Proper Proportions' for milk puddings, moulds and sauces, and her 'Marketing Hints' are all well worth reading even if some are, we would hope, now somewhat redundant:

"POULTRY. . . . Poultry should always be cooked while fresh, staleness being very objectionable and easily detected by a faint unpleasant odour. When flesh is discoloured or has begun to turn green it should be rejected . . . "

None-the-less, if you are indeed a 'worried and anxious wife or housekeeper', I am sure that you will derive comfort, amusement and, indeed, some instruction from between her pages.

Michelle Berriedale-Johnson

PREFACE

The object of this book is to offer some suggestions to worried and anxious wives and housekeepers, which it is hoped will help them solve the daily problem, 'what shall we have for dinner.'

Dinners have been arranged for every day in the year. Much thought and consideration has been given in arranging them to the methods of cooking, the accommodation of an ordinary kitchen, the powers of the cook, economy of material, and the proper seasons for obtaining the different foods.

Great care has been taken to avoid monotony, which so frequently occurs in the everyday household. Such things as roast beef, roast chicken, etc, must of a necessity be often repeated in the course of a year, but the ways of reheating and producing appetising dishes therefrom are innumerable.

With some of the dinners the cold meat dish or the dish made from the joint of the previous day may be omitted and used for luncheon.

THE NUMBER FOLLOWING EACH DISH CORRESPONDS TO THE NUMBERED RECIPE IN PART III OF THE BOOK. BY REFERRING TO THIS DETAILED DIRECTIONS WILL BE FOUND AS TO THE INGREDIENTS REQUIRED, METHOD OF PREPARATION AND, AS FAR AS POSSIBLE, THE DISHING AND GARNISHING.

PART I

MENUS

JANUARY 1

Tomato Soup, *29*
Fried Sole, *84*
Roast Beef
Horseradish Sauce
Yorkshire Pudding
Potatoes, Cauliflower
Christmas Pudding, *436*
Guard's Sauce, *661*
Mince Pies, *529*
Cheese and Celery

JANUARY 2

Brown Celery Soup, *31*
Boiled Cod, *64*
Oyster Sauce, *614*
Grilled Cutlets and Tomatoes
Cold Roast Beef
Potatoes. Winter Salad, *325*
Apple Pudding, *422*
Cheese Straws, *339*

JANUARY 3

Gravy Soup, *21*
Scalloped Fish, *90*
Fried Sweetbread, *176*
Piquante Sauce, *624*
Mince and Macaroni, *188*
Potatoes. Cauliflower, *291*
Stewed Figs and Cream
Cheese Pudding, *340*

JANUARY 4

Almond Soup, *33*
Boiled Halibut, *66*
Hollandaise Sauce, *618* or *619*
Roast Turkey, *229*
Sausages
Potatoes. Brussels Sprouts, *273*
Conservative Pudding, *600*
Cheese and Celery

NOTE

For the convenience of the reader each dish in these 365 dinners has been numbered. By turning to the indicated number in Part III full cookery instructions for the particular recipe wanted will be found.

JANUARY 5

Brown Vegetable Soup, *18*
Fish Croquettes, *93*
Fricassée of Turkey, *223*
Mashed Potatoes. Cabbage
Mince Meat Roly Poly, *425*
Caramel Custard, *541*
Swiss Eggs, *359*

JANUARY 6

Mock Turtle Soup, *24*
Fried Fillets of Plaice, *80*
Anchovy Sauce, *605*
Boiled Rabbit, *240*
Onion Sauce, *609*
Sauté Potatoes, *267*.
Cauliflower au Gratin, *292*
Apple Amber Pudding, *537*
Spanish Rice, *403*

JANUARY 7

Purée of Brussels Sprouts, *35*
Boiled Mackerel, *65*
Fennel Sauce, *612*
Mutton Cutlets, *159*
Tomato Sauce, *628*
Potatoes. Artichokes, *282*
Cabinet Pudding, *465*
Rice Fritters, *412*

JANUARY 8

Celery Soup, *31*
Eggs à la Norfolk, *404*
Roast Leg of Pork
Apple Sauce, *629*
Potatoes. Brussels Sprouts
Canary Pudding, *475*
Savoury Haddock on Toast, *383*

JANUARY 9

Clear Soup, *4*
Fried Fillets of Plaice, *80*
Anchovy Sauce, *605*
Mock Game, *145*
Shepherd's Pie, *195*
Potatoes. Sauté Tomatoes, *296*
Marmalade Pudding, *428*
Macaroni Cheese, *337*

JANUARY 10

Crécy Soup, *15*
Fried Sole, *84*
Boiled Fowl, *221*
Bacon
Potatoes. Greens
Baked Lemon Pudding, *536*
Sweet Omelet, *491*
Roes on Toast, *408*

JANUARY 11

Potato Soup, *13*
Boiled Turbot, *66*
Shrimp Sauce, *610*
Chicken Croquettes and Peas, *222*
Mashed Potatoes
Sea-kale, *288*
Sago Soufflé, *478*
Trifle, *548*
Cheese and Celery

JANUARY 12

Consommé à la Julienne, *4*
Scalloped Fish, *90*
Roast Pheasant, *233*
Salad. Potato Chips, *266*
Beresford Pudding, *467*
Honey Comb Mould, *463*
Welsh Rarebit, *346*

JANUARY 13

Palestine Soup, *30*
Fried Whiting
Anchovy Sauce
Mutton Cutlets, *159*
Salmi of Pheasant, *234*
Mashed Potatoes. Stewed Celery, *289*
Manchester Pudding, *540*
Cream Cheese

JANUARY 14

Macaroni Soup, *40*
Stuffed and Baked Plaice, *70*
Roast Goose or Duck, *228*
Apple Sauce, *629*
Potatoes. Savoury Cabbage, *308*
Banana Fritters, *489*
Chestnut Cream, *569*
Cheese Croûtons, *418*

JANUARY 15

Chestnut Soup, *36*
Boiled Halibut
Lobster Sauce, *613*
Ragoût of Goose
Potatoes. Haricot Beans, *280*
Cup Puddings, *482*
Apples and Rice, *559*
Cheese Toasts, *418*

JANUARY 16

Oxtail Soup, *27*
Halibut au Gratin
Roast Shoulder of Mutton
Onion Sauce, *609*
Baked Potatoes. Mashed Turnips, *271*
Boiled Apple Pudding, *422*
Sardines à la Suisse, *409*

JANUARY 17

Kidney Soup, *20*
Stuffed and Baked Haddock, *68*
Durham Cutlets, *189*
Tomato Sauce, *628*
Mashed Potatoes. Artichokes, *282*
Fig Pudding, *432* and *433*
Banana Charlotte, *588*
Cheese Fondu, *343*

JANUARY 18

Potato Soup, *13*
Plaice à la Bohemienne, *71*
Jugged Hare, *237*
Potatoes, Brussels Sprouts
Lemon Cheese Cakes, *522*
Milk Pudding, *441*
Cheese Straws, *339*

JANUARY 19

Hare Soup, *25*
Sole à la Colbert, *84*
Boiled Mutton, *150*
Caper Sauce, *606*
Potatoes. Carrots and Turnips
Pineapple Pudding, *535*
Chocolate Mould, *453*
Macaroni à la Milanaise, *348*

JANUARY 20

Scotch Broth, *8*
Boiled Cod and Egg Sauce, *607*
Stewed Steak, *132*
Fried Potatoes, *268*. Salsify, *283*
Apple Charlotte, *544*
Cheese Aigrettes, *342*

JANUARY 21

Tomato Purée, *29*
Coquilles de Salsifis, *284*
Bacon. Roast Fowl, *220*
Bread Sauce, *638*
Potato Chips. Brussels Sprouts, *273*
Madeira Pudding, *473*
Savoury Biscuits, *670*

JANUARY 22

Brown Vegetable Soup, *18*
Fillets of Plaice à la Maître d'Hôtel, *72*
Poulet à la Sefton, *224*
Potatoes. Savoury Rice, *338*
Stuffed Tomatoes, *297*
Apple Tart and Cream, *520*
Cheese and Celery

JANUARY 23

Rice Cream Soup, *38*
Fried Sole Knots, *85*
Tartare Sauce, *637*
Stewed Sweetbreads, *177*
Grilled Steak, *137*
Potato Ribbons.
Parsnips à la Crème, *281*
Liverpool Pudding, *427*
Apple Snow, *459*
Cheese

JANUARY 24

Purée of Brussels Sprouts, *35*
Fried Smelts, *83*
Tomato Sauce, *628*
Boiled Beef, *128*
Potatoes, Dumplings
Carrots and Turnips
Bread and Butter Pudding, *449*
Sardine Pyramids, *375*

JANUARY 25

Mulligatawny Soup, *23*
Rice
Haricot Mutton, *157*
Cold Boiled Beef
Mashed Potatoes. Winter Salad, *325*
Orange Roll, *434*
Mince Pies, *529*
Macaroni au Gratin, *419*

JANUARY 26

Barley Cream Soup, *39*
Lobster Cutlets, *81*
Ragoût of Beef, *201*
Compôte of Pigeons, *254*
Potatoes, Cauliflower
Baked Apple Dumplings, *527*
Custard Pudding, *573*
Cheese and Celery

JANUARY 27

Sago Soup, *52*
Fillets of Plaice à la Portugaise, *76*
Meat Croquettes, *190*
Tomato Sauce, *628*
Curried Rabbit and Rice
Fried Potatoes, *268*
Raisin Pudding, *431*
Stewed Pears, *547*
Cheese Straws, *339*

JANUARY 28

Oyster Soup, *28*
Fillets of Whiting à la Mornay, *119*
Mutton Cutlets à la Soubise, *161*
Potatoes. Scalloped Tomatoes, *663*
Viennoise Pudding, *464*
German Sauce, *660*
Cheese Croûtons, *418*

JANUARY 29

Celery Soup, *31*
Grilled Herrings, *101*
Mustard Sauce, *615*
Beef Olives and Mushrooms, *139*
Roast Partridge, *235*
Salad. Potato Chips, *266*
Preserved Ginger Pudding, *468*
Cheese Pyramids, *344*

JANUARY 30

Consommé à la Brunoise, *4*
Boiled Haddock
Egg Sauce, *607*
Beef Steak and Kidney Pudding, *131*
Grilled Mutton Cutlets
Cabbage. Sauté Potatoes, *267*
Dutch Apple Pudding, *528*
Cheese Soufflé, *343*

JANUARY 31

White Vegetable Soup, *14*
Fish Croquettes, *93*
Roast Hare, *236*
Potatoes. Cauliflower, *291*
Raspberry Pudding, *469*
Tartlets, *521*
Savoury Biscuits, *670*

FEBRUARY 1

Oxtail Soup, *27*
Fried Whiting
Anchovy Sauce, *605*
Boiled Turkey, *230*
Celery or Oyster Sauce, *611* or *614*
Boiled Tongue, *142*
Potatoes, Greens
Rhubarb Tart, *520*
Cheese Straws, *339*

FEBRUARY 2

Gravy Soup, *21*
Fillets of Plaice à la Maître d'Hôtel, *72*
Devilled Turkey
Stewed Ox Kidney, *141*
Chip Potatoes. Savoury Cabbage, *308*
Marmalade Pudding, *428*
Cheese Biscuits, *402*

FEBRUARY 3

Palestine Soup, *30*
Boiled Halibut, *66*
Shrimp Sauce, *610*
Roast Leg of Mutton
Baked Potatoes, Brussels Sprouts
Pancakes, *487*
Coffee Mould, *455*
Anchovy Eggs, *351*

FEBRUARY 4

Tomato Soup, *29*
Fricassée of Halibut, *92*
Meat Cakes, *196*
Stewed Rabbit, *242*
Mashed Potatoes. Braised Onions, *275*
Lemon Pie, *539*
Savoury Semolina, *347*

FEBRUARY 5

Rabbit Soup, *26*
Grilled Mackerel, *127*
Hollandaise Sauce, *618* and *619*
Beef Steak and Kidney Pie, *133*
Irish Stew, *155*
Cauliflower, *291*
Beresford Pudding, *467*
Cheese Croûtons, *418*

FEBRUARY 6

Mock Hare Soup, *22*
Curried Prawns, *104*
Fillets of Beef à la Viennoise, *199*
Mashed Potatoes. Braised Celery, *289*
Manchester Pudding, *540*
Claret Jelly, *495*
Cheese

FEBRUARY 7

Clear Soup, *4*
Scalloped Oysters, *103*
Roast Duck, *228*
Apple Sauce, *629*
Potatoes, Brussels Sprouts
Vanilla Soufflé, *479*
Compôte of Bananas, *594*
Bombay Toast, *371*

FEBRUARY 8

Potato Soup, *13*
Fried Fillets of Plaice, *80*
Anchovy Sauce, *605*
Boiled Beef, *128*
Dumplings
Potatoes. Parsnips, *281*
Rhubarb and Sago Mould, *451*
Custard
Macaroni Cheese, *337*

FEBRUARY 9

Pea Soup, *10*
Scalloped Eggs, *352*
Mutton Cutlets, *159*
Tomato Sauce, *628*
Cold Boiled Beef
Potatoes. Celery, Beetroot Salad, *324*
Haricot Beans, *280*
Chocolate Pudding, *470*
Cheese

FEBRUARY 10

Celery Soup, *31*
Fried Sole Knots, *85*
Tomato Sauce, *628*
Calf's Head, *171*
Brain Sauce, Bacon
Potatoes. Cabbage
Cabinet Pudding, *465*
Macaroon Tarts, *524*
Chutney Toast, *372*

FEBRUARY 11

Macaroni Soup, *40*
Boiled Cod, *64*
Oyster Sauce, *614*
Grilled Steak, *137*
Hashed Calf's Head
Chip Potatoes, Cauliflower
Apple Amber Pudding, *537*
Cheese Croûtons, *418*

FEBRUARY 12

Rice Cream Soup, *38*
Cod au Gratin, *90*
Stuffed and Roast Loin of Mutton, *152*
Baked Potatoes. Mashed Turnips, *271*
Half Pay Pudding, *439*
Cheese Pyramids, *344*

FEBRUARY 13

Gravy Soup, *21*
Mackerel à la Normande, *78*
Meat Croquettes, *190*
Veal Olives and Tomato Sauce, *175*
Potatoes, Brussels Sprouts
Cup Puddings, *482*
Lemon Sponge, *461*
Cheese Straws, *339*

FEBRUARY 14

Clear Soup, *4*
Whitebait, *87*
Brown Bread and Butter
Roast Loin of Pork, *179*
Apple Sauce, *629*
Baked Potatoes, Savoy Cabbage
Ostend Pudding, *593*
Cheese Omelet, *345*

FEBRUARY 15

White Vegetable Soup, *14*
Grilled Herrings, *101*
Mustard Sauce, *615*
Mutton Cutlets, *159*
Tomato Sauce, *628*
Curried Pork, *191*
Rice
Brown Bread Pudding, *472*
Cocoanut Cream, *456*
Cheese and Celery

FEBRUARY 16

Purée of Brussels Sprouts, *35*
Fillets of Plaice Portugaise, *76*
Roast Fowl, *220*
Potato Straws. Bacon, *181*
Salad, *318*
College Puddings, *567*
Wine Sauce, *656*
Cheese Balls, *341*

FEBRUARY 17

Haricot Soup, *11*
Boiled Mackerel, *65*
Fennel Sauce, *612*
Chicken Croquettes and Peas, *222*
Stewed Veal and Rice, *163*
Mashed Potatoes
Coburg Pudding, *538*
Macaroni à la Milanaise, *348*

FEBRUARY 18

Rice Cream Soup, *38*
Boiled Turbot, *66*
Lobster Sauce, *613*
Veal Cutlets and Mushrooms, *164*
Potatoes. Salsify, *283*
Chocolate Pudding, *470*
Custard Tartlets, *533*
Cheese Croûtons, *418*

FEBRUARY 19

Mulligatawny Soup, *23*
Rice
Turbot en Coquilles, *90*
Boiled Mutton, *150*
Caper Sauce, *606*
Potatoes, Carrots and Turnips
Queen of Puddings, *443*
Lemon Jelly, *493*
Cheese Aigrettes, *342*

FEBRUARY 20

Tomato Purée, *29*
Stuffed and Baked Fillets of Plaice, *70*
Rabbit à la Marengo, *225*
Fried Liver and Bacon, *167*
Potatoes, Brussels Sprouts
Rhubarb Tart, *520*
Cheese and Watercress

FEBRUARY 21

Julienne Soup, *47*
Sole au Parmesan, *75*
Roast Beef, *129*
Horseradish Sauce, *633*
Baked Potatoes. Parsnips, *281*
Yorkshire Pudding
Charlotte Russe, *510*
Sardines on Toast, *374*

FEBRUARY 22

Gravy Soup, *21*
Grilled Cod Steaks
Anchovy Sauce, *605*
Boiled Fowl, *221*
Parsley Sauce, *608*
Cold Beef
Mashed Potatoes. Tomato Salad, *319*
Swiss Apple Pudding, *671*
Cheese Balls, *341*

FEBRUARY 23

Parisian Soup, *48*
Fillets of Plaice Bohemienne, *71*
Grilled Chops
Pastry Rissoles, *197*
Mashed Potatoes. Artichokes, *282*
Raspberry Pudding, *469*
Cheese and Celery Savouries, *421*

FEBRUARY 24

Beetroot Cream Soup, *44*
Scalloped Eggs, *352*
Roast Sheep's Heart, *154*
Bacon
Blanquette of Veal, *172*
Potatoes. Cauliflower, *291*
Pineapple Fritters, *489*
Cheese and Watercress

FEBRUARY 25

Crécy Soup, *15*
Fillets of Whiting à la Mornay, *119*
Stewed Steak, *132*
Fricassée of Rabbit, *223*
Potatoes. Scalloped Tomatoes, *663*
French Pancakes, *586*
Cheese Pudding, *340*

FEBRUARY 26

Purée of Lentils, *9*
Boiled Halibut, *66*
Lobster Sauce, *613*
Roast Shoulder of Mutton
Onion Sauce, *609*
Baked Potatoes. Mashed Turnips, *271*
Conservative Pudding, *600*
Roes on Toast, *408*

FEBRUARY 27

Scotch Broth, *8*
Halibut en Coquilles, *90*
Rissoles, *197*
Tomato Sauce, *628*
Curried Veal, *165*
Rice. Potatoes Duchesse, *311.*
Cambridge Pudding, *580*
Savoury Semolina, *347*

FEBRUARY 28

Mock Hare Soup, *22*
Fillets of Plaice à la Maître d'Hôtel, *72*
Veal Cutlets, *164*
Tomato Sauce, *628*
Potatoes. Stewed Mushrooms, *295*
Monk's Pudding, *445*
Pistachio Cream, *507*
Cheese Straws, *339*

MARCH 1

White Vegetable Soup, *14*
Roast Beef, Horseradish Sauce, *633, 634*
Potatoes, Greens
Game Pie, *259*
Custard Pudding, *573*
Meat and Egg Toast, *406*

MARCH 2

Julienne Soup, *47*
Potted Perch, *124*
Durham Cutlets, *189*
Tomato Sauce, *628*
Roast Widgeon, *238*
Potato Chips. Salsify, *283*
Apples à la Crème, *574*
Macaroni Cheese, *337*

MARCH 3

Haricot Bean Soup, *11*
Sole à la Maître d'Hôtel, *72*
Mutton Cutlets à la Nelson, *212*
Scotch Kale
Scalloped Salsify, *284*
Sponge Pudding, *485*
Anchovies on Toast, *665*

MARCH 4

Imitation Hare Soup, *22*
Boiled John Dory, *6*
Lobster Sauce, *613*
Roast Wild Duck, *239*
Orange Sauce, *625*
Sea-kale, *288*
Cocoanut Pudding, *564*
Cheese Omelet, *345*

MARCH 5

Macaroni Soup, *40*
Curried Fish, *91*
Rice
Boiled Mutton, *150*
Caper Sauce, *606*
Potatoes, Greens
Maraschino Pudding, *575*
Sardine Cigarettes, *395*

MARCH 6

Onion Soup, *12*
Whitebait, *87*
Brown Bread and Butter
Stewed Rabbit, *242*
Mutton Fritters, *216*
Potatoes. Haricot Beans, *280*
Cornets à la Crème, *577*
Welsh Rarebit, *346*

MARCH 7

Oysters
Lentil Soup, *9*
Roast Pheasant, *233*
Bread Sauce, *638*
Potato Chips. Salad, *318*
Praline Soufflé, *576*
Devilled Kidneys, *362*

MARCH 8

Game Soup, *61*
Sole à la Crème, *114*
Roast Mutton
Mashed Potato. Stewed Onions, *275*
Apricot Patties, *578*
Cheese Biscuits, *402*

MARCH 9

Fish Soup, *62*
Curried Eggs, *358*
Dresden Patties, *219*
Blanquette of Rabbit, *172*
Potatoes
Swiss Pudding, *579*
Ham Toast, *373*

MARCH 10

Cabbage Soup, *43*
Boiled Salmon, *67*
Hollandaise Sauce, *618* or *619*
Roast Fowl, *220*
Bacon
Potato Chips
Celery à l'Italienne, *309*
Fig Pudding, *432*
Cheese Croûtons, *418*

MARCH 11

Mulligatawny Soup, *23*
Rice
Salmon Cutlets, *107*
Chicken Mousse, *245*
Roast Pork, *179*
Potatoes, Brussels Sprouts
Cambridge Pudding, *580*
Cheese Eclairs, *407*

MARCH 12

Parisian Soup, *48*
Stuffed and Baked Fillets of Plaice, *70*
Curry of Cold Meat, *191*
Grilled Steak, *137*
Potatoes Lyonnaise, *310*
Raspberry Cream Tart, *601*
Anchovy Straws, *393*

MARCH 13

Clear Soup, *4*
Boiled Cod, *64*
Oyster Sauce, *614*
Stewed Ox Kidney, *141*
Potatoes. Parsnips, *281*
Spanish Rice, *403*
Pineapple Soufflé, *480*
Sardines à la Suisse, *409*

MARCH 14

Oxtail Soup, *27*
Fried Smelts, *83*
Tartare Sauce, *637*
Vol au Vent of Chicken, *246*
Liver à la Française, *169*
Sea-kale, *288*
Vanilla Cream, *508*
Cheese Fondu, *343*

MARCH 15

Brown Vegetable Soup, *18*
Sole à l'Americaine, *118*
Stewed Brisket of Beef, *130*
Potatoes
Scalloped Artichokes, *284*
Leche Cream, *585*
Cheese Biscuits, *402*

MARCH 16

Tapioca Cream Soup, *52*
Egg Cutlets, *354*
Roast Duckling, *228*
Potatoes. Mashed Turnips, *271*
Coburg Pudding, *538*
Macaroni à l'Italienne, *419*

MARCH 17

Maigre Soup, *49*
Boiled Haddock
Egg Sauce, *607*
Minced Duck and Tomatoes, *252*
Grilled Mutton Cutlets
Duchess Potatoes, *311*
Normandy Pudding, *581*
Cheese Balls, *341*

MARCH 18

Oyster Soup, *28*
Bean Croquettes, *303*
Haricot Mutton, *157*
Mashed Potatoes. Salsify, *283*
Lemon Cheese Cakes, *522*
Sardines on Toast, *374*

MARCH 19

White Vegetable Soup, *17*
Fried Fillets of Plaice, *80*
Anchovy Sauce, *605*
Boiled Rabbit, *240*
Onion Sauce, *609*
Potato Croquettes, Brussels Sprouts
Marmalade Pudding, *428*
Bombay Toast, *371*

MARCH 20

Kale Brose, *59*
Dressed Cod, *105*
Beef Olives, *139*
Potatoes. Cauliflower, *291*
College Pudding, *567*
Banana Trifle, *555*
Anchovy Biscuits, *393*

MARCH 21

Palestine Soup, *30*
Sole au Gratin, *74*
Boiled Fowl, *221*
Egg Sauce, *607*
Potatoes, Parsnips
Madeira Pudding, *473*
Chutney Toast, *372*

MARCH 22

Hollandaise Soup, *53*
Egg Kromeskies, *664*
Roast Beef
Horseradish Sauce, *633*
Baked Potatoes, Greens
Chicken Patties, *248*
Maltese Pudding, *591*
Cream Cheese

MARCH 23

Tomato Soup, *29*
Fried Sole Knots, *85*
Ragoût of Beef, *201*
Curried Potatoes, *377*
Savoury Cabbage, *308*
Sultana Pudding, *583*
Cheese Straws, *339*

MARCH 24

Pea Soup, *10*
Dressed Crab, *100*
Roast Rabbit, *241*
Potatoes. Stewed Onions, *275*
Vegetable Pie, *314*
Bishop's Pudding, *572*
Eggs au Fromage, *353*

MARCH 25

Gravy Soup, *21*
Fillets of Whiting à la Mornay, *119*
Roast Fowl, *220*
Bread Sauce, *638*
Sausages
Potato Straws. Salad
Ginger Pudding, *429*
Sardine Pyramids, *375*

MARCH 26

Almond Soup, *33*
Cod Steaks
Poulet à la Sefton, *224*
Duchess Potatoes, *311*
Pigeon Pie, *232*
Canary Pudding, *475*
Cheese Fritters, *392*

MARCH 27

Kidney Soup, *20*
Kedgeree, *94*
Curry Sauce, *635*
Roast Mutton
Potatoes. Mashed Turnips, *271*
Chocolate Pudding, *470*
Macaroni à la Milanaise, *348*

MARCH 28

Mulligatawny Soup, *23*
Scalloped Eggs, *352*
Gateau of Cold Meat, *198*
Sea Pie, *134*
Prune Pudding, *571*
Anchovy Straws, *393*

MARCH 29

Haricot Soup, *11*
Plaice à la Maître d'Hôtel, *72*
Beef Steak and Kidney Pudding, *131*
Scalloped Tomatoes
Queen of Puddings, *443*
Cheese Balls, *341*

MARCH 30

Scotch Broth, *8*
Sole Portugaise, *76*
Roast Loin of Pork, *179*
Apple Sauce, *629*
Potatoes, Greens
Pineapple Pudding, *535*
Welsh Rarebit, *346*

MARCH 31

White Vegetable Soup, *14*
Fried Whiting
Anchovy Sauce, *605*
Boiled Fowl, *221*
Parsley Sauce, *608*
Potatoes, Bacon
Riz au Chou, *378*
Charlotte Russe, *510*
Sardines on Toast, *374*

APRIL 1

Oxtail Soup, *27*
Sole au Parmesan, *75*
Veal and Ham Pie, *166*
Devilled Kidneys, *362*
Potatoes à la Maître d'Hôtel, *269*
Prune Mould, *462*
Cheese Straws, *339*

APRIL 2

Potato Soup, *13*
Eggs à la Norfolk, *404*
Grilled Steak and Mushrooms, *137*
Potato Chips, *266*. Cauliflower, *291*
Boiled Batter Pudding, *438*
Anchovies on Toast, *665*

APRIL 3

Lentil Soup, *56*
Fried Smelts, *83*
Tomato Sauce, *628*
Roast Fowl, *220*
Bread Sauce
Potatoes. Bacon, *181*
Sea-kale, *288*
Chelmsford Pudding, *440*
Sardine Canapes, *401*

APRIL 4

Oysters
Curried Eggs, *358*
Fricassée of Chicken, *223*
Potato Croquettes, *265*
Sauté Tomatoes, *269*
Fig Pudding, *432*
Cheese Fritters, *392*

APRIL 5

Carrot Soup, *15*
Boiled Turbot, *66*
Hollandaise Sauce, *618* or *619*
Fillets of Beef à la Viennoise, *199*
Cauliflower au Gratin, *292*
Chocolate Mould, *455*
Anchovy Biscuits, *393*

APRIL 6

Chervil Soup, *60*
Fish Curry, *91*
Pigeon Pie, *232*
Potatoes Sauté, *267*
Grilled Mushrooms, *306*
Banana Fritters, *489*
Cheese Biscuits, *402*

APRIL 7

Clear Soup, *4*
Fillets of Sole à l'Americaine, *118*
Roast Beef, *129*
Baked Potatoes, Cauliflower, *291*
Yorkshire Pudding
French Pancakes, *586*
Sardines on Toast, *374*

APRIL 8

Mulligatawny Soup, *23*
Rice, *91*
Scalloped Fish, *90*
Stewed Lamb, *158*
Potatoes, Pea Purée, *668*
Seakale, *288*
Orange Roll, *434*
Swiss Eggs, *359*

APRIL 9

Brown Vegetable Soup, *18*
Haddock à la St Clair, *97*
Roast Loin of Pork, *179*
Apple Sauce, *629*
Baked Potatoes, Cabbage
Leche Cream, *585*
Ham Omelet, *368*

APRIL 10

Onion Soup, *12*
Sole au Gratin, *74*
Roast Fillet of Veal, *162*
Bacon
Potatoes Duchesse, *311*. Spinach, *290*
College Puddings, *567*
Cheese Straws, *339*

APRIL 11

Mock Hare Soup, *22*
Boiled Salmon and Cucumber, *67*
Mayonnaise Sauce, *636*
Cold Veal and Ham
Mashed Potatoes. Salad, *318* or *332*
Cabinet Pudding, *465*
Rosettes of Anchovies, *398*

APRIL 12

Rice Cream Soup, *38*
Salmon Cutlets, *107*
Braised Duck with Turnips, *251*
Potatoes, Cabbage
Trifle, *548*
Macaroni Cheese, *337*

APRIL 13

Spring Cream Soup, *54*
Fried Whiting
Anchovy Sauce, *605*
Grenadines of Veal, *173*
Spinach Soufflé, *313*
Marble Jelly, *584*
Cheese Biscuits, *402*

APRIL 14

Tomato Purée *29*
Plaice à la Maître d'Hôtel, *72*
Beef Steak and Kidney Pie, *133*
Sea-kale, *288*
Marmalade Pudding, *428*
Cheese Balls, *341*

APRIL 15

Oxtail Soup, *27*
Sole Rouennaise, *116*
Roast Chicken, *220*
Potatoes, Bacon
Cauliflower, *291*
Pineapple Soufflé, *480*
Œufs au Fromage, *353*

APRIL 16

Lobster Soup, *63*
Eggs au Gratin, *397*
Stewed Rabbit, *242*
Calf's Feet Fritters, *206*
Potatoes. Tomato Sauce, *628*
Cup Puddings, *482*
Sardines à la Suisse, *409*

APRIL 17

Scotch Broth, *8*
Lobster Cutlets, *81*
Roast Lamb
Mint Sauce, *632*
Baked Potatoes. Sauté Tomatoes, *296*
Coburg Pudding, *538*
Anchovy Straws, *393*

APRIL 18

Hollandaise Soup, *53*
Sole à la Colbert, *84*
Mince and Poached Eggs, *188*
Roast Sheep's Heart, *154*
Potatoes. Cabbage, *272*
Madeira Pudding, *473*
Macaroni à l'Italienne, *419*

APRIL 19

Almond Soup, *33*
Grilled Trout, *126*
Chicken à la Marengo, *225*
Potatoes. Spinach, *290*
Rhubarb and Sago Mould, *451*
Custard
Cheese Soufflé, *343*

APRIL 20

French Cheese Soup, *37*
Curried Prawns, *104*
Mutton Cutlets, *159*
Tomato Sauce, *628*
Sea-kale, *288*
Chocolate Pudding, *470*
Ham Croûtes à l'Italienne, *420*

APRIL 21

Rice and Tomato Soup, *16*
Fillets of Whiting in Batter, *79*
Roast Beef, *129*
Horseradish Sauce, *633*
Baked Potatoes, Cabbage
Yorkshire Pudding
Sago Soufflé, *478*
Anchovy Eggs, *351*

APRIL 22

Julienne Soup, *47*
Mackerel à la Normande, *78*
Durham Cutlets, *189*
Tomato Sauce, *628*
Potatoes. Peas, *277*
Veal à la Reine, *211*
Sweet Omelet, *491*
Cheese Creams, *396*

APRIL 23

Jenny Lind Soup, *50*
Boiled John Dory, *66*
Shrimp Sauce, *610*
Veal and Ham Pie, *166*
Salad
Lyonnaise Potatoes, *310*
Raisin Pudding, *431*
Welsh Rarebit, *346*

APRIL 24

Almond Soup, *33*
Fried Cod's Roe, *363*
Piquante Sauce, *624*
Beef Olives, *139*
Potatoes, Shredded Carrots
Spanish Rice, *403*
Lemon Sago, *458*
Sardine Cigarettes, *395*

APRIL 25

Brown Vegetable Soup, *18*
Sole Parmesan, *75*
Boiled Neck of Mutton, *150*
Caper Sauce, *606*
Potatoes, Scotch Kale
Vegetable Pie, *314*
Pineapple Snow, *543*
Eggs and Luxette, *394*

APRIL 26

Tomato Purée, *29*
Lobster Salad, *330*
Stewed Sweetbreads, *177*
Duchess Potatoes, *311*. Spinach, *290*
Marquise Pudding, *582*
Croûtes de Coburg, *383*

APRIL 27

Oysters
Mulligatawny Soup, *23*
Rice
Veal Cutlets à la Française, *205*
Potatoes
Cauliflower au Gratin, *292*
Bachelor's Pudding, *476*
Anchovy Fritters, *384*

APRIL 28

Chervil Soup, *60*
Fried Trout, *86*
Boiled Chicken, *221*
Parsley Sauce, *608*
Potatoes. Sea-kale, *288*
Spanish Rice, *403*
Cocoanut Cream, *456*
Chutney Toast, *372*

APRIL 29

Potato Soup, *13*
Boiled John Dory
Caper Sauce, *606*
Poulet à la Sefton, *224*
Potato Balls. Asparagus, *294*
Strawberry Cream, *506*
Ham Omelet, *368*

APRIL 30

Mock Hare Soup, *22*
Fish Scallops, *90*
Veal Olives with Tomato Sauce, *175*
Potatoes, Cabbage
Bishop's Pudding, *572*
Cheese Croûtons, *418*

MAY 1

Tapioca Cream Soup, *52*
Lobster Cutlets, *81*
Roast Sirloin of Beef, *129*
Horseradish Sauce, *633*
Baked Potatoes. Asparagus, *294*
Yorkshire Pudding
Peach Mould, *599*
Cheese and Watercress

MAY 2

Gravy Soup, *21*
Sole à la Portugaise, 76
Boiled Fowl, *221*
Bacon
Gateau of Cold Meat, *198*
Potatoes. Tomato Sauce, *628*
Spinach, *290*
Gooseberry Tart, *520*
Cheese Croûtons, *418*

MAY 3

White Vegetable Soup, *14*
Boiled Salmon and Cucumber, *67*
Tartare Sauce, *637*
Fricassée of Fowl, *223*
Mutton Cutlets and Tomatoes, *159*
Chocolate Mould, *453*
Cheese Straws, *339*

MAY 4

Tomato Purée, *29*
Salmon Coquilles, *108*
Summer Stew, *158*
Fried Calf's Liver and Bacon, *167*
Preserved Ginger Pudding, *468*
Cheese Balls, *341*

MAY 5

Kidney Soup, *20*
Fried Fillets of Plaice, *80*
Anchovy Sauce, *605*
Calf's Head, *171*
Brain Sauce
Potatoes. Cabbage
Stuffed Tomatoes, *297*
Omelette Soufflé, *590*
Cheese

MAY 6

Hollandaise Soup, *53*
Sole à la Florentine, *77*
Roast Lamb
Mint Sauce, *632*
Baked Potatoes. New Turnips
Canary Pudding, *475*
Anchovy Biscuits, *393*

MAY 7

Mock Turtle Soup, *24*
Fillets of Whiting à la Mornay, *119*
Braised Calf's Tongue with Spinach
Cold Lamb
Mint Sauce, *632*
Mashed Potatoes, Lettuce Salad
Conservative Pudding, *600*
Savoury Biscuits, *670*

MAY 8

Spring Soup, *54*
Boiled Turbot, *66*
Lobster Sauce, *613*
Roast Loin of Veal, *162*
Potatoes, Bacon
Cucumber à la Crème, *300*
Pineapple Fritters, *489*
Cheese d'Artois, *413*

MAY 9

Consommé Brunoise, *4*
Lobster Patties, *248*
Grilled Lamb Cutlets
Minced Veal and Poached Eggs, *170*
Potatoes, Cabbage
Rum Omelet, *492*
Marrow Toasts, *416*

MAY 10

American Tomato Soup, *41*
Stuffed and Baked Fillets of Plaice, *70*
Fried Sweetbread, *176*
Fricandeau of Beef, *149*
Potatoes
Asparagus, *294*
Maltese Pudding, *591*
Cheese Pyramids, *344*

MAY 11

Cucumber Soup, *34*
Baked Red Mullet, *102*
Summer Stew, *158*
Grilled Steak and Tomatoes, *137*
Potato Chips, *266*
Pancakes, *487*
Cheese Straws, *339*

MAY 12

Potato Soup, *13*
Boiled Turbot, *66*
Shrimp Sauce, *610*
Braised Duck with Turnips, *251*
Poached Eggs and Spinach, *290*
Gooseberry Tart, *520*
Cheese Ramakins, *414*

MAY 13

Clear Mulligatawny Soup
Scalloped Turbot, *90*
Veal Cutlets à la Française, *205*
Mashed Potatoes. Asparagus, *294*
Banana Charlotte, *588*
Savoury Semolina, *347*

MAY 14

French Cheese Soup, *37*
Fillets of Sole à l'Americaine, *118*
Roast Chicken, *220*
Bread Sauce, *638*
Bacon
Potatoes, Cabbage
Cocoanut Pudding, *564*
Sardine Pyramids, *375*

MAY 15

Asparagus Soup, *666*
Grilled Trout, *126*
Boiled Neck of Mutton
Caper Sauce, *606*
Chicken Croquettes and Peas, *222*
Potatoes
Caramel Custard, *541*
Cheese Croûtons, *418*

MAY 16

Scotch Broth, *8*
Boiled Salmon, *67*
Cucumber
Roast Forequarter of Lamb
Mint Sauce, *632*
Potatoes. Cauliflower, *291*
Nelson Pudding, *602*
Bombay Toast, *371*

MAY 17

Oxtail Soup, 27
Salmon Cutlets, 107
Cold Lamb
Mint Sauce, 632
Russian Salad, 335
Mashed Potatoes
Viennoise Pudding, 464
Macaroni Cheese, 337

MAY 18

Purée of Spinach, 667
Scallops en Coquilles, 121
Durham Cutlets, 189
Tomato Sauce, 628
Blanquette of Veal, 172
Potato Straws. Glazed Carrots, 270
Lemon Cheese Cakes, 522
Sardines on Toast, 374

MAY 19

Brown Vegetable Soup, 18
Fillets of Plaice à la Maître d'Hôtel, 72
Baked and Stuffed Loin of Mutton, 152
Potatoes. Asparagus, 294
Brown Bread Pudding, 294
Cheese Soufflé, 343

MAY 20

Rice Cream Soup, 38
Boiled Mackerel, 65
Fennel Sauce, 612
Mutton Collops and Tomato Sauce, 215
Roast Calf's Heart
Potato Straws. Spinach, 290
Gooseberry Fool, 546
Savoury Biscuits, 670

MAY 21

Mock Hare Soup, 22
Baked Salmon Steaks, 109
Caper Sauce, 606
Summer Stew, 158
Veal and Ham Pie, 166
Salad
Marmalade Pudding, 428
Cheese Balls, 341

MAY 22

Asparagus Soup, 666
Lobster Mayonnaise, 330
Roast Duckling, 228
Apple Sauce, 629
Potatoes, Cabbage
Cabinet Pudding, 465
Cheese Pyramids, 344

MAY 23

Oyster Soup, 28
Egg Croquettes, 354
Roast Fillet of Veal, 162
Bacon
Potatoes. Sauté Tomatoes, 296
Sago Soufflé, 478
Cheese Straws, 339

MAY 24

Spring Cream Soup, 54
Curried Prawns, 104
Mutton Cutlets and Spinach, 159
Cold Veal and Ham
Salad, 332
Cup Pudding, 482
Cream Cheese

MAY 25

Chervil Soup, 60
Boiled Halibut
Hollandaise Sauce, 618
Minced Veal and Poached Eggs, 170
Grilled Steak, 137
Potato Chips, 266
Gooseberry Tart, 520
Cheese Omelet, 345

MAY 26

Tomato Soup, 29
Fish Croquettes, 93
Roast Beef, 129
Horseradish Sauce, 633 or 634
Potatoes. Mashed Turnips, 271
Yorkshire Pudding
Gateau de Riz, 509
Macaroni à la Milanaise, 348

MAY 27

Cucumber Soup, 34
Fried Sole
Tartare Sauce, 637
Chicken à la Marengo, 225
Potatoes. Asparagus, 294
Bachelor's Pudding, 476
Cheese d'Artois, 413

MAY 28

Macaroni Soup, 40
Fillets of Whiting with Shrimps, 120
Beef Collops, 144
Veal à la Reine, 211
Potato Croquettes, 265
Madeleines, 484
Cheese Gondoles, 417

MAY 29

Bonne Femme Soup, 51
Boiled Turbot, 66
Lobster Sauce, 613
Roast Leg of Lamb
Mint Sauce, 632
Potatoes. Stewed Mushrooms, 295
Canary Pudding, 475
Welsh Rarebit, 346

MAY 30

Lettuce Soup, 42
Fish Salad, 329
Fillet of Beef à la Pompadour, 146
Lamb Curry and Rice, 191
Asparagus, 294
Spanish Puffs, 530
Cheese Pudding, 340

MAY 31

Julienne Soup, 47
Fried Whiting
Anchovy Sauce, 605
Stewed Sweetbreads, 177
Beef Steak and Kidney Pie, 133
Savoury Cabbage, 308
Sweet Omelet, 491
Cheese

JUNE 1

Spring Cream Soup, 54
Boiled Salmon, 67
Cucumber
Shrimp Sauce, 610
Chicken à la Marengo, 225
Mashed Potatoes. Spinach, 290
Cherry Tart, 520
Custard
Macaroni à la Milanaise, 348

JUNE 2

Jenny Lind Soup, 50
Salmon Mayonnaise, 99
Roast Beef, 129
Baked Potatoes. Scalloped Tomatoes, 663
Yorkshire Pudding
Asparagus, 294
Maraschino Jelly, 496
Beignets à la Turque, 411

JUNE 3

Tomato Purée, 29
Sole au Parmesan, 75
Mutton Cutlets à la Nelson, 212
Cold Beef
Salad. New Potatoes, 263
Viennoise Pudding, 464
Bombay Toast, 371

JUNE 4

Cucumber Soup, 34
Fillets of Plaice, 80
Anchovy Sauce, 605
Veal Cutlets à la Milanaise, 210
Duchess Potatoes, 311
Rice Mould, 452
Stewed Cherries
Cheese Pudding, 340

JUNE 5

Hollandaise Soup, 53
Boiled Turbot, 66
Lobster Sauce, 613
Roast Lamb
Mint Sauce, 632
New Potatoes, 263. Glazed Carrots, 270
Savoury Macaroni, 349
Gooseberry Fool, 546
Cheese

JUNE 6

Brown Vegetable Soup, 18
Fish Omelet, 122
Beef Olives and Peas, 139
New Potatoes, 263
French Raisin Pudding, 477
Ham Croûtes à l'Italienne, 420

JUNE 7

Potato Purée, 13
Lobster Cutlets, 81
Roast Duck, 228
Apple Sauce, 629
New Potatoes, 263. Peas, 277
Sponge Pudding, 485
Croûtes de Champignons, 415
Cheese

JUNE 8

Kidney Soup, 20
Fried Sole Knots, 85
Stewed Knuckle of Veal and Rice, 163
Salmi of Duck with Peas
New Potatoes, 263. Stuffed Tomatoes, 297
Pineapple Snow, 543
Cheese Gondoles, 417

JUNE 9

Veal Broth, 7
Salmon Creams, 112
Cardinal Sauce, 631
Beef Steak and Tomato Pie, 204
Poached Eggs and Spinach, 290
Fruit Salad, 550
Eggs à la Norwegienne, 405

JUNE 10

Green Pea Purée, 32
Dressed Crab, 100
Roast Chicken, 220
Bacon
New Potatoes, 263. Cabbage
Marquise Pudding, 582
Spanish Rice, 403

JUNE 11

Julienne Soup, 47
Boiled Turbot, 66
Shrimp Sauce, 610
Rissoles à la Pompadour, 364
Roast Fillet of Veal, 162
New Potatoes, 263. Mashed Turnips, 271
Compôte of Strawberries, 594
Marrow Toasts, 416

JUNE 12

Mock Hare Soup, 22
Fricassée of Fish, 92
Mutton Cutlets à la Reforme, 160
Cold Veal and Ham
Potatoes. Lettuce Salad, 318
Honey Comb Mould, 463
Macaroni à l'Italienne, 419

JUNE 13

Parisian Soup, 48
Lobster Mould and Sauce, 95
Minced Veal, 170
Grilled Steak à la Russe, 202
Potato Chips, 266
Asparagus, 294
Cherry Tart, 520
Cheese Croûtons, 418

JUNE 14

Asparagus Soup
Boiled Salmon, *67*
Cucumber
Anchovy Sauce, *605*
Roast Guinea Fowl
Bacon
Cabbage. New Potatoes, *263.*
Rhenish Cream, *460*
Cheese Omelet, *345*

JUNE 15

Mock Turtle Soup, *24*
Darioles of Salmon en Belle-Vue, *111*
Boiled Mutton
Caper Sauce, *606*
Fried Lambs' Sweetbreads, *176*
Carrots and Turnips. Potatoes, *263*
Bakewell Pudding, *534*
Cheese Straws, *339*

JUNE 16

Crécy Soup, *15*
Plaice à la Maître d'Hôtel, *72*
Roast Leg of Lamb
Mint Sauce, *632*
New Potatoes, *263*
Asparagus, *294*
Chelmsford Pudding, *440*
Anchovy Eggs, *351*
Cheese

JUNE 17

Tomato Purée, *29*
Whitebait, *87*
Brown Bread and Butter
Fillet of Beef à la Viennoise, *199*
Cold Lamb with Green Pea Salad, *213*
Chocolate Mould, *453*
Cheese Soufflé, *343*

JUNE 18

Consommé Brunoise, *4*
Sole à la Venitienne, *117*
Grenadines of Veal, *173*
Boiled Gammon, *181*
New Potatoes. Spinach, *290*
Apricot Fritters, *489*
Cream Cheese
Watercress

JUNE 19

Mock Hare Soup, *22*
Fillets of Salmon à la Tartare, *110*
Boiled Fowl, *221*
Parsley Sauce, *608*
Potato Croquettes, *265*
French Beans, *279*
Rainbow Creams, *595*
Savoury Macaroni, *349*

JUNE 20

Giblet Soup, *45*
Boiled Haddock
Egg Sauce, *607*
Curried Fowl and Rice
Stuffed and Roast Loin of Mutton, *152*
Potatoes. Mashed Turnips, *271*
Spanish Puffs, *530*
Cheese

JUNE 21

Green Pea Purée, *32*
Kedgeree, *94*
Roast Sirloin of Beef, *129*
Horseradish Sauce, *633* or *634*
Baked Potatoes. French Beans, *279*
Yorkshire Pudding, *129*
Banana Charlotte, *588*
Œufs au Fromage, *353*

JUNE 22

Tomato Purée, *29*
Curried Prawns, *104*
Fried Sweetbread, *176*
Cold Beef
Potatoes. Salad, *332*
Spinach Omelet, *669*
Ostend Pudding, *593*
Cheese Croûtons, *418*

JUNE 23

Julienne Soup, *47*
Fillets of Plaice Bohemienne, *71*
Boiled Calf's Head, *171*
Parsley Sauce, *608*
Boiled Pork
Potatoes. Peas, *277*
Gooseberry Tart, *520*
Savoury Semolina, *347*

JUNE 24

Parisian Soup, *48*
Boiled Mackerel, *65*
Fennel Sauce, *612*
Mutton Cutlets and Tomatoes, *159*
Hashed Calf's Head
Asparagus, *294*
Lemon Jelly, *493*
Cheese Soufflé, *343*

JUNE 25

Mock Turtle Soup, *24*
Sole à la Florentine, *77*
Roast Chicken, *220*
Bacon
Potatoes, Salad
Rice Fritters, *412*
Stewed Cherries
Junket, *672*
Cheese

JUNE 26

Cucumber Soup, *34*
Fried Whiting
Anchovy Sauce, *605*
Stewed Lamb and Peas, *158*
Chicken Mayonnaise, *328*
Sweet Omelet, *491*
Sardines on Toast, *374*

JUNE 27

White Vegetable Soup, *17*
Fried Eels, *82*
Tartare Sauce, *637*
Grilled Steak and Mushrooms, *137*
Compôte of Pigeons, *254*
French Beans, *279*
Raspberry Mousse, *500*
Macaroni Cheese, *337*

JUNE 28

Asparagus Soup
Boiled Halibut
Shrimp Sauce, *610*
Roast Lamb
Mint Sauce, *632*
New Potatoes. Peas, *277*
Crystal Palace Pudding, *457*
Swiss Eggs, *359*

JUNE 29

Macaroni Soup, *40*
Fish Salad, *329*
Boiled Fowl, *221*
Egg Sauce, *607*
Lamb Fritters, *216*
Potatoes, Cabbage
Pineapple Cream, *502*
Cheese d'Artois, *413*

JUNE 30

Green Pea Purée, *32*
Curried Prawns, *104*
Chicken Croquettes, *222*
Boiled Ham, *181*
Potatoes
Broad Beans and Parsley Sauce, *278*
Conservative Pudding, *600*
Cheese Biscuits, *402*

JULY 1

Macaroni Soup, *40*
Baked Red Mullet, *102*
Beef Steak and Tomato Pie, *204*
Peas, *277*
Red Current and Raspberry Tart, *520*
Lemon Jelly, *493*
Cheese

JULY 2

Lettuce Soup, *42*
Grilled Trout, *126*
Veal Cutlets à la Milanaise, *210*
Potatoes, Cabbage
Gooseberry Fool, *546*
Water Lily Savouries, *388*

JULY 3

Imitation Hare Soup, *22*
Stuffed and Baked Plaice, *70*
Roast Duck, *228*
Potatoes. Peas, *277*
Salad, *318*
Cinnamon Pudding, *562*
Anchovy Toast

JULY 4

White Vegetable Soup, *14*
Boiled Halibut
Hollandaise Sauce, *618* or *619*
Salmi of Duck
Grilled Mutton Cutlets
Duchess Potatoes, *311*
Fruit Salad, *550*
Spinach and Cheese, *399*

JULY 5

Tapioca Cream Soup, *52*
Dressed Crab, *100*
Pigeon Pie, *232*
Potato Croquettes, *265*
Boiled Cucumber, *300*
Summer Pudding, 542
Macaroni Cheese, *337*

JULY 6

Clear Soup, *4*
Boiled Salmon, *67*
Tartare Sauce, *637*
Roast Loin of Veal, *162*
Bacon
Potatoes. Spinach, *290*
Sweet Omelet, *491*
Iced Peaches, *565*
Cheese Pyramids, *344*

JULY 7

Chervil Soup, *60*
Salmon Mayonnaise, *99*
Mutton Cutlets, *159*
Tomato Sauce, *628*
Asparagus, *294*
Pineapple Pudding, *535*
Anchovy Fritters, *384*

JULY 8

Scalloped Eggs, *352*
Roast Lamb
Mint Sauce, *632*
Potatoes. Peas, *277*
Stuffed and Baked Tomatoes, *297*
Caramel Custard, *541*
Compôte of Fruit, *551*
Cheese Fritters, *392*

JULY 9

Tomato Purée, *29*
Prawns in Aspic, *647*
Durham Cutlets, *189*
Curried Eggs, *358*
Broad Beans and Parsley Sauce, *278*
Diplomatic Pudding, *592*
Cheese

JULY 10

Asparagus Soup
Whitebait, *87*
Brown Bread and Butter
Roast Fowl, *220*
Bacon
Potato Sauté, *267*. Salad, *318*
Leche Cream, *585*
Cheese Soufflé, *343*

JULY 11

Plovers' Eggs
Sole Portugaise, *76*
Fricassée of Chicken, *223*
Grilled Steak and Mushrooms, *137*
Braised Cucumber, *302*
Raspberry Cream, *505*
Cheese Biscuits, *402*

JULY 12

Gravy Soup, *21*
Kedgeree, *94*
Fricandeau of Beef, *149*
Spinach, *290*
Fruit Salad, *550*
Sponge Fingers
Anchovy Rosettes, *398*

JULY 13

Rice Cream Soup, *38*
Grilled Trout, *126*
Cold Meat Gateau, *198*
Stewed Sweetbreads, *177*
Potato Croquettes, *265*
Cherry Tart, *520*
Cheese and Biscuits

JULY 14

Curried Prawns, *104*
Braised Chicken, *225*
Asparagus, *294*
Savoury Cabbage, *308*
St Cloud Puddings, *597*
Sardine Canapés, *401*

JULY 15

Egg Kromeskies
Chicken Salad, *328*
Veal Olives and Tomato Sauce, *175*
Junket, *672*
Stewed Gooseberries
Cheese Soufflé, *343*

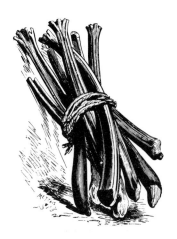

JULY 16

Hollandaise Soup, *53*
Lobster Cutlets, *81*
Stuffed and Stewed Steak, *140*
Potatoes. Peas, *277*
Italian Creams, *598*
Sardine Pyramids, *375*

JULY 17

Green Pea Purée, *32*
Sole à la Florentine, *77*
Fried Sweetbread, *176*
Piquante Sauce, *624*
Sauté Tomatoes, *296*
Strawberry Cream, *506*
Cheese Aigrettes, *342*

JULY 18

American Tomato Soup, *41*
Salmon Steaks à la Tartare, *110*
Veal Cream, *209*
Mutton Cutlets and Peas, *159*
Coffee Pudding, *566*
Rice Fritters, *412*

JULY 19

Clear Soup, *4*
Boiled Turbot, *66*
Shrimp Sauce, *610*
Roast Duck, *228*
Potatoes. Peas, *277*
Salad, *318*
Banana Charlotte, *588*
Cheese Croûtons, *418*

JULY 20

Cucumber Soup, *34*
Turbot au Gratin
Minced Duck and Tomatoes, *252*
Veal à la Reine, *211*
Asparagus, *294*
Chocolate Mould, *453*
Cheese Straws, *339*

JULY 21

Kidney Soup, *20*
Lobster au Gratin, *96*
Fillets of Beef à la Pompadour, *146*
Lyonnaise Potatoes, *310*
Sago Soufflé, *478*
Water Lily Savoury, *388*

JULY 22

Tapioca Cream Soup, *52*
Eggs à la Norfolk, *404*
Veal and Ham Pie, *166*
Cucumber Salad, *327*
Crystal Palace Pudding, *457*
Macaroni Cheese, *337*

JULY 23

Lobster Soup, *63*
Eggs and Tomatoes, *387*
Compôte of Pigeons, *254*
Potato Croquettes, *265*
Cocoanut Cream, *456*
Roes on Toast, *408*

JULY 24

Sole au Parmesan, *75*
Stuffed and Roast Loin of Mutton, *152*
Potatoes. Peas, *277*
Stuffed Tomatoes, *297*
Leche Cream, *585*
Sardine Pyramids, *375*

JULY 25

Cabbage Soup, *43*
Baked Red Mullet, *102*
Potatoes. Chicken à la Marengo, *225*
Broad Beans and Parsley Sauce, *278*
Rhubarb and Sago Mould, *451*
Custard, *657*
Cheese Biscuits, *402*

JULY 26

Jenny Lind Soup, *50*
Lobster Mayonnaise, *330*
Summer Stew, *158*
Peas, *277*
Lemon Sponge, *461*
Rice and Cheese, *338*

JULY 27

Lettuce Soup, *42*
Boiled Turbot, *66*
Shrimp Sauce, *610*
Galantine of Chicken, *226*
Russian Salad, *335*
Queen of Puddings, *443*
Cheese Straws, *339*

JULY 28

Whitebait, 87
Brown Bread and Butter
Roast Lamb
Mint Sauce, 632
Potatoes. Asparagus, 294
Macaroni Cutlets, 350
Maraschino Jelly, 496
Tartlets, 521
Sardines à la Suisse, 409

JULY 29

Cucumber Soup, 34
Fried Fillets of Plaice, 80
Anchovy Sauce, 605
Blanquette de Veau, 172
Cold Lamb with Green Pea Salad, 213
Potato Croquettes, 265
Coffee Cream, 501
Cheese Soufflé, 343

JULY 30

Clear Soup, 4
Curried Eggs, 358
Mutton Cutlets à la Reforme, 160
Spinach Omelet, 669
Cold Lemon Pudding, 545
Croûtes a l'Italienne, 420

JULY 31

White Vegetable Soup, 14
Sole à la Turque, 73
Fillets of Beef à la Viennoise, 199
Asparagus, 294
Lemon Jelly, 493
Tomatoes with Cheese Cream, 381

AUGUST 1

Vegetable Marrow Soup, 17
Lobster Mould, 95
Mutton Cutlets à la Nelson, 212
Chicken Pie, 250
Salad, 318
Cauliflower au Gratin, 292
Summer Pudding, 542
Sardines on Toast, 374

AUGUST 2

Green Pea Purée, 32
Boiled Salmon, 67
Cucumber
Tartare Sauce, 637
Veal Cutlets and Mushrooms, 164
Duchess Potatoes, 311
Strawberry Cream, 506
Savoury Semolina, 347

AUGUST 3

Julienne Soup, 47
Fillets of Whiting à la Mornay, 119
Roast Neck of Mutton
Fried Calves' Brains, 208
Tomato Sauce, 628
Mashed Potatoes. French Beans, 279
Dantzic Jelly, 596
Cheese Straws, 339

AUGUST 4

Jenny Lind Soup, 50
Salmon Mayonnaise, 99
Roast Lamb
Mint Sauce, 632
Potatoes. Peas, 277
Apricot Mousse, 500
Cheese Omelet, 345

AUGUST 5

Gravy Soup, 21
Sole à la Florentine, 77
Beef Collop, 144
Cold Lamb
Mint Sauce, 632
Potato Croquettes.
Green Pea Salad, 322
Stuffed Tomatoes, 297
Ambrosia, 454
Sardines à la Suisse, 409

AUGUST 6

Chervil Soup, 60
Sole à la Colbert, 84
Fricassée of Chicken, 223
Stuffed Vegetable Marrow, 287
French Beans, 279
Greengage Tart, 520
Cheese Croûtons, 418

AUGUST 7

Purée à la Reine, 46
Boiled Turbot, 66
Lobster Sauce, 613
Grilled Steak, 137
Veal and Ham Pie, 166
Potato Chips, 266. Lettuce Salad, 318
Pineapple Cream, 502
Cheese Fondu, 343

AUGUST 8

Tomato Soup, 29
Fish Salad, 329
Roast Duck, 228
Apple Sauce, 629
Potatoes. Peas, 277
Cauliflower in Batter, 293
Fruit Salad, 550
Beignets à la Turque, 411

AUGUST 9

Cucumber Soup, 34
Fried Fillets of Plaice, 80
Anchovy Sauce, 605
Boiled Mutton
Caper Sauce, 606
Salmi of Duck
Potatoes. Vegetable Marrow, 286
Diplomatic Pudding, 592
Macaroni à l'Italienne, 419

AUGUST 10

Brown Vegetable Soup, 18
Fillets of Red Mullet
Tartare Sauce, 637
Mutton Cutlets, 159
Potatoes. Boiled Gammon, 181
Broad Beans with Parsley Sauce, 608
Peach Fritters, 489
Cheese Straws, 339

AUGUST 11

Rice Cream Soup, *38*
Lobster Cutlets, *81*
Roast Beef, *129*
Horseradish Sauce, *633*
Baked Potatoes. French Beans, *279*
Yorkshire Pudding
Compôte of Strawberries, *594*
Cheese Ramakins, *414*

AUGUST 12

Potato Purée, *13*
Grilled Herrings, *101*
Mustard Sauce, *615*
Braised Sweetbreads
Piquante Sauce, *624*
Cold Beef
Russian Salad, *335*
St Cloud Puddings, *597*
Spanish Rice, *403*

AUGUST 13

Carrot Soup, *15*
Sole au Parmesan, *75*
Chicken à la Cimiez, *247*
Beef Croquettes, *190*
Potatoes, Cabbage
Italian Creams, *598*
Ham Toasts, *373*

AUGUST 14

Vermicelli Soup, *40*
Boiled Haddock
Anchovy Sauce, *605*
Veal Cutlets à la Milanaise, *210*
Broad Beans with Parsley Sauce, *278*
Egg Salad, *326*
Raspberry Cream Tart, *601*
Roes on Toast, *408*

AUGUST 15

Bonne Femme Soup, *51*
Fillets of Salmon à la Tartare, *110*
Roast Lamb
Mint Sauce, *632*
Baked Potatoes. Marrow, *286*
Spinach Soufflé, *313*
Gooseberry Charlotte, *588*
Cheese Pudding, *340*

AUGUST 16

Julienne Soup, *47*
Boiled Halibut
Shrimp Sauce, *610*
Roast Grouse, *238*
Cold Lamb
Mint Sauce, *632*
Potato Chips, *266*. Salad, *318*
Peach Darioles à la Reine, *599*
Cheese Croûtons, *418*

AUGUST 17

Parisian Soup, *48*
Fish Salad, *329*
Beef Steak and Kidney Pie, *133*
Salmi of Grouse, *234*
French Beans, *279*
Rhenish Cream, *460*
Savoury Semolina, *347*

AUGUST 18

Kidney Soup, *20*
Plaice à la Maître d'Hôtel, *72*
Roast Loin of Veal, *162*
Bacon
Potatoes. Peas, *277*
Scalloped Tomatoes, *663*
Ground Rice Mould, *450*
Stewed Greengages
Cheese Balls, *341*

AUGUST 19

Tomato Purée, *29*
Grilled Trout, *126*
Eggs à la Norfolk, *404*
Cold Veal
Ham and Egg Salad, *336*
Savoury Cabbage, *308*
Raspberry and Red Currant Pudding, *422*
Cheese

AUGUST 20

Cucumber Soup, *34*
Lobster Mayonnaise, *330*
Grilled Steak à la Russe, *202*
Minced Veal, *170*
Potato Straws. Broad Beans, *278*
Omelette Soufflé, *590*
Anchovy Eggs, *351*

AUGUST 21

Vegetable Marrow Soup, *17*
Stuffed and Fried Fillets of Plaice, *80*
Boiled Mutton
Caper Sauce, *606*
Potatoes. French Beans, *279*
Savoury Rice Fritters, *412*
Fruit Salad, *550*
Cheese Straws, *339*

AUGUST 22

Scotch Broth, *8*
Sole à la Portugaise, *76*
Roast Fowl, *220*
Bacon
Sauté Potatoes, *267*. Salad, *318*
Spanish Rice, *403*
Summer Pudding, *542*
Beignets à la Turque, *411*

AUGUST 23

Jenny Lind Soup, *50*
Fried Fillets of Plaice, *80*
Anchovy Sauce, *605*
Poulet à la Sefton, *224*
Veal Olives with Tomato Sauce, *175*
Duchess Potatoes, *311*. Peas, *277*
Pistachio Cream, *507*
Cheese Soufflé, *343*

AUGUST 24

Brown Vegetable Soup, *18*
Boiled Turbot, *66*
Shrimp Sauce, *610*
Mutton Cutlets and Spinach, *159*
Sauté Potatoes, *267*
Cauliflowers au Gratin, *292*
Maraschino Jelly, *496*
Cheese Cakes, *525*
Sardine Fritters, *409*

AUGUST 25

Hollandaise Soup, *53*
Turbot au Gratin, *90*
Roast Duck, *228*
Apple Sauce, *629*
Potatoes. Peas, *277*
Macaroni à la Milanaise, *348*
Cabinet Pudding, *465*
Bombay Toast, *371*

AUGUST 26

Giblet Soup, *45*
Boiled Salmon, *67*
Cucumber
Melted Butter Sauce, *617*
Blanquette of Veal, *172*
Hashed Duck
Sauté Potatoes, *267*. French Beans, *279*
Greengage Tart, *520*
Cheese Gondoles, *417*

AUGUST 27

Green Pea Purée, *32*
Salmon Croquettes, *108*
Roast Beef, *129*
Potatoes. Vegetable Marrow, *286*
Yorkshire Pudding
Crystal Palace Pudding, *457*
Tomatoes with Cheese Cream, *381*

AUGUST 28

Crécy Soup, *15*
Sole à la Florentine, *77*
Calf's Feet Fritters, *206*
Tomato Sauce, *628*
Cold Beef
Mashed Potatoes
Cauliflower Salad, *323*
Raspberry Cream, *505*
Cheese Pudding, *340*

AUGUST 29

Vermicelli Soup, *40*
Fillets of Whiting à la Mornay, *119*
Durham Cutlets, *189*
Stuffed and Stewed Shoulder of Veal, *207*
Mashed Potatoes. Braised Onions, *275*
Pineapple Pudding, *535*
Cheese

AUGUST 30

Rice Cream Soup, *38*
Lobster Salad, *330*
Roast Lamb
Mint Sauce, *632*
Potatoes. Mashed Turnip, *271*
Diplomatic Pudding, *592*
Macaroni à la Milanaise, *348*

AUGUST 31

White Vegetable Soup, *14*
Fried Sole Knots, *85*
Fillets of Beef à la Pompadour, *146*
Cold Lamb
Mint Sauce, *632*
Potato Salad, *320*
Chocolate Mould, *453*
Œufs au Fromage, *353*

SEPTEMBER 1

Gravy Soup, *21*
Fried Whiting
Anchovy Sauce, *605*
Boiled Fowl, *221*
Duchess Potatoes, *311*. Beans, *279*
Eggs baked in Tomatoes, *360*
Plum Tart, *520*
Welsh Rarebit, *346*

SEPTEMBER 2

Tapioca Cream Soup, *52*
Boiled Cod, *64*
Oyster Sauce, *614*
Chicken Croquettes and Peas, *222*
Liver à la Française, *169*
Potatoes, Cabbage
Maltese Pudding, *591*
Cheese Croûtons, *418*

SEPTEMBER 3

American Tomato Soup, *41*
Fish Cakes, *88*
Boiled Calf's Head, *171*
Brain Sauce
Potatoes, Beans
Cauliflower au Gratin, *292*
Brown Bread Pudding, *472*
Chutney Toast, *372*

SEPTEMBER 4

Mock Turtle Soup, *24*
Fillets of Plaice Bohemienne, *71*
Roast Partridge, *235*
Bread Sauce, *638*
Potato Chips, *266*. Salad, *318*
Macaroni à l'Italienne, *419*
Madeira Pudding, *473*
Bombay Toast, *371*

SEPTEMBER 5

Celery Soup, *31*
Scalloped Eggs, *352*
Mutton Cutlets, *159*
Tomato Sauce, *628*
Zephires of Game à la Chasseur, *261*
Potato Croquettes, *265*. Salad, *318*
Cup Puddings, *482*
Cheese d'Artois, *413*

SEPTEMBER 6

Consommé Brunoise, *4*
Boiled Haddock
Egg Sauce, *607*
Roast Hare, *236*
Potatoes, Brussels Sprouts
Braised Celery, *289*
Marquise Pudding, *582*
Savoury Semolina, *347*

SEPTEMBER 7

Hare Soup, *25*
Lobster Cutlets, *81*
Boiled Leg of Mutton
Caper Sauce, *606*
Potatoes, Carrots and Turnips
Riz au Chou, *378*
Sponge Pudding, *485*
Sardine Cigarettes, *395*

SEPTEMBER 8

Barley Cream Soup, *39*
Fillets of Whiting with Shrimps, *120*
Stewed Veal and Rice, *163*
Mutton Collops and Tomato Sauce, *215*
Mashed Potatoes, Beans
Plum Tart, *520*
Baked Custard
Cheese Aigrettes, *342*

SEPTEMBER 9

Potato Purée, *13*
Œufs à la Norfolk, *404*
Irish Stew, *155*
Grilled Steak and Chips, *137*
Savoury Cabbage, *308*
Bachelor's Pudding, *476*
Sardines à la Royal, *376*

SEPTEMBER 10

Julienne Soup, *47*
Boiled Halibut
Shrimp Sauce, *610*
Roast Fillet of Veal, *162*
Boiled Bacon, *181*
Potatoes, Cabbage
Savoury Macaroni, *349*
Viennoise Pudding, *464*
Cheese

SEPTEMBER 11

Tomato Purée, *29*
Fish Croquettes, *93*
Stewed Ox Kidney and Macaroni, *141*
Cold Veal
Ham and Egg Salad, *336*
Potatoes Lyonnaise, *310*
Orleans Pudding, *466*
Cheese Straws, *339*

SEPTEMBER 12

Hollandaise Soup, *53*
Sole à la Turque, *73*
Roast Fowl, *220*
Bacon
Potatoes, Artichokes, *282*
Risotto à l'Italienne, *379*
Macaroon Tarts, *524*
Sardines on Toast, *374*

SEPTEMBER 13

Gravy Soup, *21*
Scalloped Oysters, *103*
Curried Fowl and Rice, *191*
Mutton Cutlets, *159*
Stewed Onions, *275*
Spanish Puffs, *530*
Cheese Pudding, *340*

SEPTEMBER 14

Almond Soup, *33*
Grilled Cod Steaks
Anchovy Sauce, *605*
Roast Shoulder of Mutton
Onion Sauce, *609*
Baked Potatoes
Celery à l'Italienne, *303*
Raisin Pudding, *431*
Spanish Rice, *403*

SEPTEMBER 15

Kidney Soup, *20*
Sole à la Florentine, 77
Mutton Olives, *214*
Beef Steak and Tomato Pie, *204*
Cauliflower, *291*
French Pancakes, *586*
Marrow Toasts, *416*

SEPTEMBER 16

Purée of Lentils, *9*
Stuffed and Baked Fillets of Plaice, *70*
Roast Pork, *179*
Apple Sauce, *629*
Stewed Partridges, *257*
Potatoes, Beans
Savoury Cabbage, *308*
Conservative Pudding, *600*
Cheese and Celery

SEPTEMBER 17

Vegetable Marrow Soup, *17*
Fried Whiting
Anchovy Sauce, *605*
Pork Cutlets, *217*
Tomato Sauce
Roast Sheep's Heart, *154*
Potatoes. Mashed Turnips, *271*
Cocoanut Cream, *456*
Œufs au Fromage, *35*

SEPTEMBER 18

Brown Vegetable Soup, *18*
Boiled Mackerel, *65*
Fennel Sauce, *612*
Roast Beef, *129*
Horseradish Sauce, *633*
Baked Potatoes. Leeks, *285*
Yorkshire Pudding
Canary Pudding, *475*
Anchovy Biscuits, *393*

SEPTEMBER 19

Rice Cream Soup, *38*
Stuffed and Baked Haddock, *68*
Grilled Mutton Cutlets and Tomatoes
Cold Beef
Potatoes Sauté, *267*
Beetroot and Celery Salad, *324*
Riz au Chou, *378*
Orange Roll, *434*
Chutney Toast, *372*

SEPTEMBER 20

Macaroni Soup, *40*
Sole Portugaise, *76*
Haricot Mutton, *157*
Potatoes, Brussels Sprouts
Stuffed Vegetable Marrow, *287*
Plum Tart, *520*
Custard, *657* or *658*
Cheese Fritters, *392*

SEPTEMBER 21

Tomato Purée, *29*
Whitebait, *87*
Brown Bread and Butter
Beef Steak and Kidney Pudding, *131*
Stewed Celery, *289*
Pineapple Pudding, *535*
Cheese Omelet, *345*

SEPTEMBER 22

Potato Soup, *13*
Fried Sole à la Colbert, *84*
Grilled Steak, *137*
Boiled Rabbit, 240
Onion Sauce, *609*. Potato Chips, *266*
Savoury Macaroni, *349*
Tartlets, *521*
Caramel Custard, *541*
Cheese

SEPTEMBER 23

Rabbit Soup, *26*
Boiled Turbot, *66*
Lobster Sauce, *613*
Roast Leg of Mutton
Baked Potatoes. Cabbage
Stuffed Tomatoes, *297*
Lemon Pudding, *471*
Cheese Aigrettes, *342*

SEPTEMBER 24

Purée of Brussels Sprouts, *35*
Fish Curry, *91*
Boiled Fowl, *221*. Parsley Sauce, *608*
Mutton Fritters, *216*
Duchess Potatoes, *311*
Cauliflower au Gratin, *292*
Chocolate Mould, *453*
Sardine Cigarettes, *395*

SEPTEMBER 25

Celery Soup, *31*
Grilled Herrings, *101*
Chicken Croquettes, *222*
Jugged Hare, *237*
Potatoes, Beans
Marquise Pudding, *582*
Cheese Straws, *339*

SEPTEMBER 26

Hare Soup, *25*
Fillets of Whiting à la Mornay, *119*
Boiled Mutton
Caper Sauce, *606*
Veal Cutlets and Bacon, *164*
Sauté Potatoes, *267*
Damson Tart, *520*
Custard, *657*
Cheese and Celery Savouries, *421*

SEPTEMBER 27

Scotch Broth, *8*
Lobster Cutlets, *81*
Stewed Steak, *132*
Mutton Collops and Tomato Sauce, *215*
Potatoes, Brussels Sprouts
Manchester Pudding, *540*
Savoury Omelet, *367*

SEPTEMBER 28

Clear Soup, *4*
Fillets of Plaice Bohemienne, *71*
Roast Duck, *228*
Apple Sauce, *629*
Potatoes, Mashed Turnips, *271*
Braised Celery, *289*
Maltese Pudding, *591*
Rice Fritters, *412*

SEPTEMBER 29

Palestine Soup, *30*
Boiled Cod, *64*
Oyster Sauce, *614*
Roast Fillet of Veal, *162*
Boiled Ham, *181*
Salmi of Duck
Potatoes, Beans
Peach Fritters, *489*
Cheese Croûtons, *418*

SEPTEMBER 30

Mock Hare Soup, *22*
Fish Pie, *89*
Fillets of Beef à la Viennoise, *199*
Cold Veal and Ham
Nut Salad, *331*
Scalloped Tomatoes, *663*
Rum Omelet, *492*
Cheese and Celery

OCTOBER 1

Jenny Lind Soup, *50*
Sole au Vin Blanc, *115*
Roast Venison, *262*
Red Current Jelly.
Potatoes, Cabbage
Stewed Lentils, *304*
Damson Pudding, *422*
Cheese Aigrettes, *342*

OCTOBER 2

Clear Soup, *4*
Oyster Patties, *248*
Curry of Veal and Rice, *165*
Hashed Venison
Scalloped Artichokes, *284*
Queen of Puddings, *443*
Cheese Pyramids, *344*

OCTOBER 3

Oyster Soup, *28*
Eggs à la Norfolk, *404*
Chicken à la Marengo, *225*
Potatoes Duchesse, *311*
Macaroni à l'Italienne, *419*
Preserved Ginger Pudding, *468*
Sardines on Toast, *374*

OCTOBER 4

Brown Vegetable Soup, *18*
Boiled Halibut
Hollandaise Sauce, *618* or *619*
Fillets of Beef à la Pompadour, *146*
Savoury Cabbage, *308*
Swiss Apple Pudding
Cheese Omelet, *345*

OCTOBER 5

Oxtail Soup, *27*
Fricassée of Fish, *92*
Roast Pheasant, *233*
Bread Sauce, *638*
Potato Chips, *266*. Salad, *318*
Spinach and Poached Eggs, *290*
Sago Soufflé, *478*
Welsh Rarebit, *346*

OCTOBER 6

Windsor Soup, *57*
Fried Smelts, *83*
Tomato Sauce, *628*
Boiled Leg of Mutton
Caper Sauce, *606*
Salmi of Pheasant, *234*
Potatoes
Banana Charlotte, *588*
Macaroni Cheese, *337*

OCTOBER 7

Scotch Broth, *8*
Baked Red Mullet, *102*
Beef Olives, *139*
Gateau of Cold Meat, *198*
Potato Croquettes, *265*
Cauliflower, *291*
Raspberry Pudding, *469*
Sardine à la Suisse, *409*

OCTOBER 8

Kidney Soup, *20*
Stuffed Herrings, *69*
Potato straws. Boiled Rabbit, *240*
French Beans. Parsley Sauce, *608*
Mutton Cutlets Reforme, *160*
Damson Tart, *520*
Custard, *657* or *658*
Roes on Toast, *408*

OCTOBER 9

Vegetable Marrow Soup, *17*
Whitebait, *87*
Brown Bread and Butter
Horseradish Sauce, *633*
Yorkshire Pudding. Roast Beef, *129*
Brussels Sprouts, *273*
Spinach Omelet, *669*
Caramel Custard, *541*
Cheese

OCTOBER 10

Gravy Soup, *21*
Sole à la Florentine, *77*
Veal Cutlets and Mushrooms, *164*
Cold Beef
Mashed Potatoes. Nut Salad, *331*
Beresford Pudding, *467*
Swiss Eggs, *359*

OCTOBER 11

Haricot Soup, *11*
Fried Fillets of Plaice, *80*
Anchovy Sauce, *605*
Compôte of Pigeons, *254*
Cauliflower, *291*
French Pancakes, *586*
Cheese Pudding, *340*

OCTOBER 12

Mock Hare Soup, *22*
Boiled Cod, *64*
Egg Sauce, *607*
Roast Shoulder of Mutton
Onion Sauce, *609*
Potatoes, Cabbage
Stewed Celery, *289*
Half Pay Pudding, *439*
Macaroni Cutlets, *350*

OCTOBER 13

Celery Soup, *31*
Fish Cakes, *88*
Grilled Steak à la Russe, *202*
Curried Mutton, *191*
Potato Chips, *266*
Vegetable Marrow, *286*
Damson Pudding, *422*
Cheese Ramakins, *414*

OCTOBER 14

Clear Soup, *4*
Fillets of Sole à l'Americaine, *118*
Roast Pheasant, *233*
Bread Sauce, *638*
Potatoes, French Beans
Savoury Vegetable Marrow, *307*
Nelson Pudding, *602*
Sardines on Toast, *374*

OCTOBER 15

Tomato Purée, *29*
Mackerel à la Normande, *78*
Rissoles of Pheasant, *194*
Veal à la Reine, *211*
Duchess Potatoes, *311*
Scalloped Artichokes, *284*
Apple and Cranberry Tart, *520*
Anchovy Toasts

OCTOBER 16

Purée of Brussels Sprouts, *35*
Eggs à la Norwegienne, *405*
Beef Steak and Kidney Pudding, *131*
Curried Potatoes, *377*
Stuffed Tomatoes, *297*
Pancakes, *487*
Water-Lily Savoury, *388*

OCTOBER 17

Rabbit Soup, *26*
Grilled Herrings, *101*
Mustard Sauce, *615*
Boiled Fowl, *221*
Sausages
Potatoes, Cabbage
Macaroni à la Milanaise, *348*
Apple Charlotte, *544*
Cheese and Celery Savouries, *421*

OCTOBER 18

Giblet Soup, *45*
Scalloped Oysters, *103*
Rissoles à la Pompadour, *364*
Haricot Mutton, *157*
Potatoes. Leeks, *285*
Spanish Rice, *403*
Cup Puddings, *482*
Chutney Toast, *372*

OCTOBER 19

Brown Vegetable Soup, *18*
Haddock à la St Clair, *97*
Roast Loin of Veal, *162*
Boiled Ham, *181*
Potatoes, Beans
Cauliflower au Gratin, *292*
Marmalade Pudding, *428*
Anchovy Biscuits, *393*

OCTOBER 20

Parisian Soup, *48*
Fried Sole Knots, *85*
Tartare Sauce, *637*
Mutton Cutlets and Spinach, *159*
Cold Veal and Ham
Mashed Potatoes. Nut Salad, *331*
Conservative Pudding, *600*
Cheese Croûtons, *418*

OCTOBER 21

Haricot Soup, *11*
Boiled Haddock
Egg Sauce, *607*
Roast Duck, *228*
Apple Sauce, *629*
Minced Veal, *170*
Potatoes. Artichokes, *282*
Sweet Omelet, *491*
Cheese Balls, *341*

OCTOBER 22

Tomato Purée, *29*
Fried Cod's Roe, *363*
Piquante Sauce, *624*
Fillets of Beef à la Pompadour, *146*
Salmi of Duck
Savoury Vegetable Marrow, *307*
Madeira Pudding, *473*
Cheese Pyramids, *344*

OCTOBER 23

Kidney Soup, *20*
Fried Fillets of Plaice, *80*
Anchovy Sauce, *605*
Boiled Mutton. Caper Sauce, *606*
Potatoes, Carrots, Turnips
Savoury Macaroni, *349*
Apple Tart, *520*
Cheese

OCTOBER 24

Scotch Broth, *8*
Oyster Patties, *248*
Grilled Steak, *137*
Mutton Collops and Tomato Sauce, *215*
Lyonnaise Potatoes, *310*
Spinach, *290*
Viennoise Pudding, *464*
Chutney Toast, *372*

OCTOBER 25

Windsor Soup, *57*
Lobster Cutlets, *81*
Roast Partridges, *235*
Bread Sauce, *638*
Potato Chips. Beans
Scalloped Artichokes, *284*
Honey Comb Mould, *463*
Cheese Pudding, *340*

OCTOBER 26

Clear Soup, *4*
Sole Parmesan, *75*
Jugged Hare, *237*
Potatoes. Celery, *289*
Stuffed Tomatoes, *297*
Canary Pudding, *475*
Ham Croûtes à l'Italienne, *420*

OCTOBER 27

Hare Soup, *25*
Boiled Cod, *64*
Oyster Sauce, *614*
Stewed Veal and Rice, *163*
Grilled Cutlets
Mashed Potatoes
Cauliflower in Batter, *293*
Pineapple Pudding, *535*
Cheese and Celery

OCTOBER 28

Potato Purée, *13*
Fish Cakes, *88*
Boiled Calf's Head, *171*
Brain Sauce
Potatoes, Cabbage
Vegetable Pie, *314*
Swiss Apple Pudding
Savoury Biscuits, *670*

OCTOBER 29

Mock Turtle Soup, *24*
Fillets of Whiting with Shrimps, *120*
Boiled Pork
Onion Sauce, *609*
Liver à la Française, *169*
Potatoes, Brussels Sprouts
Lemon Cheese Cakes, *522*
Macaroni à la Milanaise, *348*

OCTOBER 30

White Vegetable Soup, *14*
Sole à la Colbert, *84*
Stuffed and Baked Loin of Mutton, *152*
Potatoes, Mashed Turnips
Curried Lentils, *305*
Damson Pudding, *422*
Cheese and Celery Savouries, *421*

OCTOBER 31

Palestine Soup, *30*
Fillets of Plaice Bohemienne, *71*
Roast Fowl, *220*
Sausages
Potato Chips, *266*
Braised Celery, *289*
Maltese Pudding, *591*
Savoury Semolina, *347*

NOVEMBER 1

Carrot Soup, *15*
Sole à la Crème, *114*
Saddle of Mutton
Roast Potatoes. Boiled Chestnuts, *299*
Sprouts and Cheese, *400*
Marmalade Pudding, *428*
Anchovy Eggs, *351*

NOVEMBER 2

Oxtail Soup, *27*
Mutton Fritters, *216*
Roast Fowl, *220*
Bread Sauce, *638*
Potato Chips, *266*
Sahara Salad, *334*
Rice Soufflé, *556*
Cheese Croûtons, *418*

NOVEMBER 3

Mulligatawny Soup, *23*
Fillets of Turbot
Sauce Italienne, *626*
Chicken Croquettes, *222*
Potato Soufflé, *312*
Almond Pudding, *557*
Swiss Eggs, *359*

NOVEMBER 4

Purée of Brussels Sprouts, *35*
Dressed Crab, *100*
Fillets of Beef à la Béarnaise, *200*
Artichokes, *282*
Bombe of Fruits, *561*
Rice and Cheese, *338*

NOVEMBER 5

Almond Soup, *33*
Fried Whiting
Anchovy Sauce, *605*
Roast Hare, *236*
Potatoes, Chicory
Canary Pudding, *475*
Cheese Biscuits, *402*

NOVEMBER 6

Celery Soup, *31*
Devilled Shrimps, *386*
Ragoût of Hare
Boiled Neck of Mutton
Caper Sauce, *606*
Potatoes. Cauliflower, *291*
Banana Pudding, *563*
Cheese

NOVEMBER 7

Scotch Broth, *8*
Fried Smelts, *83*
Tomato Sauce, *628*
Liver à la Française, *169*
Grilled Pheasant, *256*
Celeriac Salad
Chestnut Cream, *569*
Sardines on Toast, *374*

NOVEMBER 8

Rice Cream Soup, *38*
Angels on Horseback, *410*
Roast Beef, *129*
Baked Potatoes, Carrots
Yorkshire Pudding
College Puddings, *567*
Celery and Cheese Savouries, *421*

NOVEMBER 9

Clear Soup, *4*
Curried Lentils, *305*
Boiled Fowl, *221*
Celery Sauce, *611*
Potatoes, Brussels Sprouts
Apples and Rice, *559*
Sardines à la Suisse, *409*

NOVEMBER 10

Mock Turtle Soup, *24*
Sole Bohemienne, *71*
Mutton Cutlets à la Nelson, *212*
Poulet à la Sefton, *224*
Spinach and Cheese, *399*
Bishop's Pudding, *572*
Anchovy Straws, *393*

NOVEMBER 11

Tomato Purée, *29*
Curried Eggs, *358*
Beef Olives, *139*
Fried Sweetbreads, *176*
Duchess Potatoes, *311*
Apple Charlotte, *544*
Cheese Croûtons, *418*

NOVEMBER 12

Chestnut Soup, *36*
Boiled Skate
Shrimp Sauce, *610*
Rabbit Pie, *243*
Cauliflower au Gratin, *292*
Chocolate Pudding, *470*
Bombay Toast, *371*

NOVEMBER 13

Parisian Soup, *48*
Sole au Gratin, *74*
Stewed Steak and Vegetables, *132*
Potatoes. Artichokes, *282*
Prune Pudding, *571*
Macaroni Cheese, *337*

NOVEMBER 14

Mock Hare Soup, *22*
Boiled Cod, *64*
Oyster Sauce, *614.* Roast Grouse, *238*
Potato Chips, *266.* Salad, *318*
Snowden Pudding, *558*
Cream Cheese

NOVEMBER 15

Game Soup, *61*
Spinach and Poached Eggs, *290*
Beef Collops, *144*
Potatoes. Stewed Onions, *275*
Bachelor's Pudding, *476*
Ham Toast, *373*

NOVEMBER 16

Tapioca Cream Soup, *52*
Lobster Cutlets, *81*
Haricot Mutton, *157*
Fried Potato. Mashed Turnips, *271*
Bakewell Pudding, *534*
Kidney Omelet, *369*

NOVEMBER 17

Barley Cream Soup, *39*
Baked Red Mullet, *102*
Chicken à la Marengo, *225*
Cauliflower, *291*
Chelmsford Pudding, *440*
Herring Roes on Toast, *408*

NOVEMBER 18

Chervil Soup, *60*
Egg Croquettes, *354*
Raised Game Pie, *260*
Braised Celery, *289*
Spanish Fritters, *589*
Chutney Toast, *372*

NOVEMBER 19

American Tomato Soup, *41*
Herring Sauté, *123*
Veal Cutlets à la Milanaise, *210*
Tomatoes and Eggs, *387*
Brown Bread Pudding, *472*
Savoury Omelet, *367*

NOVEMBER 20

Boiled Turbot, *66*
Lobster Sauce, *613*
Scalloped Salsify, *284*
Roast Pheasant, *233*
Potato Chips, *266.* Bread Sauce, *638*
Banana Trifle, *555*
Welsh Rarebit, *346*

NOVEMBER 21

Game Soup, *61*
Timbales of Haddock Genoise, *382*
Roast Shoulder of Mutton
Baked Potatoes. Onion Sauce, *609*
Cauliflower au Gratin, *292*
Orleans Pudding, *466*
Foie-Gras in Pastry, *385*

NOVEMBER 22

Kidney Soup, *20*
Lobster au Gratin, *96*
Stewed Rabbit, *242*
Potatoes. Savoury Cabbage, *308*
Pineapple Pudding, *535*
Cheese Aigrettes, *342*

NOVEMBER 23

Rabbit Soup, *26*
Curried Eggs, *358*
Stuffed and Stewed Steak, *140*
Potato Straws. Parsnips, *281*
Baroness Pudding, *560*
Devilled Almonds

NOVEMBER 24

Hollandaise Soup, *53*
Fish Cakes, *88*
Roast Duck, *228*
Potato Chips, *266.* Apple Sauce, *629*
Salad, *318*
Lemon Pudding, *471*
Œufs Norwegienne, *405*

NOVEMBER 25

Purée of Brussels Sprouts, *35*
Grilled Herrings, *101*
Mustard Sauce, *615*
Minced Duck and Tomatoes, *252*
Mutton Cutlets, *159*
Spinach, *290*
Cup Puddings, *482*
Sardines à la Suisse, *409*

NOVEMBER 26

French Cheese Soup, *37*
Sole au Gratin, *74*
Roast Beef, *129*
Baked Potatoes. Artichokes, *282*
Yorkshire Pudding
Maltese Pudding, *591*
Anchovy Biscuits, *393*

NOVEMBER 27

Tomato Purée, *29*
Fillets of Whiting à la Mornay, *119*
Curry of Cold Meat, *191*
Liver à la Française, *169*
Sweet Omelet, *491*
Cheese and Celery Savouries, *421*

NOVEMBER 28

Soubise Soup, *12*
Grilled Mackerel, *127*
Hollandaise Sauce, *618*
Roast Partridge, *235*
Bread Sauce, *638*
Potato Chips, *266*
Scalloped Artichokes, *284*
Viennoise Pudding, *464*
Savoury Semolina, *347*

NOVEMBER 29

Potato Soup, *13*
Fried Plaice, *80*
Anchovy Sauce, *605*
Stewed Steak, *132*
Potatoes
Cauliflower in Batter, *293*
Stuffed Tomatoes, *297*
Preserved Ginger Pudding, *468*
Cheese Biscuits, *402*

NOVEMBER 30

Celery Soup, *31*
Sole à la Florentine, *77*
Beef Steak and Kidney Pudding, *131*
Brussels Sprouts and Cheese, *400*
Monk's Pudding, *445*
Anchovy Toast

DECEMBER 1

Potage à la Royale, *55*
Scallops of Egg, *352*
Game Pie, *259*
Artichokes, *282*
Brown Bread Pudding, *472*
Canapés Fumés, *389*

DECEMBER 2

White Lentil Soup, *56*
Sole Gascoyne, *113*
Jugged Hare, *237*
Potatoes. Stewed Celery, *289*
Princess Pudding, *568*
Savoury Eggs, *397*

DECEMBER 3

Carrot Soup, *15*
Dressed Cod, *105*
Savoury Rolled Steak, *140*
Potatoes. Stewed Lentils, *304*
Liverpool Pudding, *427*
Macaroni Cheese, *337*

DECEMBER 4

Purée à la Reine, *46*
Sole à la Crème, *114*
Beef Steak and Kidney Pie, *133*
Potatoes. Kale
Chocolate Soufflé, *481*
Savoury Biscuits, *670*

DECEMBER 9

Mulligatawny Soup, *23*
Rice
Lobster Cutlets, *81*
Roast Fowl, *220*
Sausages. Potato Chips, *266*
Salad, *318*
Dutch Apple Pudding, *528*
Parmesan Soufflé, *343*

DECEMBER 5

Windsor Soup, *57*
Kedgeree, *94*
Casserole of Cold Meat, *218*
Veal Cutlets à la Française, *205*
Mashed Potatoes, Brussels Sprouts
Monk's Pudding, *445*
Cheese and Celery Biscuits, *421*

DECEMBER 10

Hollandaise Soup, *53*
Sole Maître d'Hôtel, *72*
Chicken Croquettes and Peas, *222*
Potatoes. Sea-kale, *288*
Queen of Puddings, *443*
Canapés Fumés, *389*

DECEMBER 6

Sole à la Bohemienne, *71*
Sea-kale, *288*
Roast Leg of Mutton
Baked Potatoes. Boiled Chestnuts, *299*
French Raisin Pudding, *477*
Anchovy Eggs, *351*

DECEMBER 7

Chestnut Soup, *36*
Stuffed and Baked Fillets of Plaice, *70*
Grilled Steak, *137*
Potato Chips, *266*. Winter Salad, *325*
Apple Pudding, *422*
Cheese Custard, *390*

DECEMBER 11

Steamed Fish Pudding, *125*
Curried Lentils, *305*
Roast Hare, *236*
Potatoes, Cabbage
Vanille Soufflé, *479*
Kidney Toast, *370*

DECEMBER 8

Macaroni Soup, *40*
Boiled Cod, *64*. Oyster Sauce, *614*
Beef Steak Pudding, *131*
Potatoes, Scotch Kale
Viennoise Pudding, *464*
Savoury Omelet, *367*

DECEMBER 12

Hare Soup, *25*
Fried Fillets of Plaice, *80*
Anchovy Sauce, *605*
Mutton Cutlets à la Réforme, *160*
Potatoes. Salsify, *283*
French Pancakes, *586*
Bombay Toast, *371*

DECEMBER 13

Lobster au Gratin, *96*
Cauliflower in Batter, *293*
Roast Beef, *129*
Horseradish Sauce
Baked Potatoes
Brussels Sprouts
Yorkshire Pudding
Chestnut Cream, *569*
Cheese

DECEMBER 14

Lentil Soup, *9*
Boiled Mackerel, *65*
Fennel Sauce, *612*
Curry of Cold Meat, *191*
Cabbage, Rice
Rum Omelet, *492*
Savoury Semolina, *347*

DECEMBER 15

Gravy Soup, *21*
Scalloped Eggs, *352*
Roast Pheasant, *233*
Bread Sauce, *638*
Potato Chips, *266*
Salad, *318*
Pineapple Snow, *543*
Macaroni à la Milanaise, *348*

DECEMBER 16

Game Soup, *61*
Boiled Cod, *64*
Egg Sauce, *607*
Stewed Steak, *132*
Potatoes, Greens
Madeira Pudding, *473*
Welsh Rarebit, *346*

DECEMBER 17

Oyster Soup, *28*
Scotch Eggs, *357*
Beef Steak and Kidney Pie, *133*
Boiled Celery, *289*
Beresford Pudding, *467*
Farced Olives, *391*

DECEMBER 18

Purée of Turnips, *58*
Boiled Brill
Shrimp Sauce, *610*
Roast Grouse, *238*
Potato Straws, *266*. Stuffed Tomatoes, *297*
Cup Puddings, *482*
Ham Omelet, *368*

DECEMBER 19

Purée of Brussels Sprouts, *35*
Cod à la Provençale, *106*
Egg Croquettes, *354*
Salmi of Grouse
Coffee Cream, *501*
Caviare

DECEMBER 20

Kale Brose, *59*
Fish Pie, *89*
Boiled Fowl, *221*
Ham Sauce
Potatoes, Cabbage
Apple Tart, *520*
Sardines à la Royal, *376*

DECEMBER 21

Tomato Purée, *29*
Sole au Gratin, *74*
Devilled Chicken, *249*
Stewed Veal and Rice, *163*
Potatoes
Beignets Soufflé, *570*
Cheese and Celery Savouries, *421*

DECEMBER 22

Mock Turtle Soup, *24*
Halibut Steaks
Tartare Sauce, *637*
Roast Duck, *228*
Apple Sauce, *629*
Potatoes. Mashed Turnips, *271*
Fig Pudding, *432* or *433*
Cheese Croûtons, *418*

DECEMBER 23

Celery Soup, *31*
Fried Smelts, *83*
Tomato Sauce, *628*
Duck au Gratin, *253*
Mashed Potatoes, Kale
Charlotte Russe, *510*
Swiss Eggs, *359*

DECEMBER 24

Brown Vegetable Soup, *18*
Fillets of Whiting with Shrimps, *120*
Stewed Partridges, *257*
Brussels Sprouts. Potato Chips, *266*
Chocolate Pudding, *470*
Cheese d'Artois, *413*

DECEMBER 25

Clear Soup, *4*
Boiled Halibut
Lobster Sauce, *613*
Roast Turkey, *229*
Sausages
Potatoes, Brussels Sprouts
Christmas Pudding, *436*
Guard's Sauce, *661*
Mince Pies, *529*
Cheese Straws, *339*

DECEMBER 26

Gravy Soup, *21*
Scallops of Fish, *90*
Roast Goose, *228*
Apple Sauce, *629*
Potatoes, Cabbage
Bachelor's Pudding, *476*
Mince Pies, *529*
Cheese Ramakins, *414*

DECEMBER 27

White Vegetable Soup, *14*
Sole au Vin blanc, *115*
Ragoût of Turkey
Potatoes. Haricot Beans, *280*
Orange Roll, *434*
Mince Pies, *529*
Savoury Biscuits, *670*

DECEMBER 28

Grilled Cod Steaks
Stewed Lentils, *304*
Salmi of Goose
Potatoes. Cauliflower au Gratin, *282*
Trifle, *548*
Meringues, *554*
Cheese and Celery

DECEMBER 29

Purée of Brussels Sprouts, *35*
Boiled Haddock
Egg Sauce, *607*
Jugged Hare, *237*
Potatoes Sauté, *267*
Forcemeat Balls
Savoury Cabbage, *308*
Preserved Ginger Pudding, *468*
Cheese Gondoles, *417*

DECEMBER 30

Hare Soup, *25*
Sole au Parmesan, *75*
Sea Pie, *134*
Mutton Cutlets à la Nelson, *212*
Apple Tart, *520*
Baked Custard Pudding
Roes on Toast, *408*

DECEMBER 31

Brown Vegetable Soup, *18*
Fish Curry, *91*
Rice
Pheasant en Cocotte, *255*
Potato Chips, *266*
Poached Eggs and Spinach, *290*
Sweet Omelet, *491*
Cheese and Celery

PART II

BASIC GUIDELINES

METHODS OF COOKING

BOILING

Boiling is one of the simplest and most common forms of cooking food. To boil with success plenty of time must be allowed. To use the expression to *boil* with regard to meat is misleading, as after the first five minutes it must simmer only, and not boil. The object is to soften the fibres of the meat and to retain all its nourishing juices; this can only be accomplished by hardening or coagulating the albumen on the outside of the meat, to prevent the juices escaping. This takes place during the first five minutes' boiling. The temperature must then be reduced and the meat simmered gently until cooked (boiling-point of liquid is 212°F, 100°C; simmering-point 180°F, 90°C.)

Both fresh and salt meat are boiled. Fresh meat must be put into boiling water and salt meat into tepid water. This draws out some of the salt.

The time for boiling meat depends on the size, shape and quality. A rough guide is fifteen minutes to the pound (0.5 kg) and fifteen minutes over. For salt and immature meat (veal and lamb) twenty minutes to the pound (0.5 kg) and twenty minutes over. For pork twenty-five minutes must be allowed. The liquor fresh meat is boiled in should be saved for the stock-pot; that in which salt meat has been boiled is usually too rank for use. Always keep the lid on the pan when boiling meat and skim well.

Fish must be carefully boiled. The size, shape and quality must be taken into consideration, as in boiling meat. As a rule six minutes to every pound (0.5 kg) and six minutes over is sufficient; but very large cod, turbot, salmon, etc., will take as much as ten minutes. All white fish must be put into water well below boiling-point with salt and vinegar or lemon juice. Allow 2 oz (50 g) salt and 2 tablespoons vinegar to every gallon (4.5 litres) of water.

There are different methods for different fish. Salmon is put into boiling water to set the curd between the flakes, and then reduced to a lower temperature. No vinegar is added, as this draws out the colour. Mackerel is put into tepid water and must cook very gently or the skin will crack and its appearance be spoiled.

Plenty of water must be used when boiling green vegetables, with 1 oz (25 g) salt to each gallon (4.5 litres) of water and a small quantity of carbonate of soda to keep the colour. The lid must always be left off the pan, and the scum removed as it rises. The coarsest kinds of green vegetables, such as cabbage, must be boiled quickly; delicate vegetables, such as peas, asparagus, cauliflower, etc., must be boiled gently. Root vegetables must be cooked slowly with the lid on the pan, and be well skimmed. Salt must be added in the same proportion as for green vegetables, and all roots and tubers are put into boiling water except old potatoes, which are put into cold water. When boiling a pudding, allow plenty of water to cover it, and it must boil rapidly all the time. A kettle should always be kept boiling near at hand, to replenish as the water boils away. The basin or mould must be quite full and well greased to ensure success in turning out. A piece of buttered paper should be put over the pudding before tying on the cloth. If a cloth only is used, and no basin, it must be well scalded and floured.

ROASTING

Roasting in front of the fire. 1 – Roasting is nicest when done in front of the fire. The flavour is superior to that roasted in any other way. It is an extravagant method of cooking meat, as only prime joints are suitable and a large fire is needed.

2 *In the oven* – This is termed also baking and is the more usual method in these days.

It is advisable to turn a joint at least once when roasting in the oven. The gravy should be made in the tin, first pouring off the dripping, and then poured *round* the meat, not *over* it, or the crispness will be destroyed.

STEWING

Stewing is cooking in a small quantity of liquid in a closed vessel for a long time. It is an economical method because by it the toughest meat can be rendered tender, digestible and savoury; but success cannot be attained without long slow cooking. Another advantage to a busy housewife is that a stew requires little attention and little fuel.

There are two ways – 1 *On the stove*; 2 *In the oven*.

In both cases the vessel in which the stew is cooked must be covered closely.

Contrary to boiling, where the meat is plunged into boiling water to close the pores and retain the juices, a stew is made with cold or tepid liquid to draw out some of the juices, which with the added liquid form the gravy which is served with it. Meat is often lightly fried or seared before it is stewed. This prevents all the juices going into the gravy and makes the stew more savoury and a better colour. Meat can be stewed either in a thick or a thin liquid. If good meat is used, it is better to put it in already thickened gravy. The colour of the stew will be better as the thickening medium or liaison is flour and that is browned. In this way all the trouble is over at first, a great point when time is an object. If tough and inferior meat is used, it is better to stew it in a thin liquid. It penetrates and softens the meat better than a thick gravy. A little vinegar added softens the fibres of tough meat. The liquid of a stew should never boil during the whole process, only simmer very gently; and to make a stew successfully it must not be hurried. Long slow cooking is essential. The disadvantage of stewing is that it is rich, and cannot be digested by some people. Meat, fish, vegetables and fruit can be cooked by this method.

STEAMING

Steaming is cooking by moist heat or heated vapour rising from boiling water. It is a slower process than boiling, and is especially useful in invalid cookery because the cooking though slow is thorough and the loss of nutritive properties of the food, as well as flavour, is less than by boiling.

Steaming can be done in various ways. A proper steamer (with holes to admit the steam) can be fitted to a saucepan. A saucepan can be converted into a steamer by having only enough water to come one-third of the way up the vessel containing what is being steamed. In both cases the pan must be closely covered, to keep in the steam. This method requires care, as the water evaporates. In that case more must be added. It is an economical way of cooking, because two things can be cooked at the same time in the same vessel. For example, a pudding can be boiled in the lower part and potatoes steamed on the top.

Meat, fish, vegetables, puddings, can all be cooked by steam; but as a rule, with the exception of a chop for an invalid, which can be cooked between two buttered plates over boiling water, steamed meat is very tasteless.

FRYING

Frying is cooking by direct contact with hot fat, and can be divided into two methods – 1 *Deep or wet frying*; 2 *Shallow or dry frying*.

Dry frying is usually adopted by the untrained English cook for everything, and if carelessly done the food is sodden with fat, most unwholesome and highly indigestible. The fat is seldom of use afterwards, as it quickly becomes burnt and discoloured. It has its advantages, however, and is useful for food that requires slow and thorough cooking, such as sausages, cutlets, liver and bacon, kidneys, potatoes, etc. This method is also called sautéing. A small quantity of fat should be put into a frying or sauté pan and heated until a faint blue smoke rises before the frying is commenced. Frequent turning is necessary to prevent the food from becoming hard or burnt.

Deep frying is the French method and is best adapted for fish, rissoles, croquettes, fritters, etc., because the material for rissoles, etc., usually requires reheating only. All food that is fried in deep fat must have a coating either of egg and bread crumbs, flour and milk, or batter. This prevents the juices coming out into the fat, spoiling both the food and the fat. A proper frying bath is necessary to carry out this method successfully; for an ordinary household it must be large enough to take 2 or 3 lb (1–1.5 kg) of fat; the best being a mixture of beef and mutton fat rendered down. A frying basket is a great advantage, but not an absolute necessity. It must be bought to fit the fat bath. It can be used on most occasions, but not for fritters or any food coated with batter.

The most important point is the temperature of the fat. It must be brought to the required heat slowly. There are three useful tests for telling when the fat is hot enough. 1 When a faint blue smoke rises. 2 If when a crumb of bread is dropped in bubbles form round it. 3 When it is quite still; if it bubbles it shows the presence of water. If the fat is at the correct heat the outside coating coagulates immediately and the juices and flavour cannot escape, and then the fat can be used for all kinds of food – fish, meat, sweets, cheese, savouries, etc. The fat requires replenishing and clarifying occasionally, and it must always be strained into a pan after using, and on no account be left in the fat bath till used the next time.

Too much must not be put in the fat at once. This cools it and reduces the temperature. It must be reheated between each batch of food that is put in. Everything fried should be well drained on paper to free it from all fat, otherwise it has a most unappetizing appearance.

GRILLING

Grilling is a modified form of roasting, and is the quickest method of cooking. The food to be grilled should be brushed over with oil or liquid butter before being put on the gridiron and over the fire. This method is only suitable for small pieces of meat and fish, joints of poultry and game, etc. Frequent turning is necessary. Avoid sticking in a fork or skewer when turning, as this allows the juices to escape. It is best to use two spoons. Small tongs can be bought for the purpose. A double gridiron is useful for fish, as it breaks so easily when turned. A steak for grilling should be cut thick; the outside should be well browned, and when cut into the juices should flow from the meat if properly cooked. No gravy is served with grilled meat; but frequently a pat of maître d'hôtel butter (see no 137) is put on the top. The time for cooking depends on the size and thickness of the meat. From six to eight minutes for a chop or small steak; ten to twelve minutes for a moderate-sized steak. Fish must always be well done.

Broiling is the same thing as grilling; but it is usually done in front of the fire. An advantage of grilling and broiling is that it can be done and served very quickly.

BRAISING

Braising is a combination of stewing and roasting, and is applied generally to small pieces of meat, poultry and game. It is a Continental method of cooking, especially popular in France. It is a most appetizing method, a particularly good flavour is imparted to the meat by the vegetables and herbs used.

The process is as follows: Prepare some vegetables (carrot, turnip, onion, leek, celery, tomato and herbs), cut in rough pieces and place them at the bottom of a stewpan in which is some hot fat; brown them lightly, lay on the meat, cover tightly and cook for fifteen minutes; then add enough stock to barely cover the vegetables, place a greased paper on the top, cover closely and cook till the meat is tender. The meat should be browned in the oven before dishing and the gravy reduced to a glaze and brushed over the meat.

A proper braising pan should be used if possible. These have a sunken lid in which hot coal or charcoal is placed. The meat is thus subjected to two heats – above and below. Then there is no necessity to brown the meat in the oven, as when using a stewpan.

PROPER PROPORTIONS

MILK PUDDINGS:

2 oz (50 g) cereals to 1 pint (600 ml) milk.

1 oz (25 g) semolina to 1 pint (25 g) milk.

MOULDS:

3 oz (75 g) whole cereals to 1 pint (600 ml) milk.

2 oz (50 g) ground cereals to 1 pint (600 ml) milk.

SAUCES:

1   Foundation Sauces:

2 oz (50 g) butter, 2 oz (50 g) flour to 1 pint (600 ml) liquid.

2   Thickened Gravies:

1 oz (25 g) butter, 1 oz (25 g) flour to 1 pint (600 ml) liquid.

3   Stiff Binding Mixtures (Panada):

1 oz (25 g) butter, 1 oz (25 g) flour to 1 gill (150 ml) liquid.

SOUPS:

1   Stock:

1 lb (450 g) bones or bones and meat to 1 quart (1.1 litres) cold water and 1

quart (1.1 litres) over for evaporation.

2   Thick Soups:

1 oz (25 g) flour to 1 quart (1.1 litres) soup.

1 oz (25 g) sago, rice, etc., to 1 quart (1.1 litres) soup.

3   Purées:

2 oz (50 g) butter and 2 oz (50 g) flour to 1 quart (1.1 litres) purée.

CREAMS:

1   Whole Creams:

½ oz (15 g) gelatine to 1 pint (600 ml) cream.

2   Custard and Fruit Creams:

¾ oz (20 g) gelatine to 1 pint (600 ml) cream.

JELLIES:

2 oz (50 g) gelatine to 1 quart (1.1 litres) liquid.

Aspic Jelly: 2½ oz (65 g) gelatine to 1 quart (1.1 litres) liquid.

Increase the proportion in hot weather.

CUSTARDS:

1 Plain:

2 yolks of eggs and 1 oz (25 g) cornflour to 1 pint (600 ml) milk.

2   Rich:

4 yolks of eggs to ¾ pint (450 ml) milk.

BREAD:

1 *Fermented:*

½ oz (15 g) yeast to 1 lb (450 g) flour.

1 oz (25 g) yeast to 3½ lb (1.6 kg) flour.

2 *Baking Powder Bread (unfermented):*

2 teaspoonfuls baking powder to 1 lb (450 g) flour.

PASTRY:

1 *Suet Crust:*

8 oz (225 g) suet to 1 lb (450 g) flour (good).

6 oz (175 g) suet to 1 lb (450 g) flour and 1 teaspoonful baking powder
(cheaper).

2 *Short Crust:*

8 oz (225 g) fat to 1 lb (450 g) flour.

6 oz (175 g) fat to 1 lb (450 g) flour and 1 teaspoonful baking powder.

3 *Flaky:*

10 oz (275 g) shortening to 1 lb (450 g) flour.

4 *Puff Pastry:*

1 lb (450 g) shortening to 1 lb (450 g) flour.

BATTER:

Pancake Batter:

8 oz (225 g) flour, 1 pint (600 ml) milk, 2 eggs.

More eggs and less milk for richer batter.

MARKETING HINTS

Economy should be studied when marketing. The real meaning of the word in this case is getting full value for the money spent. To achieve this always buy provisions when in season, and in exactly suitable quantities.

Store-rooms, whether for dry or fresh goods, must always be cool, dry and well-ventilated. In buying fresh goods a rule to remember is that they are best when in season. The flavour is fullest then. They are most plentiful, wholesome and nutritious, as well as cheapest; but now most things can be purchased all the year round if one can afford to pay the price for them.

MEAT

Good meat is firm and not flabby; when pressed the mark quickly disappears. There is no disagreeable smell. It should be free from moisture. To test meat put in a skewer close to the bone and if it comes out clean and smells sweet the meat is in good condition.

BEEF

The flesh should be deep red in colour, smooth grained, the lean and fat intermixed. The fat should be of a pale straw colour and somewhat soft. If very yellow it generally denotes the animal was fed on oil-cake. It is rich and greasy and wastes in cooking, but is quite wholesome.

MUTTON

The flesh of mutton should be fine grained and firm, paler in colour than beef; the fat white and firm. Mutton is finest when it is between four and five years old; but it is seldom met with.

Sheep are generally killed when between two and three years old. Mutton should be moderately fat. If very lean it will be poor in flavour and tough.

LAMB

Lamb is judged as mutton, but the flesh is paler in colour. It is best when about twelve weeks old.

VEAL

Veal should always be chosen from a small animal; if large it is coarse and tough. The flesh should be fine in grain and dry; it is not fit for food if moist and clammy. The lean should be pale pink and firm in the fibre; the fat firm and white. When buying veal two useful tests as to the condition are the state of the liver and the fat round the kidneys. The former must be clear and free from spots, and the latter firm, sweet and dry.

PORK

Pork must be more carefully chosen than any other butcher-meat. The lean of good pork is pale pink and firm; the fat white and clear; the skin thin and smooth and cool to the touch.

HAM and BACON

The fat of ham and bacon should have a clear pinky appearance; the lean firm; the rind, like the skin of good pork, should be thin. If it looks yellow and the salt is crusted on it, it should be rejected, as it will be rancid and unpalatable.

   To test a ham insert a bright steel skewer near the bone. If it comes out clean and free from any unpleasant smell it proves the ham is in good condition. On the other hand if the skewer is not clean and smells unpleasant, the ham should be rejected.

POULTRY

Always buy poultry when young, except for soup and stock. If young the breast-bone and the tips of the pinions will be pliable. If in good condition the flesh should be firm, the breast plump, and there should be some fat. If too fat the flavour is rank and the flesh greasy. Poultry should always be cooked while fresh, staleness being very objectionable and easily detected by a faint unpleasant odour.

When the flesh is discoloured or has begun to turn green it should be rejected, and it is not advisable to purchase fowls with the skin torn in plucking or the breast-bone broken. This spoils the appearance when served.

GAME

Most of the tests for the age of poultry can be applied to game; but game should always be bought in its feathers, never after it is plucked. Game is greatly improved in tenderness and flavour by hanging; it is not considered worth eating while fresh. The length of time for hanging depends on the weather and the larder. In cold dry windy weather it will keep for some weeks, according to the taste of the consumer; but if the atmosphere is moist and warm it decomposes quickly and becomes unwholesome and unfit to eat. Birds should be hung by the neck and sprinkled with pepper to keep away the flies and hung in a safe in the open air if possible.

Waterfowl, such as wild duck, snipe, teal, etc., should not hang more than a day or two. Pheasant are in season from October 1 to February 1; Partridge, September 1 to February 1; Grouse, August 12 to December 10; Blackcock, August 20 to December 10; Ptarmigan, August 12 to December 10; Hares, September 1 to March 1; Wild Duck, Teal, Snipe, Widgeon, August 1 to March 1; Buck Venison, June to September; Doe Venison, November to February.

FISH

It is most essential that fish should be fresh and in full season; it decomposes more quickly than any food. It is in best condition, most plentiful and cheapest when in season. When fish is kept on ice it is difficult to detect if it is stale; but after it has been removed it quickly loses its apparent freshness and can be judged by its smell and appearance. No one can mistake the smell of stale fish. If in good condition the flesh should be firm and plump, of a good even colour, eyes bright, gills and spots red. There are a few kinds that can be kept for a short time, such as turbot, cod and halibut; but it must be kept in a cool place in a current of air, and not in water. Fish may need soaking before cooking, but must not lie long in water, as this impoverishes the flavour and the fish becomes flabby. If fish is slimy especially fresh-water fish, rub it with dry salt, as well as thoroughly wash it. Mackerel is unfit for food unless quite fresh. Salmon is best cooked as soon as possible after it is caught. The price varies with the supply and the season.

VEGETABLES

The same rule applies as to fish and other foods. Vegetables are always best and cheapest when in season. The flavour is never so good when they are forced and are out of season.

Vegetables can never be too fresh; when stale they become unwholesome and indigestible. Absolute freshness cannot be obtained unless they are procured straight from the garden. This is impossible to those living in towns, so it is advisable to buy from a shop that has a good constant supply. Cabbage and green vegetables of all kinds should be bright in colour and crisp; a leaf or pod should break with a sharp crack when bent. If soft, flabby and a faded yellow colour they are stale.

Certain vegetables, such as cucumbers, vegetable marrows and asparagus keep fresh for a day or two if the stalks are put in water. Root vegetables are stored for winter use; but the flavour is not so good as when fresh. They must not be stored until fully ripe, and must be carefully arranged in a cool dry place and protected from the frost.

DISHES AND THEIR ACCOMPANIMENTS

FISH

BOILED COD – Oyster, Egg, or Parsley Sauce
BOILED SALT COD – Egg Sauce and Parsnips
COD'S ROE – Italian or Piquante Sauce
BOILED EELS – Parsley Sauce and Lemon
FRIED EELS – Tartare Sauce
BOILED HADDOCK – Anchovy or Egg Sauce and Lemon
GRILLED HERRINGS – Mustard Sauce
BOILED MACKEREL – Fennel, Parsley or Gooseberry Sauce
OYSTERS – Cut Brown Bread and Butter and Lemon
PLAICE – Any suitable sauce, Cut Lemon and Parsley
BOILED SALMON – Dressed Cucumber, Lobster, Caper Hollandaise, Shrimp or Melted Butter Sauce
COLD SALMON – Mayonnaise, Tartare, or Anchovy Cream Sauce, Salad, Cucumber
GRILLED SALMON – Tartare, Italienne, Maître d'Hôtel, Piquante, Tomato or Béarnaise Sauce
SMELTS – Tomato or Anchovy Sauce
SOLES – Any suitable Sauce, Cut Lemon
BOILED TURBOT – Shrimp, Lobster or Hollandaise Sauce, Garnish Lobster Coral and Cut Lemon
WHITING – Anchovy, Parsley or Caper Sauce, Lemon
WHITEBAIT – Lemon, Cut Brown Bread and Butter

MEAT

ROAST BEEF – Yorkshire Pudding, Roast Potatoes, Scraped Horseradish and Horseradish Sauce
BOILED BEEF – Suet Dumplings, Carrots, Turnips, Parsnips
COLD BEEF – Salad, Pickles, Beetroot, Mashed Potatoes
GRILLED STEAK – Oysters, Maître d'Hôtel Butter, Horseradish Sauce, Potato Chips
CALF'S HEAD – Parsley Sauce, Bacon, Lemon, Garnish with Brains and Tongue (sliced)
BOILED MUTTON – Carrots and Turnips, Caper or Parsley Sauce
ROAST MUTTON – (Shoulder) Onion Sauce
ROAST MUTTON – (Saddle and Haunch) Baked Potatoes, Gravy, Red Current Jelly
ROAST PORK – Sage and Onion Stuffing, Apple Sauce, Gravy
BOILED PORK – Pease Pudding, Boiled Green Vegetables

ROAST VEAL – Veal Forcemeat, Bacon or Pork, Melted Butter Sauce and Gravy

VENISON – Red Currant Jelly, Port Wine Sauce

VEGETABLES

ARTICHOKES – (Jerusalem) White Sauce

ASPARAGUS – Toast underneath and Melted Butter

BROAD BEANS – Parsley Sauce

CAULIFLOWER – White Sauce or Cheese Sauce

CELERY – White or Brown Sauce

HARICOT BEANS – Butter and Chopped Parsley or Parsley Sauce

ONIONS – Butter, White or Brown Sauce

NEW POTATOES – Butter and Chopped Parsley

SEA-KALE AND SALSIFY – White Sauce

SPINACH – Hard-boiled Egg and Fried Bread

VEGETABLE MARROW – White Sauce

POULTRY AND GAME

BLACKCOCK – Toast, Good Gravy, Bread Sauce, Watercress

WILD DUCK – Orange Sauce or Good Gravy and Orange Salad, Watercress

GROUSE – Toast, Bread Sauce, Gravy, Browned Crumbs, Salad, Potato Chips

ROAST HARE – Forcemeat Balls, Good Gravy, Red Currant Jelly

ROAST PARTRIDGE – Bread Sauce, Gravy, Browned Crumbs, Salad, Potato Chips

ROAST PHEASANT – Bread Sauce, Gravy, Browned Crumbs, Salad

TEAL, – etc. Orange Sauce or Salad, Lemon Quarters, Watercress

QUAILS, SNIPE, PLOVERS, –etc. Toast spread with Trail, Good Brown Gravy

BOILED FOWL – Parsley, Egg, Celery, or White Sauce, Lemon

ROAST FOWL – Bread Sauce, Bacon, Gravy, Watercress

ROAST DUCK – Sage and Onion Stuffing, Gravy, Apple Sauce, Green Peas

ROAST GOOSE – Sage and Onion Stuffing, Gravy, Apple Sauce

GUINEA FOWL – Bread Sauce, Good Brown Gravy

PIGEONS – Bread or Piquante Sauce

BOILED RABBIT – Onion or Parsley Sauce

ROAST RABBIT – Bread Sauce and Gravy, or Brown Sauce and Red Currant Jelly

BOILED TURKEY – Celery, Chestnut or Oyster Sauce, Boiled Ham or Tongue

ROAST TURKEY – Veal and Sausage or Chestnut Stuffing, Bread Sauce, Gravy, Sausages

How to Use Up
Cold Meat and Fish

It is a great advantage to know how to produce savoury and appetizing dishes from cold meat, fish, game and poultry, etc. A good and economical manager, with a little care and forethought, can produce many dainty dishes from scraps and odds and ends that some would consider useless.

As warmed-up meat has less flavour than that which is freshly cooked, special care must be taken with the flavouring and seasoning. Garnishing, too, in cold meat cookery is of importance; the garnish not only improves the appearance of a dish but adds materially to the quantity; the addition of a border of rice, macaroni, haricot beans, etc, often makes a small portion of meat into a good and substantial dish.

In preparing to recook a cold joint, cold poultry or game, all the meat should be carefully removed from the bones. These should be chopped, put into a pan with the skin, gristle, and some prepared vegetables, covered with water, and boiled. The stock, or gravy, will then be a valuable help in producing a well-flavoured dish. All the fat that is not required can be rendered down and used for frying and other purposes. Extract of meat or the gravy found under the dripping from a roast joint can be used to flavour when there are no bones to boil down and no stock available. Underdone meat is far more satisfactory for reheating than meat that is well cooked and dry. The most important point of all to remember is that the meat is already cooked, and that it only needs *reheating*. It is now recommended that all food that is reheated should be brought to a temperature of 100°C throughout in order to destroy any bacteria which might cause digestive upsets. Chicken can be prone to these, as can anything bound with raw egg. Mince, curries, hash and made-up dishes of that description, must not *boil* after the meat is added. Meat should be chopped for a mince instead of passing it through a mincing machine; it should be cut in thin slices for a hash and in dice for a curry. Borders of macaroni, well-boiled rice, haricot beans, mashed potatoes, French beans can all be used for stews, minces, hash, etc. Poached eggs make a suitable garnish for those of white meat, such as veal and chicken. Chopped parsley, yolk of hard-boiled egg sieved, slices of egg, croûtons of fried bread, sippets of toast, all add to the tempting appearance of a dish if used tastefully. Curry is one of the most successful ways of using up cold meat, especially white meat, such as veal, pork, chicken and rabbit. The sauce should be made first and thoroughly cooked, then the meat put in and allowed to reheat very slowly, so that it becomes impregnated with the flavour and seasoning. The remains of any meat, poultry or game can be made into rissoles, croquettes, cutlets, meat cakes, cannelons, balls, etc., the name varies according to the shape, but the binding sauce or panada is the same in all cases. This mixture is made by cooking together 1 oz (25 g) of butter and 1 oz (25 g) of flour and adding 1 gill (150 ml) of liquid, stirring till it boils and leaves the sides of the pan; it is then ready to mix with the meat, which should be finely minced, well flavoured and seasoned, with breadcrumbs or mashed potato added if necessary. This mixture will, when cool, be firm enough to shape and when reheated will become moist and creamy again. Rissoles, croquettes, etc., should be coated with egg and breadcrumbs or crushed vermicelli and fried. The same mixture can be enclosed in very thin light pastry coated and fried. Small portions of meat or fish can be dipped in batter and fried in hot fat. Cold fish with the skin and bone removed and very finely flaked added to a well-flavoured panada can be made in the same way into cutlets, croquettes, cakes, etc. In making all these dishes the mixture must be divided into portions of uniform size and shaped alike, otherwise the appearance of the dish will be spoilt.

Another appetizing method for using up cold meat is serving it "au gratin" or "scalloped." The correct and daintiest way is by using the real scallop shells or those made of china or plate. Failing these a fancy fireproof gratin dish can be used or an ordinary pie-dish. The fish or meat must be prepared, mixed with a good sauce, put in the buttered shells with layers of breadcrumbs, tiny bits of butter on the top and sprinkled with grated cheese if liked (it is a good plan to keep the dry rinds and grate for this purpose). The scallops should then be nicely browned in a quick oven or under the gas and served on a folded serviette. Cold vegetables such as Jerusalem artichokes, salsify and sea-kale are excellent served in this way. Remains of meat, poultry and game are very appetizing when "devilled." This method is a "hot" one and is very suitable when the meat is somewhat flavourless. There are a variety of devil pastes and sauces. They usually contain mustard, chutney, curry powder and other hot ingredients and they are added either before or after grilling, and are termed wet or dry devils accordingly. If scraps of meat or fish are too small to be used in any other way they can be pounded smooth, well seasoned and potted.

How to Arrange a Menu

When giving a dinner the first thing to be done is to arrange the menu. This requires both skill and judgement, for upon this to some extent will depend the success of the meal. For a complete dinner the courses are as follows:

Hors d'œuvres
Potages
Poissons
Entrées
Relevés
Rôti
Entremets
Dessert
Café

Sometimes one or more of the courses is omitted, but the order of serving them is the same. Fewer dishes are served in each course than formerly, but it is a good plan to have an alternative dish at one or two of the courses. The time at the table should not exceed an hour and a half, and the service must be quick, but on no account hurried.

In arranging a menu it is a good plan to decide first of all what food shall comprise the dinner and then how that food shall be dressed and served. This simplifies matters and ensures better results. Great care must always be taken to avoid repetition, either with regard to material, colour, garnishing, or taste. Choose foods which are in season, as they are then at their best, and alternate the methods of cooking them. The following hints can be remembered with advantage when compiling a menu:

HORS D'ŒUVRES

This is not, strictly speaking, a course. They are intended to stimulate the appetitie, and are usually served cold, very small and very daintily dished, and should consist of highly flavoured articles of food, such as anchovies, olives, sardines, oysters, caviare, tiny salads, marinaded herrings, etc.

POTAGES

If two soups are served the clear should come before the thick or purée. If only one is served a clear soup is preferable. In choosing the soup for a dinner care should be taken that it does not consist of anything which will appear later on in the menu.

POISSONS

When two kinds of fish are included in the course one may be plainly cooked and the other dressed; the one cooked by a dry method such as frying, grilling or broiling should be served first. If the fish is dressed it should be in small portions, tastefully garnished and hot fish should always be served before cold. Great care should be taken in the preparation of the sauces so as to avoid sameness in composition and colour. For instance, Hollandaise and Béarnaise should not be served in the same dinner as they are similar, nor mayonnaise and tartare, as one includes the other. If a small, light dinner only is required, a fish soup, such as bisque of lobster or oyster, may be served to include the first two courses.

ENTRÉES

The term entrée is applied to a "made" dish, one that is complete in itself. It is invariably handed at the table, so that it is very necessary that it should be dished tastefully, and it is in this course that the cook has the best chance to show her skill both in taste and in garnishing. If two entrées are served one should be brown and the other white, which of the two comes first depends on the dishes that precede and follow and also on the composition of the dishes themselves. A light entrée should always precede a heavy and highly flavoured one, and hot entrées always be served before cold. In the choice of sauces the same rules apply as for the fish course. Repetition in colour and flavour must be carefully avoided.

RELEVÉS (OR REMOVES)

This course constitutes the substantial part of the dinner and consists usually of a joint either boiled, roasted or braised. It is served from the side à la Russe and the vegetables and correct accompaniments handed round. Two vegetables are sufficient, and great care should be taken in their preparation. Sorbets or water-ices are served after this course.

RÔTI OR ROAST

This consists of poultry or game, either plainly roasted or otherwise prepared and dressed. It is necessary that nothing inferior should be served in this course. The greatest care should be taken with choice, preparation and cooking of it, as the choicest game or poultry loses its flavour if badly roasted. The correct accompaniments should be sent to table with the dish, a salad is always served and usually potato chips.

ENTREMETS

This course is divided into three:

1 *A dressed vegetable*, which immediately follows the roast and is served as a separate course.

2 *Sweet entremets* served either hot or cold.

3 *A Savoury* – This precedes the desert, is usually served hot and generally consists of cheese.

The dressed vegetable as a course is often omitted by English cooks, who know little as a rule of vegetable cookery, but it is a distinct feature in a French dinner, and is of more importance than the sweet course. It should consist of a choice vegetable in season, simply but well cooked and tastefully served so as to preserve its distinctive flavour. Great attention should be paid to the choice of sweets; they must be light and delicate, colour and taste well considered, and everything of a solid nature carefully avoided. They may be served hot or cold, but hot dishes should always precede cold ones. Ices may be included in this course or be served after with the dessert. The savoury which completes the dinner is generally served hot and more often than not includes cheese in its composition. It is invariably handed round and may be served in small portions, one for each guest, and should always be well flavoured and daintily dished.

DINNERS FOR INVALIDS

COOKING for invalids is often looked upon as a disagreeable necessity only, and very little care is bestowed upon it. During convalescence when small and light meals are allowed, and also in the cases of confirmed invalids, it means so much to find care and thought has been given to the preparation of their meals. Not only in the actual cooking of the food, but in the dainty manner of serving it. These few hints may prove of use in helping in the planning of the daily meals of an invalid.

The serving of the food is of great importance, and the greatest care must be taken with the tray – these details add to the tempting appearance of the meal and to the patient's enjoyment of it.

Only the very freshest and best materials should be used and served – there is less flavour and nourishment in inferior food.

In cases of serious illness the doctor's orders must be carried out to the letter, very little or no seasoning added without instructions. If liquid food alone is given it should be as varied as possible.

Food should be given only in small quantities, and made to look as tempting as possible, and served at once when cooked, otherwise it will lose its freshness and fail to tempt the appetite. A dish should not be served the second time if it can be avoided, and recooked meat is unsuitable. All food should be covered when carried from the kitchen to the sick room, and all remains of or untouched food be thrown away, especially in the case of infectious diseases. The invalid should never be consulted about a meal, it will then come as a pleasant surprise and be more enjoyable. All medicine should be put out of sight at meal times, and the meals themselves be punctual – the food should be absolutely hot or cold as the case may be; lukewarm food is most unappetizing.

Vegetables should not be given except with the doctor's consent, and then they must be of the freshest. Fruit should be fresh and sound, and not over-ripe.

The method of cooking employed is of importance – steaming is the best, as it is light and thorough, and food cooked in that way loses less of its nourishment than in any other way. It is inclined to be tasteless, but that is a fault a cook can easily remedy. Fried foods are generally avoided owing to their richness. Soups can be made from meat, game, poultry, or fish, but they should contain no root or starch substances and thickened with yolks of eggs. Oysters are considered excellent when taken raw, as they contain a self-digesting ferment. If they cannot be afforded a good and cheap substitute is tripe, which is digested in an hour. The following are Specimens of suitable light dinners for an invalid:

Chicken Broth
Steamed Fillets of Sole
Bread and Butter Pudding
•
Oysters
Boiled Chicken and Parsley Sauce
Rusk Pudding
•
Mutton Broth
Minced Chicken
Port Wine Jelly
•
Boiled Whiting, Anchovy Sauce
Steamed Chop and Rice
Arrowroot Pudding
•
Veal Broth
Beef Quenelle
Apple Snow
•
Meat Tea
Stewed Calf's Foot
Prune Mould
•
Rice Soup
Tripe and Tomato Sauce
Savoury Custard
•
Fried Whiting
Stewed Lambs' Sweetbreads
Orange Jelly
•
Gravy Soup
Chicken Fricassée
Custard Pudding
•
Fish Soup
Boiled Mutton and Caper Sauce
Sago Soufflé
•
Fish Eggs
Fried Sweetbread
Rice Jelly
•
Baked Fillets of Plaice
Chicken Soufflé
Prune Pudding

Recipes for these dishes are included in Part III and can be found by turning to the index. The cook should remember to reduce the seasoning.

DIGESTION TABLE OF VARIOUS FOODS

FOOD	HOW COOKED	HOURS IN STOMACH
Apples	Raw	1½ to 2
Apple Dumpling	Boiled	3
Beans	Boiled	2½
Beef	Boiled	2¾
Beef	Roasted	3½
Beef	Fried	4
Beefsteak	Broiled	3
Brains	Boiled	1¾
Bread	Baked	3½
Butter	Melted	3½
Cabbage	Boiled	4½
Carrots	Boiled	3¼
Cheese	Raw	3½
Chicken	Fricassée	2¾
Custard	Baked	2¾
Duck	Roasted	4
Eggs	Raw	1½
Eggs	Boiled (soft)	3
Eggs	Boiled (hard)	3½
Eggs	Fried	3½
Fowl	Boiled	4
Fowl	Roasted	4
Hash, with meat and vegetables	Heated	2½
Lamb (fresh)	Broiled	2½
Milk	Boiled	2
Milk	Raw	2½
Mutton	Boiled	3
Mutton	Roasted	3½
Oysters	Raw	2.55
Pork (salt)	Boiled	4½
Pork	Roasted	5¼
Potatoes	Baked	2½
Potatoes	Boiled	3½
Rice	Boiled	1
Sago	Boiled	1¾
Salmon	Boiled	4
Sponge Cake	Baked	2½
Suet (Beef)	Boiled	5.3
Suet (Mutton)	Boiled	4½
Tapioca	Boiled	2
Tripe	Boiled	1
Turkey	Boiled	2.25
Turkey	Roasted	2½
Turnips	Boiled	3½
Veal	Broiled	4

FRENCH COOKERY TERMS

ALLEMANDE, a rich white sauce.

ALLSPICE, the dried berries of an evergreen plant.

ASPIC, a savoury jelly.

A L'INDIENNE, curried dishes.

AU BLEU, a term used for fish cooked in wine.

AU FOUR, baked in the oven.

AU GRATIN, a term applied to dishes served in the dish in which it is cooked.

AU MAIGRE, any dish in which meat is not used; Lenten dishes.

AU JUS, any dish prepared with gravy or meat stock.

AU NATUREL, food served raw or plainly cooked.

BABA, a very light cake-mixture.

BAIN-MARIE, a large vessel containing boiling water in which small saucepans containing sauces are put to keep hot without boiling.

BARDER, to bard or cover the breasts of game or poultry with thin slices of bacon.

BATTERIE DE CUISINE. A complete set of kitchen apparatus.

BAVAROISE, a rich kind of cold custard pudding.

BEARNAISE, a sauce similar to Hollandaise flavoured with tarragon and other herbs.

BÉCHAMEL, a white sauce.

BEIGNETS, fritters, pieces of meat, fish, vegetables or fruit dipped in batter and fried.

BISQUE, a rich soup made of shell fish.

BOMBE, an iced pudding filled with cream.

BLANCHE, to blanch, to put meat or vegetables in cold water and bring to the boil to cleanse or remove any strong flavour.

BLANQUETTE, meat or poultry served in a white sauce, thickened with yolks of eggs.

BORAGE, an aromatic plant used to flavour "cups" and iced drinks.

BOUCHÉES, mouthfuls, tiny patties of puff pastry.

BOUILLI, fresh boiled beef.

BOUILLON, a plain clear soup, unclarified beef broth.

BOUQUET GARNI, a small bunch of herbs with peppercorns and cloves, etc., tied in muslin, used to flavour soups and stews and removed before serving.

BRAISE, to cook meat or poultry slowly with vegetables and herbs in a closely covered pan; an elaborate form of stewing.

BRIOCHE, a light French yeast cake.

BRUNOISE, a clear soup with garnish of vegetables cut in dice.

CAISSE, little paper cases in which soufflées and many other things are served.

CANNELONS, small rolls of puff pastry stuffed with meat.

CASSEROLE, a stew pan or a shape of pastry or potato for ragoûts or fricassées.

CHARLOTTE, a mould of biscuits filled with cream or custard.

CHARTREUSE, name applied to a mould of jelly filled with cream or bavaroise, also a savoury jelly mould with ragoût of meat or vegetables in centre.

CHERVIL, an aromatic plant used for flavouring.

COMPÔTE, fruit stewed in syrup; also a stew of game.

COLCANNON, mashed potatoes and cabbage fried together.

CONSOMMÉ, a clear, strong soup.

COQUILLES, shells; shell-shaped dishes, such as scalloped oysters are served in.

COURONNE, crown; to arrange cutlets, fritters, etc., in a ring round a dish, one overlapping the other.

CROQUETTES, minced meat or fish formed cork shapes, coated and fried.

CROUSTADES, cases of fried bread in which various ragoûts are served.

CROÛTONS, thin slices of bread cut into shapes and used for garnishing.

CHAUDFROID, a cold entrée; a sauce used for masking cold meat.

DARIOLES, small moulds used for jellies or puddings, etc.

DEMI-GLACE, a rich brown sauce.

DRAGÉES, sugar plums.

ENTRÉE, a made or side dish.

ENTREMETS, dishes either sweet or savoury served after the roast in a dinner.

ESPAGNOLE, Spanish sauce; a rich brown sauce the foundation for many others.

FARCE, forcemeat or stuffing.

FEUILLETAGE, puff pastry.

FENNEL, an aromatic plant used for flavouring served with mackerel.

FILET, fillet, the undercut of a loin of beef, mutton, veal, pork, or game. Also breasts of poultry and the flesh of fish taken from the bone.

FINANCIÈRE, a ragoût of truffles, olives, sweetbread, cockscombs, used as a garnish for entrées.

FONDU, a light baked cheese pudding.

FRICANDEAU, a fillet of beef or veal larded and braised.

FOIE-GRAS, fat goose liver.

FRICASSÉE, a white stew of chicken, veal, rabbit or fish.

FRITTERS, small pieces of meat, fish, vegetables or fruit, dipped in batter and fried.

GALANTINE, meat or poultry boned, stuffed with forcemeat, rolled, boiled, and served cold.

GARNITURE, garnish-accessories required for a dish.

GIBLETS, neck, liver, heart, gizzard and pinions of poultry.

GLACE, icing.

GLAZE, stock reduced by boiling to a stiff jelly.

GRENADINES, small fillets of veal or beef larded and braised.

HARICOT, a stew of fried mutton served with vegetables.

HÂTELETS, small silver or plated skewers.

HOMINY, prepared maize, used for milk puddings.

HORS D'ŒUVRES, small relishes served at the beginning of a dinner.

IRISH MOSS, a kind of seaweed.

JUGGING, a term used for stewing meat or game in a jar in the oven.

JULIENNE, finely shredded vegetables used as a garnish to clear soup.

KROMESKIES, minced meat or game rolled in thin slices of bacon dipped in batter and fried.

KEDGEREE, an Indian dish of fish, rice, and hard-boiled eggs, served with curry sauce.

LARD, to insert small pieces of fat bacon in lean meat and breasts of poultry and game.

LIAISON, a mixture of yolks of eggs and cream used for thickening soups and sauces.

LUTING, a paste used for fastening the lids on pie-dishes for potted game, etc.

MACÉDOINE, a garnish of various kinds of vegetables or a mixture of fruits.

MADELEINE, a kind of small cake.

MAÎTRE D'HÔTEL, a flavouring butter, mixed with chopped parsley and lemon juice.

MARASCHINO, a liqueur used for flavouring jellies and ices.

MARINADE, a kind of pickle in which meat and fish is steeped to heighten the flavour before cooking.

MATELOTE, a rich fish stew with wine and herbs.

MIREPOIX, a rich, highly flavoured sauce, flavoured strongly with herbs and vegetables, used for entrées.

MIROTON, slices of meat or poultry recooked and served in the same dish.

MULLIGATAWNY, an Indian soup flavoured with curry powder.

NOUILLES, paste made of flour, salt, eggs and water, cut into fancy shapes and used to garnish soups, etc.

NOYEAU, a liqueur flavoured with peach kernels.

PANADA, a thick sauce used for binding meat or fish mixtures.

PANURETTE, browned crumbs used for coating or garnishing.

PARBOIL, to partly cook.

PÂTÉ, a pie.

PAPILLOTES, the papers in which fish or meat is wrapped before grilling or broiling.

PETITS FOURS, small pastries, iced and decorated.

PIÈCE DE RESISTENCE, the principal joint or other important dish of a dinner.

PILAU, an Eastern dish made of rice, onions and highly flavoured meat.

POTAGE, soup.

POT AU FEU, a dish of beef broth and vegetables.

PRINTANIER, a clear soup with new spring vegetables.

QUENELLES, small shapes of pounded white meat mixture, poached.

QUINCE, a fruit similar to an apple used for marmalade, jelly and tarts.

RAGOÛT, a rich, highly flavoured stew or hash.

RAMAQUINS, small cheese soufflées served in china or paper cases.

RAVIGOTE, a sauce or butter flavoured with green herbs.

RATAFIA, essence of almonds; a small almond biscuit.

RECHAUFFÉ, a dish served a second time, or made from cold remains.

RELEVÉ, the remove, or the course of a dinner consisting of the joint.

RÉMOULADE, a cold sauce flavoured with mustard and herbs, used as a salad dressing.

RISSOLES, a mixture of minced meat or fish wrapped in thin pastry, coated and fried.

RÔTI, roast game; the term applied to any dish served in the game course of a dinner.

ROUX, butter and flour cooked together, used for thickening soups and sauces.

SALAMANDER, a flat piece of iron which is made red hot and used to brown the tops of scallops, puddings, etc.

SALMI, a rich brown hash of game or poultry.

SAUTÉ PAN, a shallow pan used for frying.

SAVARIN, a light spongy yeast cake.

SORBET, a half frozen water ice, flavoured with liqueur, served between the joint and the game course.

SOUFFLÉ, a very light pudding, either sweet or savoury; it can be steamed or baked.

SUPRÊME, a rich white sauce made from chicken, stock, cream, etc.

TAMMY, a cloth through which sauces and soups are pressed to make them smooth.

TIMBALE, a mould lined with boiled macaroni or pastry and filled with a savoury mixture of meat and poultry.

TOURNEDOS, small fillets of beef served as entrées.

VELOUTÉ, a rich white sauce, made from chicken stock, cream, etc.

MENU TERMS IN FRENCH AND ENGLISH

MEAT

Bacon	Lard
Beef	Bœuf
Brains	Cervelles
Calf's head	Tête de veau
Chicken	Poulet, volaille
Clear soup	Consommé
Curries	Kari
Cutlets	Côtelettes
Ducks	Canards
Forcemeat	Farce
Fowl	Volaille
Game	Gibier
Goose	Oie
Gravy	Jus
Guinea Fowl	Pintade
Ham	Jambon
Hare	Lièvre
Kidney	Rognon
Lamb	Âgneau
Leg of mutton	Gigot de mouton
Liver	Foie
Meat	Viande
Mutton cutlets	Côtelettes de mouton
Oxtail	Queue de bœuf
Partridges	Perdreaux
Pheasant	Faisan
Pigeon	Pigeon
Pullet	Poularde
Rabbit	Lapin
Ribs of beef	Côtes de bœuf
Roast	Rôti
Saddle of mutton	Selle de mouton
Sausages	Saucisses
Sirloin of beef	Aloyau de bœuf
Sweetbread	Ris de veau
Tongue	Langue
Turkey	Dindon
Veal	Veau
Venison	Venaison
Woodcock	Bécasse

FISH

Anchovies	Anchois
Brill	Barbue
Cod	Cabillaud
Cray fish	Écrivisses
Eels	Anguilles
Fish	Poissons
Grey mullet	Mulet
Gurnet	Gournal
Haddock	Aiglefin, merleuche
Halibut	Flétan
Herrings	Harengs
Mackerel	Macquereau
Mullet (red)	Rougets
Oysters	Huîtres
Pike	Brochet
Plaice	Plie
Prawns	Crevettes
Roes (fish)	Laitances
Salmon	Saumon
Skate	Raie
Smelts	Éperlans
Sprats	Melettes
Trout	Truite
Turtle	Tortue
Whitebait	Blanchailles
Whiting	Mérlan

VEGETABLES

Artichokes	Artichauts
Asparagus	Asperges
Barley	Orge
Beans	Haricot
Beetroot	Betterave
Brussels sprouts	Choux de Bruxelles
Cabbage	Chou
Capers	Câpres

Cauliflower	Choufleur
Celery	Céleri
Cress	Cresson
Cucumber	Concombre
Endive	Chicorée
French beans	Haricots verts
Garlic	Ail
Gherkin	Cornichon
Horseradish	Raifort
Leek	Poireau
Lettuce	Laitue
Mushrooms	Champignons
Onions	Oignons
Parsley	Persil
Parsnip	Panais
Peas	Pois
Potatoes	Pommes de terre
Sea-kale	Choux marins
Sorrel	Oseille
Spinach	Épinards
Truffles	Truffes
Turnips	Navets
Vegetables	Légumes
Vegetable marrow	Courge à la moelle

FRUIT

Almonds	Amandes
Apples	Pommes
Apricots	Abricots
Cherries	Cerises
Chestnuts	Marrons
Figs	Figues
Gooseberries	Groseilles
Lemon	Citron
Peaches	Pêches
Raspberry	Framboise
Pineapple	Annas
Plum	Prune
Prunes	Pruneaux
Strawberries	Fraises
Walnuts	Noix
Currants	Raisin de Corinthe
Grapes	Raisins
Melon	Melon
Pear	Poire

MISCELLANEOUS

Bread	Pain	Milk	Lait	Sugar	Sucre
Butter	Beurre	Mustard	Moutarde	Tarts	Tartes
Cheese	Fromage	Pickled	Mérine	Tartlets	Tartelettes
Coffee	Café	Pie	Pâté	Tea	Thé
Forcemeat	Farce	Potted	En terrine	Vanilla	Vanille
Fritters	Beignets	Sago	Sagou	Breakfast	Déjeuner
Game	Gibier	Salt	Sel	Luncheon	Déjeuner à la fourchette
Gravy	Jus	Smoked	Fumé		
Ices	Glaces	Stewed	Étuvée	Dinner	Diner
Jelly	Gelée	Stuffed	Farcie	Supper	Souper

PART III

RECIPES

SOUPS

1 FIRST STOCK

2 lb (900 g) bones	bunch of herbs
2 lb (900 g) shin of beef	peppercorns
2 carrots	1 oz (25 g) fat
2 onion	2 teaspoonfuls salt
1 turnip	6 pints (3.4 litres) water
1 stick of celery	

Melt the fat in a large saucepan and brown the bones, cut the meat into small pieces and allow to soak for half an hour or longer. Put the meat, bones, water and salt into the pan, bring slowly to boiling-point, skim well, add vegetables cut in large pieces and herbs and peppercorns tied in muslin. Simmer for five hours, strain.

2 SECOND STOCK

bones	1 bay leaf
any trimmings from fresh	bunch of herbs
meat or poultry	12 peppercorns
1 carrot	2 cloves
2 onions	1 oz (25 g) fat
stick of celery	2 teaspoonfuls salt
ham or bacon bones	water

Chop and wash the bones, fry a nice brown in a little fat, add the trimmings of meat or poultry, ham bone or bacon bones, salt and water. Bring to the boiling-point, then add the vegetables, well cleaned, the herbs and peppercorns tied in muslin. Boil gently from four to five hours, skim well, strain, remove the fat when cold.

3 FISH STOCK

bones and trimmings from	small piece of carrot
fish	1 small onion
water to cover	salt
bouquet garni (see No 648)	

Put bones and trimmings into a saucepan, cover with cold water, bring to the boiling-point, add vegetables and bouquet garni and salt. Boil for fifteen to twenty minutes, strain, and use for fish sauces and soups.

4 CONSOMMÉ

good stock (recipe No. 1)	2 whites of eggs
1 carrot	2 shells
1 turnip	½ lb (225 g) lean beef
1 onion or shallot	sherry
stick of celery	

Shred the beef finely, removing all the fat, put in basin with some of the stock, add the white of the eggs and crushed shells, whisk all well together, put the remainder of stock in a white-lined pan, add well prepared vegetables and the clearing ingredients, whisk well together, remove the whisk and allow to boil gently for twenty minutes, when clear pour gently through a cloth which has had boiling water poured through first; the sherry must be passed through the cloth; the garnish, from which the soup takes its name, must be carefully prepared; cooked vegetables must be rinsed with hot water and put in the soup tureen, and the consommé poured in gently.

Consommé as above with strips of vegetables, *Consommé à la Julienne;* with fancy shapes of custard, *Consommé à la Royal;* with small cubes of vegetables, *Consommé à la Brunoise;* with French plums and leeks, *Consommé à la Portugaise;* with vegetables cut in small fancy shapes, *Consommé à la Jardinière.*

5 WHITE STOCK

2 lb (900 g) veal bones	stick celery
1 lb (450 g) lean veal	salt
1 turnip	2 quarts (2.3 litres) water
1 onion	bouquet garni

Put bones chopped and washed in a white-lined pan with meat cut in small pieces. Bring to the boil, add the vegetables, skim well. Boil gently for three to four hours and strain. This stock is suitable for white soups, purées and sauces.

6 MUTTON BROTH

2 lb (900 g) scrag of mutton	1 stick celery
1 quart (1.1. litres) water	1 oz (25 g) pearl barley or rice
1 onion	1 teaspoonful parsley
1 carrot	salt and pepper
1 turnip	
(Enough for four people)	

Cut the meat from the bones, chop the bones, put into a stewpan with the water and a little salt, bring to the boil and remove the scum as it rises, add the vegetables, well cleaned, and simmer for an hour and a half, strain it and add the rice or pearl barley; the latter must be previously blanched; season well, sprinkle over chopped parsley and serve.

7 VEAL BROTH

small knuckle veal	4 cloves
3 quarts (3.4 litres) water	slice of lemon peel
2 onions	salt and pepper
4 oz (100 g) rice	
(Enough for ten people)	

Wash the veal, put it in a stewpan with the cold water. When it boils remove the scum thoroughly, add a little salt, this causes the scum to rise better, simmer for an hour

and a half, then add the onions stuck with cloves and the rice, which must be well washed, and the lemon peel; cook again for an hour and a half; remove the vegetables and the knuckle, cut the meat into neat pieces, return to the pan, flavour to taste, serve the broth with rice and meat in it.

8 SCOTCH BROTH

2 lb (900 g) neck mutton	2 oz (50 g) pearl barley
1 quart (1.1 litres) water	bouquet garni
1 onion	seasoning
1 carrot	1 teaspoonful chopped parsley
1 turnip	

(Enough for four people)

Cut meat up finely, removing fat and skin, chop the bones, add to the water with onion seasoning and bouquet garni, allow to simmer gently for one hour, strain and remove bones, return to the saucepan with the blanched barley, carrot and turnip cut in tiny dice, simmer till carrot is tender, put back some of the meat cut in neat pieces, season and add parsley just before serving.

9 LENTIL SOUP

½ pint (300 ml) lentils	1 oz (25 g) dripping
1 quart (1.1 litres)	2 potatoes
3 onions	bunch of herbs
2 small carrots	salt and pepper
1 small turnip	

(Enough for four people)

Wash the lentils and soak for twelve hours with a little carbonate of soda in the water. Cut the vegetables into small pieces, put the dripping into the pan with them and cook for five minutes with the lid on. Add the lentils, water and flavourings, boil gently till reduced to a pulp, pass through a sieve, season and serve with small squares of toast or croûtons of fried bread.

10 PEA SOUP

1 quart (1.1 litres) water	small piece turnip
½ pint (300 ml) split peas	stick of celery
1 onion	salt and pepper
small piece of carrot	

Soak the peas for twelve hours with a pinch of carbonate of soda added to the water, put them in a saucepan with the water and vegetables, cut up in small pieces, simmer for two or three hours till tender, pass through a sieve, season and serve with croûtons of toast or fried bread, sprinkle dried mint over just before serving.

11 HARICOT SOUP

1 ½ pints (900 ml) water	1 onion
½ pint (300 ml) milk	½ oz (15 g) dripping
½ pint (300 ml) haricot beans	salt and pepper

(Enough for four people)

Soak the beans for twelve hours in cold water with a pinch of carbonate of soda, melt the dripping in a saucepan, add onion and beans, cook for twelve minutes with the lid on, add the water and simmer for three or four hours until the beans are tender. Pass through a sieve, add the milk, season well, reheat, serve with croûtons of fried bread.

12 ONION SOUP

3 Spanish onions	2½ pints (1.4 litres) water
2 small onions	¼ pint (150 ml) milk
1 oz (25 g) dripping	salt
2½ oz (65 g) flour	pepper

(Enough for four or five people)

Peel and cut up the onions. Put into a saucepan with the dripping and cook for five minutes with the lid on. Add the water and salt. Boil until the onion is quite tender, mix the flour smoothly with the milk, add to the soup and boil well. Season to taste and serve.

13 POTATO SOUP

1 lb (450 g) potatoes	1 oz (25 g) fat
2 onions	½ oz (15 g) sago
1 pint (600 ml) water	salt and pepper
½ pint (300 ml) milk	

(Enough for three people)

Peel and cut the potatoes into slices, chop the onions, melt the fat in a saucepan, add potatoes and onions and cook for five minutes with the lid on; add the water and boil gently till reduced to a pulp; add the washed sago and the milk. Cook till the sago is transparent. Season and serve.

14 WHITE VEGETABLE SOUP

2 carrots	1 oz (25 g) butter or dripping
2 turnips	1 quart (1.1 litres) water
1 leek	(boiling)
1 onion	1 oz (25 g) flour
1 stick celery	½ pint (300 ml) milk
1 bay leaf	½ teaspoonful sugar
	salt and pepper

(Enough for four or five people)

Clean, prepare and cut vegetables into strips, put them into a pan with the butter or dripping and cook for five minutes with the lid on, shaking occasionally, add the boiling water, bay leaf and sugar, boil gently until the carrot is tender, mix the flour smoothly with the milk, stir into the soup, boil well and season.

15 CARROT SOUP

4 carrots	1 quart (1.1 litres) stock
2 or 3 sticks of celery	1 slice of ham or ham bone
2 onions	2 lumps of sugar
1 turnip	salt and pepper
1 oz (25 g) butter	

(Enough for four people)

Prepare and slice the vegetables, put them into a saucepan with the butter and cook ten minutes with the lid on, pour over the stock, add the ham, a bouquet garni and the sugar, simmer for two hours. Pass the soup through a sieve, season, and serve with fried croûtons of bread.

16 RICE AND TOMATO SOUP

4 large tomatoes or small tin	1½ oz (40 g) rice
1 oz (25 g) dripping	salt
1 onion	pepper
1 quart (1.1 litres) water	

(Enough for four people)

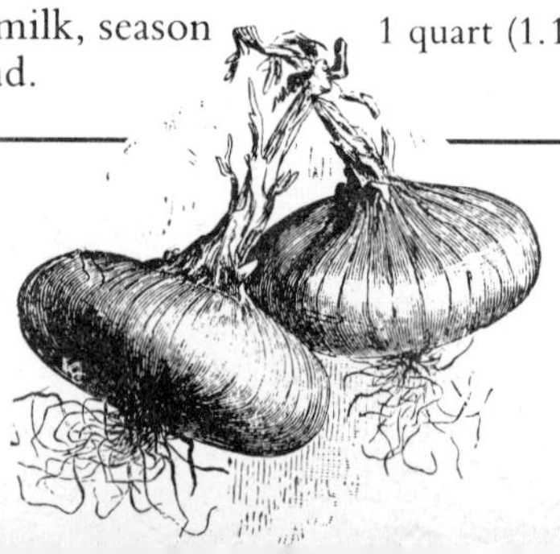

Melt the dripping in the saucepan, lightly brown the chopped onion, add the tomatoes cut in slices, water and rice, boil gently till cooked, add the seasoning and serve.

17 VEGETABLE MARROW SOUP

1 vegetable marrow	½ oz (15 g) flour
1½ pints (900 ml) milk	chopped parsley
1 onion	salt and pepper
½ oz (15 g) butter	

(Enough for four people)

Peel and slice the marrow, boil with the onion till tender, drain and rub through sieve, add the milk, butter and flour mixed smoothly with a little of the milk, boil up, season, sprinkle the chopped parsley over and serve with croûtons of fried bread.

18 BROWN VEGETABLE SOUP

1 quart (1.1 litres) water	bunch of herbs
1 carrot	1 oz (25 g) flour
1 turnip	1 oz (25 g) dripping or butter
1 onion	salt and pepper
1 stick of celery	

(Enough for four people)

Melt the dripping in a stewpan, prepare and chop the vegetables and brown them carefully in the fat, remove them, add the flour to the fat and brown it, taking care it does not burn; add the water gradually, stir till it boils, return the vegetables and the herbs to the stewpan and simmer gently for an hour, strain, season well and serve with squares of toast.

19 MELT SOUP

1 ox melt or 2 sheeps's melts	1 carrot
1 onion stuck with cloves	salt and pepper
1 quart (1.1 litres) water	1 oz (25 g) rice or sago

(Enough for four people)

Well wash and cut up the melt, put with the salt and pepper into a saucepan, add the water and vegetables, bring slowly to the boil, remove the scum, simmer gently for about two hours, strain, return to the pan and thicken with rice or sago, or some short lengths of cooked macaroni.

20 KIDNEY SOUP

1 ox kidney	1 oz (25 g) dripping
1 carrot	3 pints (1.7 litres)
½ turnip	1 teaspoonful vinegar
1 onion	½ tablespoonful ketchup
3 small potatoes	salt
1 oz (25 g) flour	pepper

(Enough for five or six people)

Wash and cut up the kidney, prepare and slice the vegetables, melt the dripping in the saucepan and fry the onion, dip the kidney pieces in the flour and fry lightly, add the water and vegetables, simmer for three hours, rub all through a sieve and reheat and add the seasoning and flavourings. Some of the kidney may be kept back before sieving and served in the soup as a garnish.

21 GRAVY SOUP

1 quart (1.1 litres) stock	bouquet garni
1 small carrot	salt and pepper
1 onion	1 oz (25 g) cooked macaroni
turnip	

(Enough for four people)

Cut up the vegetables and add with the bouquet garni to the stock, simmer gently for thirty minutes, strain, season well, add the cooked macaroni cut in small rings, vermicelli can be added as the garnish if preferred.

22 MOCK HARE SOUP

1 quart (1.1 litres) stock or	bouquet garni
water	1 dessertspoonful mushroom
¼ lb (100 g) gravy beef	ketchup
1 carrot	1 dessertspoonful Worcester
1 onion	sauce
1 small turnip	1 wineglass port
1 oz (25 g) flour	½ teaspoonful red-currant jelly
1½ oz (40 g) butter	salt and pepper

(Enough for four people)

Cut up the meat, dip in flour and brown in the butter with the onion whole stuck with cloves, remove the meat and onion and carefully brown the flour, add the water or stock gradually, allow to boil, put back the meat and onion, the vegetables cut up, and the flavourings, simmer for one and a half to two hours, strain and return to the stewpan, add the forcemeat balls (see below), cook gently for ten minutes, season well and add last the port and red-currant jelly.

Forcemeat Balls

2 tablespoonfuls bread crumbs	1 egg
1 teaspoonful chopped parsley	1 tablespoonful chopped suet
little grated lemon rind	½ teaspoonful chopped herbs
	little nutmeg

Mix all the ingredients together, bind with the egg, form into small balls.

23 MULLIGATAWNY SOUP

2 quarts (2.3 litres) stock	2 oz (50 g) curry powder
1 chicken or rabbit	½ pint (300 ml) cream
1 onion	lemon juice
1 apple	pinch of sugar
4 oz (100 g) butter	salt
4 oz (100 g) flour	4 oz (100 g) Patna rice

(Enough for seven or eight people)

Prepare the chicken or rabbit and cut it into neat joints, fry them a golden brown in the butter, remove the joints and add to the butter the finely-chopped apple and onion. Cook with the lid on for twenty minutes, add the curry powder and flour and cook well, add the stock, stir till it boils, put back the joints, simmer till tender, pass the soup through a sieve, add the flavourings and the cream, cut the best of the meat from the bones into small neat pieces and serve in the soup.

The rice must be well cooked and served separately.

24 MOCK TURTLE SOUP

4 quarts (4.5 litres) water	½ lb (225 g) ham (raw)
½ calf's head	bunch of herbs
1 shallot	blade of mace
1 onion	6 cloves
1 carrot	3 oz (75 g) butter
1 turnip	3 oz (75 g) flour
2 sticks celery	2 wineglasses sherry
6 mushrooms	salt and pepper

(*Enough for twelve or fourteen people*)

Wash the calf's head thoroughly, cut the flesh from the bones and tie in a cloth, place in a stewpan with the bones and simmer gently for three and a half hours, take out the head, strain the stock, and let it get cold, then remove the fat. Melt the butter in a stewpan and fry the vegetables and ham, add the flour and brown it carefully, add all the flavourings, pour in the stock and simmer for two hours, removing the fat as it rises, strain, return to the stewpan, add some of the calf's head cut into neat pieces, with the sherry; season well, and serve with small forcemeat balls made with veal stuffing and previously fried, or with egg balls.

Egg Balls

2 hard-boiled eggs	½ an egg
salt	cayenne

Pound the hard-boiled eggs and mix to a paste with the raw egg, add salt and cayenne, form into small balls using some flour, poach in boiling water for five or six minutes.

25 HARE SOUP

3 quarts (3.4 litres) water	1 blade of mace
1 hare	12 peppercorns
1 lb (450 g) gravy beef	bunch of herbs
1 carrot	3 oz (75 g) flour
1 turnip	3 oz (75 g) butter
1 onion	salt and pepper
2 oz (50 g) ham or bacon	2 glasses port wine

(*Enough for ten or twelve people*)

Cut the hare into joints and fry them with the ham in butter, prepare the vegetables, cut in pieces and fry lightly, put the hare, vegetables, spices and herbs into a stewpan and pour over the water, simmer gently from four to five hours, strain it and let the liquid get cold, then remove the fat, add the thickening of flour and cook well, add the seasoning and the port wine, serve with forcemeat balls in the soup.

Some of the hare can be pounded and passed through a sieve and added to the soup if liked.

Forcemeat Balls

2 oz (50 g) bread crumbs	1 oz (25 g) finely chopped suet
1 teaspoonful parsley	½ teaspoonful herbs
little grated lemon peel	salt
1 egg	pepper

Mix all the ingredients together, add the liver of the hare, cooked and chopped, bind with the egg, form into small balls and fry them in butter.

26 RABBIT SOUP

1 rabbit	1½ oz (40 g) flour
3 onions	1 quart (1.1 litres)
2 carrots	12 peppercorns
1 oz (25 g) butter or dripping	salt
1 tablespoonful mushroom ketchup	bunch of herbs

(*Enough for four people*)

Skin and cleanse the rabbit, cut into neat joints and dip in flour, melt the butter or dripping in a saucepan, lightly fry the chopped onions and the joints of rabbit, pour in a quart (1.1 litres) of water, bring to the boil and skim well, slice the carrots and add with the peppercorns and bunch of herbs; simmer for four to five hours, strain and thicken with the remainder of the flour mixed with the ketchup. Cook for five minutes, season well and serve with croûtons of fried bread.

27 OXTAIL SOUP

1 oxtail	bouquet garni
2 quarts (2.3 litres) water	2 oz (50 g) butter
2 onions	2 oz (50 g) flour
2 carrots	salt and pepper
1 turnip	wineglass of port

(*Enough for six or seven people*)

Joint the tail, fry it with the vegetables in a little butter, add the water and herbs, bring to the boil and skim well, simmer from three to four hours and strain it, cook the butter and flour together, carefully browning the flour, add the stock and boil, put back some of the best pieces of the oxtail, season well, add the port and serve.

28 OYSTER SOUP

1 quart (1.1 litres) white stock (made from chicken, veal, or cod's head and shoulders).	blade of mace
	½ pint (300 ml) cream
	few peppercorns
2 doz oysters	3 or 4 sprigs parsley
1 small whiting	1 oz (25 g) butter
1 onion	1 oz (25 g) flour
2 sticks of celery	1 yolk of egg
	salt and cayenne

(*Enough for five or six people*)

Put into a saucepan the stock, whiting (cut in pieces, not skinned), mace, parsley, onion, peppercorns and oyster beards, simmer for one hour, strain through a hair sieve, cook butter and flour together, add the strained stock and boil, season and add oyster liquor, yolk of egg mixed with the cream and the oysters cut into three or four pieces, reheat and serve.

29 TOMATO PURÉE

1½ pints (900 ml) white stock	1 gill (150 ml) cream
1 lb (450 g) tomatoes	1 small onion
1½ oz (40 g) butter	small piece of carrot
1 oz (25 g) flour	salt and pepper
1 teaspoonful sugar	

(*Enough for three or four people*)

Put the sliced tomatoes, chopped onion, sugar and carrot in a saucepan with the stock and simmer till tender, pass through a hair sieve, make a roux with the flour and

butter, add the purée, stirring well till it boils, season, put the cream in the tureen, pour the soup over and stir gently, serve with croûtons of fried bread; if necessary a little tomato ketchup added improves the colour.

30 PALESTINE SOUP

1½ pints (900 ml) white stock	1 oz (25 g) butter
1 lb (450 ml) artichokes	1 oz (25 g) flour
1 onion	2 tablespoonfuls cream
½ pint (300 ml) milk	salt and pepper
bouquet garni	

(*Enough for three or four people*)

Peel the artichokes under water with a little lemon juice or vinegar added, put the stock in a saucepan, add the chopped onion and sliced artichokes, simmer till tender, pass through a hair sieve, make a roux with the butter and flour, add the purée and stir till it boils, add the milk, season well, put the cream in the tureen, pour the soup over and stir gently, serve with croûtons of fried bread.

31 CELERY SOUP

1 head celery	1 oz (25 g) butter
1 onion	bouquet garni
1½ pints (900 ml) white stock	2 tablespoonfuls cream
½ pint (300 ml) milk	salt and pepper
1 oz (25 g) flour	

(*Enough for three or four people*)

Wash the celery carefully, adding lemon juice to the water to preserve the colour, cut up and add with chopped onion and bouquet garni to the stock, simmer gently till tender, pass through a sieve, make a roux with the butter and flour, add the purée and milk, stir till it boils, season well, put the cream in the tureen and pour the soup over, serve with croûtons of fried bread.

32 GREEN PEA PURÉE

2 pints (1.1 litres) peas	1 small onion
sprig of mint	1 teaspoonful castor sugar
sprig of parsley	salt and pepper
1 quart (1.1 litres) white stock	1 gill (150 ml) cream

(*Enough for four people*)

Boil the stock, add the peas and the shells, mint, parsley and onion, boil till peas are tender, pass through a hair sieve, return to the saucepan, add the cream, sugar and seasoning, reheat it, but do not allow it to boil, serve with croûtons of fried bread.

33 ALMOND SOUP

3 oz (75 g) sweet almonds	1 gill (150 ml) cream
6 bitter almonds	1 small onion
1 head of celery	1 oz (25 g) butter
1½ pints (900 ml) white stock	1 oz (25 g) flour
½ pint (300 ml) milk	salt and pepper

(*Enough for four people*)

Blanch and pound the almonds, put on to boil with the cut-up celery and onion in the stock, simmer gently for one hour, rub through a sieve, cook the butter and flour together, add the purée and the milk, bring to the boil, stirring all the time, add the seasoning, put the cream in the tureen, pour the soup over, stirring gently and serve.

34 CUCUMBER SOUP

1 cucumber (large)	1 oz (25 g) flour
1 quart (1.1 litres) white stock	1 gill (150 ml) cream
1 oz (25 g) butter	2 yolks of eggs
1 small onion	salt and pepper

(*Enough for four or five people*)

Peel the cucumber, cut in inch (2.5 cm) lengths, put in a saucepan with onion and boiling stock, cook till tender, pass through a sieve, cook the flour in the butter, add the purée, bring to the boil, stirring all the time, add the yolks and the cream, but do not allow the soup to boil again, season and serve with croûtons of fried bread. A little green colouring may be added to this soup if required.

35 PURÉE OF BRUSSELS SPROUTS

1 lb (450 g) sprouts	1 gill (150 ml) cream
1 shallot	pinch of carbonate of soda
1½ pints (900 ml) white stock	salt and pepper

(*Enough for four people*)

Wash and prepare the sprouts, put in a saucepan with the boiling stock, carbonate of soda and shallot, cook gently till tender, pass through a hair sieve, return to the pan (if not thick enough, a little cornflour smoothly mixed can be added and boiled up), add the cream, season and serve with croûtons of fried bread.

36 CHESTNUT SOUP

1 quart (1.1 litres) white stock	salt and pepper
1 lb (450 g) peeled chestnuts	cayenne
1 gill (150 ml) cream	

(*Enough for four people*)

Wipe the chestnuts, split the shells across, put them in a saucepan of boiling water and boil ten minutes, peel them and put them in a stewpan with the stock and cook slowly until quite soft. Pass the soup through a hair sieve, add the seasoning and cream, reheat and serve with croûtons of fried bread.

37 FRENCH CHEESE SOUP

1 pint (600 ml) white stock	1 oz (25 g) butter
½ pint (300 ml) milk	1 oz (25 g) flour
1 onion	3 oz (75 g) Gruyère cheese
1 bay leaf	salt and pepper

(*Enough for three people*)

Chop the onion, fry lightly in the butter, add the milk and boil up, add the bay leaf and the flour mixed smoothly with a little milk, allow it to boil for fifteen minutes, stirring well; then add the grated cheese and season, boil again and serve.

38 RICE CREAM SOUP

1½ pints (900 ml) stock	2 potatoes
½ pint (300 ml) milk	1 stick celery
1 oz (25 g) ground rice	½ oz (15 g) butter
1 onion	salt and pepper

(*Enough for four people*)

Slice the vegetables, put on with the stock and boil till tender, rub through a sieve, add the ground rice mixed smoothly with a little milk, return to the pan and boil for five minutes. A little cream is an improvement, season well, and serve with croûtons of fried bread.

39 PEARL BARLEY CREAM

1 quart (1.1 litres) stock	chopped parsley
1 pint (600 ml) pearl barley	1 yolk of egg
1 onion	a little milk
1 carrot	salt and pepper

(Enough for four or five people)

Simmer the barley in the stock with the onion and carrot for two hours, having previously blanched it; remove the carrot, stew till reduced to a pulp, rub it through a sieve, add enough stock or water till it is the consistency of thick cream, boil up, allow it to cool and add the yolk of egg beaten with a little milk, season and serve with the chopped parsley sprinkled on the top.

40 MACARONI SOUP

2 oz (50 g) macaroni	1 quart (1.1 litres) clear soup
½ oz (15 g) butter	(see No 4).
1 onion	salt and pepper
4 cloves	grated cheese (Parmesan).

(Enough for four people)

Cook the macaroni in fast-boiling water with the butter and onion stuck with cloves till quite tender, drain well, cut into small rings or half-inch (1 cm) lengths, heat the clear soup, add the macaroni and simmer from eight to ten minutes, season and serve with grated Parmesan cheese.

41 AMERICAN TOMATO SOUP

3 pints (1.7 litres) stock	1 oz (25 g) butter
1 lb (450 g) tomatoes	trimmings of ham
1 onion	1 blade of mace
1 oz (25 g) flour	salt and pepper
1 oz (25 g) sago	

(Enough for five or six people)

Chop the onion and fry in the butter, cut the tomatoes into pieces and add with the stock, ham trimmings and mace; cook for twenty minutes, skimming occasionally. When the tomatoes are cooked pass through a sieve, return to the pan, boil up, sprinkle in the sago, season and boil for ten to fifteen minutes, and serve with small squares of toast.

42 LETTUCE SOUP

1 quart (1.1 litres) stock (white)	1 gill (150 ml) cream
3 lettuces	salt and pepper
1 shallot	

(Enough for four people)

Shred the lettuces finely, blanch them in boiling water, boil the stock, and lettuce, finely chopped shallot, simmer for fifteen minutes, add the cream, season well and serve.

43 CABBAGE SOUP

1 quart (1.1 litres) water	1 oz (25 g) butter
2 cabbages	1 pint (600 ml) milk
1 onion	chopped parsley
2 oz (50 g) sago	salt and pepper

(Enough for five or six people)

Cleanse and shred the cabbage finely, throw into boiling water, bring to the boil and strain, return to the saucepan with one quart (1.1 litres) boiling water, chopped onion, butter, parsley, milk, salt and pepper. Boil gently for fifteen minutes, sprinkle in the sago, cook about ten minutes till transparent and serve.

44 BEETROOT SOUP

1 quart (1.1 litres) stock	1 stick celery
1 oz (25 g) butter	½ gill (75 ml) cream
1 oz (25 g) flour	salt and pepper
1 cooked beetroot	

(Enough for four or five people)

Melt the butter in a saucepan, stir in the flour and cook without browning, add stock, or if no stock, milk and water; stir till it boils, cut the celery and beet into shreds, add to the soup and boil for fifty minutes to an hour.

Pass the soup through a sieve, rub through only enough beetroot to give a good colour and consistency, add the cream and seasoning, reheat and serve with small croûtons of fried bread.

45 GIBLET SOUP

3 pints (1.7 litres) stock	bouquet garni
2 sets of fowls' giblets	1½ oz (40 g) butter
2 onions	1 oz (25 g) flour
1 carrot	2 oz (50 g) rice
1 leek	chopped parsley
1 stick celery	salt and pepper

(Enough for five or six people)

Carefully clean the giblets (heart, gizzard, liver, wings and neck) and cut into small pieces. Prepare and slice the vegetables, melt the butter in a saucepan, add the onions and giblets, fry a nice brown, stir in the flour, cook gently for three or four minutes, add the stock and vegetables, boil up and simmer gently for forty minutes, skimming occasionally. Cook the 2 oz (50 g) rice, drain and add, remove some of the giblets and keep to garnish, pass through a sieve, return to the pan, season well and add a little sherry if liked, reheat and put in pieces of giblets and chopped parsley and serve.

46 WHITE CHICKEN SOUP

3 pints (1.7 litres) white stock	1 onion
1 chicken	bunch of herbs
2½ oz (65 g) butter	mace
2 oz (50 g) flour	1 gill (150 ml) cream
½ pint (300 ml) milk	salt and pepper

(Enough for five or six people)

Cut the chicken into joints, wash well and cook in a stewpan with some of the butter, mace, onion and herbs, with the lid on the pan, taking care it does not brown; add the stock and simmer for an hour. Remove the joints, take off the flesh and pound well in a mortar, put back the bones and simmer till required. Make a roux with the remainder of the butter and flour, strain in the stock, add the pounded chicken and simmer for about twenty minutes, rub through a sieve, add the cream, reheat, season and serve.

47 JULIENNE SOUP

1 quart (1.1 litres) water	3 tomatoes
2 onions	some meat essence or gravy
1 carrot	chopped parsley
1 turnip	salt and pepper
Celery	

(Enough for four or five people)

Prepare the vegetables and cut into thin shreds, boil the water, throw in the vegetables with some salt, and boil quickly till tender, add the meat essence or strong gravy, season well, add the tomatoes cut into small neat pieces and the chopped parsley, boil up and serve.

48 PARISIAN SOUP

1 quart (1.1 litres) white stock	½ gill (75 ml) cream
2 oz (50 g) tapioca	lemon juice
2 yolks of eggs	salt and pepper
½ oz (15 g) grated cheese	

(Enough for four people)

Boil the stock, which should be well flavoured with vegetables, and remove the scum as it rises, shake in the finely crushed tapioca and simmer for fifteen minutes. Beat the yolks of eggs, add a little lemon juice and grated cheese, stir into the soup, cook gently, but do not let it boil, add the cream and serve at once.

49 MAIGRE SOUP

3 pints (1.7 litres) water	2 oz (50 g) pearl barley
2 carrots	celery
2 turnips	½ pint (300 ml) milk
2 onions	salt and pepper

(Enough for five or six people)

Chop the vegetables and put into a saucepan with three pints (1.7 litres) of water, simmer for two hours, blanch the barley and add to the soup, and simmer for one hour, add the milk, season well and serve.

50 JENNY LIND SOUP

1 quart (1.1 litres) white stock	1½ oz (40 g) sago
1 gill (150 ml) milk	pinch of sugar
yolks of 2 eggs	salt and pepper

(Enough for four people)

Wash the sago and add it to some boiling well-flavoured white stock, simmer for an hour, beat up the yolks of eggs with the milk, strain into the soup and cook, but do not allow it to boil or the eggs will curdle, season well and serve at once.

51 BONNE FEMME SOUP

1 quart (1.1 litres) white stock	1 oz (25 g) flour
1 lettuce	2 yolks of eggs
1 cucumber	¼ pint (150 ml) milk
3 onions	salt and pepper
3 oz (75 g) butter	a French roll

(Enough for four or five people)

Shred the lettuce finely, cut the cucumber into strips and chop the onions, melt the butter in a saucepan, add the vegetables and cook lightly without browning them with the lid on the pan, mix the flour with a little cold stock, add to the vegetables with the remainder of the stock, which should be boiling. Cook together from fifteen to twenty minutes, season with salt, pepper and a grate of nutmeg, beat up the yolks of the eggs and strain into the soup and cook, but do not let it boil. Break up some French roll in the tureen and pour the soup over and serve.

52 TAPIOCA CREAM SOUP

1 quart (1.1 litres) white stock	yolks of 2 eggs
1 oz (25 g) tapioca	salt and pepper
1 gill (150 ml) milk or cream	

(Enough for four people)

Put the stock well flavoured with vegetables into a stew-pan, let it boil up, remove any scum that rises, and put in finely crushed tapioca, boil till this is transparent, beat the yolks, add the gill (150 ml) milk or cream, pour into the soup, stir until it thickens, but do not let it boil, season to taste and serve.

53 HOLLANDAISE SOUP

1 quart (1.1 litres) white stock	2 turnips
1 oz (25 g) butter	1 gill (150 ml) green peas
1 oz (25 g) flour	1 gill (150 ml) cream
3 yolks of eggs	pinch of castor sugar
2 carrots	seasoning

(Enough for four or five people)

Prepare and cut the vegetables in fancy shapes and cook till tender in salted water, melt the butter in a pan and add the flour, cook together for a few minutes without browning, add the stock, stir till boiling and cook slowly for five minutes. Allow the soup to cool, strain in the cream and yolks of eggs and reheat, but on no account should you allow the soup to boil, add sugar and seasoning to taste, put the vegetables in a tureen and pour the soup over and serve; the vegetables can be omitted, but a well-flavoured stock must be used.

54 SPRING CREAM SOUP

1 quart (1.1 litres) white stock	½ gill (75 ml) green peas
1 oz (25 g) ground rice	asparagus heads
1 oz (25 g) butter	¼ lb (100 g) French beans
1 gill (150 ml) cream	2 carrots
1 gill (150 ml) milk	2 turnips
pinch castor sugar	little parsley, chervil and
salt and pepper	tarragon

(Enough for four or five people)

Prepare and cut the vegetables into fancy shapes and cook them separately in salted water, they must not be over-done. Heat the stock, remove the scum as it rises, thicken with the ground rice, stir until boiling, and simmer for fifteen minutes, add the vegetables and cook gently for five minutes, pour in the cream, add butter in small pieces, sugar and seasoning, and lastly two teaspoonfuls of mixed chopped parsley, tarragon and chervil.

55 POTAGE À LA ROYALE

3 pints (1.7 litres) white stock	1 oz (25 g) cheese
2 oz (50 g) cooked macaroni	croûtons of toast
2 yolks of eggs	salt and pepper

(Enough for four or five people)

Boil the stock, which should be well flavoured, add the macaroni cut in small pieces, and the grated cheese, mix in the yolks of eggs, but do not allow the soup to boil, season well and serve with small squares of toast.

56 WHITE LENTIL SOUP

1 quart (1.1 litres) water	1 oz (25 g) flour
½ pint (300 ml) lentils	½ pint (300 ml) milk
1 carrot	pepper and salt
1 turnip	croûtons of fried bread
1 onion	

(Enough for four people)

Wash and soak the lentils, put them into a saucepan with the waer, carrot, turnip and onion, simmer gently for several hours, remove the carrot, rub the soup through a sieve, return to the saucepan, season and thicken it with the flour, boil up, add the milk but do not boil again, serve with croûtons of fried bread.

57 WINDSOR SOUP

1 quart (1.1 litres) stock	½ pint (300 ml) cream
2 oz (50 g) flour	3 oz (75 g) pearl barley
3 oz (75 g) butter	salt and pepper
3 yolks of eggs	

(Enough for four people)

Blanch the barley, add the flour and cook gently in the butter, stir in the stock and simmer for two and a half hours, pass through a sieve, add the yolks and cream, season well, reheat and serve with croûtons of fried bread.

58 PURÉE OF TURNIPS

1 quart (1.1 litres) white stock	1 oz (25 g) sago
6 large turnips	½ pint milk
1 onion	salt and pepper

(Enough for four people)

Peel turnips thickly, cut into slices and cook for two and a half hours in the stock, rub through a sieve, add the sago, allow it to thicken, add the milk, season and serve with croûtons of fried bread.

59 KALE BROSE

Scotch kale	1 turnip
2 quarts (2.3 litres) water or stock	2 oz (50 g) pearl barley
2 onions	salt and pepper
2 carrots	

(Enough for six or seven people)

Blanch the kale and cut into small pieces, boil the stock, add the barley and vegetables, cut into small pieces, let the brose simmer very gently from two to three hours, season and serve.

60 CHERVIL SOUP

1 quart (1.1 litres) white stock	½ tablespoonful chopped
½ oz (15 g) crème de riz	parsley
½ tablespoonful chopped	salt and pepper
chervil	

(Enough for four people)

Cook some chervil in the white stock for fifteen minutes, strain it, mix the crème de riz with a little cold water, add to the soup and stir till it boils and thickens, season well; just before serving sprinkle in the chervil and parsley very finely chopped, serve with fried croûtons of bread.

61 GAME SOUP

1 quart (1.1 litres) game stock	vegetables
2 oz (50 g) ham	1 oz (25 g) sago
½ lb (225 g) lean beef	salt and pepper

(Enough for four people)

The stock should be made from boiling down game bones, mince the beef and cook with the ham and the vegetables in the stock for three hours, strain, add the sago and boil for five minutes, season and serve.

62 FISH SOUP

1 quart (1.1 litres) fish stock	½ pint (300 ml) milk
1 oz (25 g) sago	1 teaspoonful parsley
½ oz (15 g) cornflour	salt and pepper

(Enough for four people)

Boil the stock, thicken with the cornflour mixed smoothly, and the sago, simmer for fifteen minutes, add the milk, chopped parsley, and seasoning, serve with small croûtons of fried bread.

63 LOBSTER SOUP

1 lobster	1 strip lemon rind
1 quart (1.1 litres) stock	½ pint (300 ml) milk
1 onion	bunch of herbs
2 oz (50 g) butter	mace, salt and pepper
1 oz (25 g) flour	little cream

(Enough for four or five people)

Take the meat from the shell of the lobster, put in a pan with the stock, herbs, mace and lemon rind, simmer from one and a half to two hours till all the flavour has been extracted, strain through a sieve, melt the butter in a saucepan, add the flour, cook together, then add the milk and the soup, and stir till it boils, season well and colour if necessary, drop in a few neat pieces of lobster meat and add a little cream just before serving.

FISH

64 BOILED COD

4 lb (1.8 kg) cod	vinegar or little lemon juice
salt	lemon and parsley

(Enough for eight people)

Well wash the fish in salt and water, place it in hot water with a little vinegar or lemon juice and salt, simmer very slowly until cooked, skimming occasionally, and allowing ten minutes to the pound (0.5 kg) and ten minutes over.

Drain well, serve on a hot dish and folded serviette, garnish with cut lemon and parsley and serve with oyster, anchovy, or any suitable sauce.

65 BOILED MACKEREL

4 mackerels parsley or fennel sauce (see
salt No. 612)
(*Enough for six or seven people*)

Open the fish just enough to take out the roe, thoroughly cleanse the fish and the roe and replace it, remove the eyes. Place into salted water just below boiling point, simmer eight to ten minutes according to the size, taking care not to break the skin, which will happen if cooked too fast. Dish on a folded serviette, garnish with lemon and parsley and serve with parsley or fennel sauce.

66 BOILED TURBOT

turbot, 4 lb (1.8 kg) parsley
vinegar or lemon juice lobster coral
1 lemon
(*Enough for eight people*)

Well wash the fish but do not remove the fins, these are considered a great delicacy; place in a fish-kettle of hot water with salt and vinegar added, bring to the boil and simmer very gently until cooked, allowing six to eight minutes to the pound (0.5 kg) and six to eight minutes over, according to size and thickness. Drain the fish, dish on a folded serviette on a hot dish and garnish with lobster coral and lemon and parsley, serve with lobster or shrimp sauce (see No. 610 or 613).

Note. — Halibut, Brill, John Dory are cooked in the same way.

67 BOILED SALMON

4 lb (1.8 kg) salmon cucumber
salt
(*Enough for eight people*)

Well wash the fish, put it in boiling water with salt, allow it to boil for a few minutes, then simmer very slowly till cooked; if a large thick piece allow eight minutes to the pound (0.5 kg) and eight minutes over, if a thin piece six minutes. Drain well, put on a hot dish with a folded serviette, garnish with sliced cucumber and parsley, serve with dressed cucumber and a suitable sauce, such as hollandaise, mayonnaise, tartare (see sauces in the index).

68 STUFFED AND BAKED HADDOCK

1 fresh haddock brown crumbs
veal stuffing dripping or butter
1 egg or little milk
(*Enough for three or four people*)

Thoroughly cleanse the fish, fill the inside with veal stuffing. Sew up the opening and truss the fish in the shape of the letter S, place it in a baking tin, brush it with beaten egg and a little milk, sprinkle with brown crumbs and bake it slowly, basting it frequently with dripping or butter, serve it on a hot dish, garnish with parsley and cut lemon and anchovy or any other suitable sauce poured round.

69 STUFFED HERRINGS

3 or 4 herrings brown crumbs
veal stuffing
(*Enough for three people*)

Cut off the head and tail, wash well in salted water, make an incision down the back and carefully remove the backbone, lay some stuffing on the tail end and roll up, bake on a greased tin, brush over with milk and sprinkle with brown crumbs. Serve on a hot dish with fancy paper★, garnish with parsley and cut lemon.

★ Fatty foods were often served on a cake doily.

70 STUFFED AND BAKED FILLETS OF PLAICE

1 plaice salt and pepper
½ oz (15 g) butter chopped parsley
½ oz (15 g) flour coraline pepper
1 gill (150 ml) milk veal stuffing (see No. 643)
little lemon juice
(*Enough for three or four people*)

Fillet the plaice, skin the fillets, if large cut in half lengthways, place a little stuffing on each half fillet, roll up, place on a greased tin, squeeze over each a little lemon juice and bake slowly for fifteen to twenty minutes, dish on a hot dish, make a sauce with the butter, flour and milk, coat the fillets with it, garnish with coraline pepper and chopped parsley.

71 FILLETS OF FISH À LA BOHEMIENNE

fillets of sole or plaice 1 tablespoonful cream
2 oz (50 g) butter lemon juice
1 oz (25 g) flour salt and pepper
1 gill (150 ml) milk parsley
½ lb (225 g) tomatoes
(*Enough for three or four people*)

Lay the fillets, cut in half or rolled, on a greased tin, sprinkle a little lemon juice and pepper on each, cover with greased paper and bake in the oven from fifteen to twenty minutes, cook the sliced tomatoes in 1 oz (25 g) butter. When tender pass them through a sieve, make a sauce with the remainder of the butter, flour, milk and tomato purée, boil, then add seasoning and cream. Put the fillets on a hot dish, coat with the sauce and garnish with cut lemon and parsley.

72 FILLETS OF FISH À LA MAÎTRE D'HÔTEL

fillets of plaice or sole chopped parsley
1 oz (25 g) flour lemon juice
1 oz (25 g) butter salt and pepper
½ pint (300 ml) milk
(*Enough for three or four people*)

Skin and fillet the fish, bake in the oven on a greased tin sprinkled with lemon juice and pepper. Make a sauce with the flour, butter and milk, add the chopped parsley and lemon juice, season well, place the fillets on a hot dish, coat them with the sauce, garnish with cut lemon and parsley.

73 SOLE À LA TURQUE

1 sole	1 shallot
1 tablespoonful bread crumbs	½ teaspoonful herbs
½ oz (15 g) suet	1 teaspoonful chopped parsley
1 gill (150 ml) picked shrimps	¼ oz (10 g) butter
1 egg	few brown bread crumbs
grated rind of ½ lemon	pepper and salt
½ pint (300 ml) stock	

(Enough for four people)

Skin the sole, remove head, tail and fins, wash thoroughly, make an incision down the fish on one side and raise the fillets, chop the shrimps, make a stuffing with the other ingredients, moisten with the beaten egg, place it in the fish, put in some small bits of butter, bake in a fireproof dish with the stock round for twenty minutes. Add a little sherry to the liquor; if liked sprinkle over a few brown crumbs and garnish with cut lemon and parsley.

74 SOLE AU GRATIN

1 sole	some Italian sauce
4 mushrooms	little sherry or white wine
lemon juice	½ oz (15 g) butter
parsley	brown bread crumbs
1 small shallot	salt and pepper

(Enough for four people)

Chop the shallot, parsley and mushrooms finely, grease a fireproof dish, lay in some of the seasoning, skin and score the sole, place it in the dish, moisten with lemon juice and a little sherry or white wine, place on the rest of the seasoning and cover with Italian sauce (see No. 626), sprinkle over a few brown crumbs and put some small pieces of butter on top and bake for twenty minutes, sprinkle over a little finely-chopped parsley and serve.

75 SOLE AU PARMESAN

2 medium-sized soles	1½ oz (40 g) Parmesan cheese
1 oz (25 g) flour	little lemon juice
2 oz (50 g) butter	salt, pepper, and nutmeg
1 gill (150 ml) milk	

(Enough for five or six people)

Skin, trim and wipe soles, place them in a greased tin or fireproof dish, season them and squeeze over some lemon juice, cover with greased paper and bake for twenty minutes, make a sauce with the butter, flour and milk, cooking the flour in the butter till a pale fawn colour, add the grated cheese, stir till it boils and cook for ten minutes, season with salt, pepper and nutmeg. Strain the sauce over the soles, brown under the gas or in a quick oven and serve.

76 SOLE À LA PORTUGAISE

sole	1 oz (25 g) butter
1 Spanish onion	1 oz (25 g) grated cheese
2 or 3 tomatoes	salt and pepper

(Enough for four people)

Skin the sole, place it in a greased fireproof dish, slice the onion very thinly, place on the top of the sole with the tomatoes sliced, sprinkle over salt and pepper and the grated cheese, put the butter in small pieces on the top and bake from twenty to thirty minutes, the sole can be filleted if prefered and tomato sauce used instead of sliced tomato; fillets of any fish can be "à la Portugaise."

77 SOLE À LA FLORENTAINE

fillets of sole (2 soles)	1 tablespoonful cream
½ lb (225 g) cooked spinach	1 oz (25 g) butter
good white sauce	½ glass white wine
2 oz (50 g) Parmesan cheese	lemon juice
1 shallot	salt and pepper

(Enough for six or seven people)

Cook and sieve the spinach, melt the butter and brown in it the finely-chopped shallot, add this to spinach with cream and seasoning. Place it in a layer in a greased fireproof dish, dry and knot the fillets of sole, poach them for ten minutes in a greased sauté pan with a little lemon juice, white wine and fish stock with a small piece of butter on each fillet; when cooked place the fillets on the spinach, sprinkle over some of the grated cheese, add the rest to the white sauce with the liquor the fillets were cooked in, coat the fillets with the sauce, sprinkle over more cheese and brown under the griller, or in a quick oven, and serve.

78 MACKEREL À LA NORMANDE

2 mackerels	½ teaspoonful chopped herbs
2 tablespoonsful bread crumbs	½ small onion
1 teaspoonful chopped parsley	salt and pepper

(Enough for four people)

Thoroughly cleanse the mackerel, split and remove the backbone, also the head and fins, mix the stuffing which should not be moistened, place it on one fish and lay over the other skin side upwards. Sprinkle over a few brown crumbs, dot on some pieces of dripping, bake in a greased tin, serve on a fancy paper with a garnish of cut lemon and parsley.

79 FISH FRIED IN BATTER

fillets of whiting or plaice	2 tablespoonfuls tepid water
2 oz (50 g) flour	white of 1 egg
1 tablespoonful oil or dissolved butter	salt and pepper

(Enough for five or six people)

Wash and dry the fillets and dip in flour, place the flour in a basin, add salt, add the oil, then mix smoothly with the tepid water, beat it well, and if possible stand aside for some time; just before using add the beaten white of egg. Dip in each fillet, fry them in deep fat without using a basket. Drain well, garnish with fried parsley.

80 FRIED FILLETS OF PLAICE

fillets of plaice	salt and pepper
a little flour	egg and bread crumbs

(Enough for three or four people)

Wash and thoroughly dry the fillets, dip them in flour seasoned with salt and pepper, beat up the egg, dip in the fillets, drain and roll them in the crumbs, shaking off any loose ones, fry a golden brown in hot fat, drain well, and serve garnished with lemon and parsley.

81 LOBSTER CUTLETS

1 lobster or small tin	lemon juice
1 oz (25 g) flour	salt and pepper
1 oz (25 g) butter	egg and bread crumbs
1 gill (150 ml) milk	parsley

(Enough for six people)

Cut open lobster, crack the claws, take out the meat and chop it finely, make a roux with the flour and butter, add the milk in which the shells have been simmered, add the lobser meat, lemon juice, salt and pepper, put the mixture on a wet plate, divide it into equal portions and allow to cool, form into cutlet shapes, coat with egg and bread crumbs, fry a golden brown in hot fat, place a small piece of claw in each cutlet as a bone, place the head in the centre of the dish on a bed of fried parsley and place the cutlets round; if tinned lobster is used a croûton of fried bread can take the place of the head, to support the cutlets.

82 FRIED EELS

2 eels	salt and pepper
little flour	egg and bread crumbs

(Enough for seven or eight people)

Skin and thoroughly cleanse the eels and allow to soak in salt and water some time. Cut in three-inch (7.5 cm) lengths, dip them in seasoned flour, coat in egg and bread crumbs and fry in deep fat, serve on a hot dish on a fancy paper, garnish with fried parsley, serve with tartare or piquante sauce (see No. 624 or 637).

83 FRIED SMELTS

1 doz. smelts	egg and bread crumbs
flour	lemon
salt and pepper	parsley

(Enough for four people)

Wash the smelts, they require gentle handling in cleaning, trim with scissors, dip in seasoned flour, coat with egg and bread crumbs, roll on board to make them a nice shape, fry a golden brown in hot fat, arrange on a hot dish with fancy paper, garnish with quarters of lemon and fried parsley. Serve with tartare or tomato sauce (see No. 637 or 628).

84 FRIED SOLE À LA COLBERT

1 sole	½ oz (15 g) butter
egg and bread crumbs	1 teaspoonful chopped parsley
little flour	lemon juice
salt and pepper	

(Enough for three people)

Skin and trim the sole, make an incision down the centre and remove a piece of the backbone two inches (5 cm) long and slightly raise the fillets, dip in seasoned flour and coat with egg and bread crumbs, fry a golden brown in hot fat, drain well, dish on a fancy paper and place in the opening a square of maître d'hôtel butter made by mixing on a plate the butter, chopped parsley and lemon juice; if quite firm this can be cut in fancy shapes with a small cutter.

85 SOLE KNOTS

1 sole	egg and bread crumbs
flour	parsley
pepper and salt	

(Enough for four people)

Skin and fillet a sole, cut each fillet in half lengthways, tie each piece in a knot, dip in seasoned flour, coat with egg and bread crumbs, fry a golden brown in hot fat, drain on paper, dish on fancy paper and garnish with fried parsley, serve with tomato or any suitable sauce.

86 FRIED TROUT

trout	egg and bread crumbs
lemon	parsley

Wash and cleanse the trout and dry them in a clean cloth, dip them in seasoned flour, then coat them with egg and bread crumbs, fry a golden brown in hot fat, drain thoroughly and dish them on a hot dish on a serviette, garnish with cut lemon and fried parsley. Send cut lemon to table with them.

87 WHITEBAIT

1 pint (600 ml) whitebait	pepper and salt
flour	brown bread and butter
lemon	

(Enough for four people)

Drain the fish, shake them lightly in flour so as to separate them, turn on to a sieve and gently shake away all loose flour. Plunge at once into very hot fat, shaking the basket gently all the time, remove the fish, reheat the fat and plunge them in again to crisp them, drain them well and dish on a hot dish with a fancy paper, season well and serve with quarters of lemon and the thin brown bread and butter.

88 FISH CAKES

½ lb (225 g) each of cold fish and potatoes	little butter
	salt and pepper
½ teaspoonful anchovy	egg and bread crumbs
½ teaspoonful chopped parsley	

(Enough for ten or twelve cakes)

Remove all bones and skin, flake the fish finely, mash the potatoes, mix them together, add the butter and flavourings, form in small cakes, using a little flour; coat with egg and bread crumbs, fry in hot fat, garnish with fried parsley.

89 FISH PASTY

equal quantities cold fish and potatoes	some anchovy sauce or white sauce
pepper and salt	

Remove skin and bones from fish, flake and add it to the sauce, season well and place mixture in a greased pie dish,

mash the potatoes smoothly, place it on the top of the fish, decorate it nicely and brush over with egg or milk, cook till a nice brown in a hot oven.

90 SCALLOPED FISH

any cold fish	few bread crumbs
little butter	

For Sauce

1 oz (25 g) butter	1 oz (25 g) flour
½ pint (300 ml) milk	salt and pepper

Remove the skin and bones from fish and flake it, make a white sauce and flavour it nicely, add it to the dish, butter some scallop shells, put in some of the mixture, sprinkle over some bread crumbs, put small pieces of butter on the top, bake till a nice brown in a quick oven; a little grated cheese can be sprinkled over before baking if liked.

91 FISH CURRY

1 lb (450 g) cooked fish	1 oz (25 g) dessicated cocoanut
1 apple	lemon juice
1 small onion	salt
2 oz (50 g) butter	1 dessertspoonful curry paste
1 oz (25 g) flour	4 oz (100 g) Patna rice
½ oz (15 g) curry powder	

(Enough for four or five people)

Boil the rice and dry it thoroughly, melt the butter in a stewpan, well cook the apple and onion finely chopped, add the flour and curry powder and cook for fifteen to twenty minutes, then add the milk and stir till it boils, infuse the cocoanut in a little of the milk for some minutes, then strain it into the curry, add the curry paste, lemon juice and salt and a pinch of sugar, flake the fish and stir in gently not to break the flakes, serve on a hot dish with a border of the rice and garnish with cut lemon and parsley.

To boil the rice. — Well wash the rice, put in fast-boiling water to which has been added salt and a little lemon juice, when tender drain on to a sieve, pour cold water over to separate the grains and dry thoroughly.

92 FRICASSÉE OF FISH

1 lb (450 g) cold cooked fish	1 gill (150 ml) cream
1 oz (25 g) butter	lemon juice
1 oz (25 g) flour	salt and pepper
1 gill (150 ml) milk	mashed potatoes

(Enough for four or five people)

Remove skin and bones from fish and roughly flake it, make a white sauce with butter, flour, milk and cream, season well and add lemon juice, make a border of mashed potato, using a rose tube and forcing bag, place the mixture in the centre, garnish the fish with lemon and parsley. Another suitable garnish is the flaked yolk of hard-boiled egg.

93 FISH CROQUETTES

¾ lb (350 g) cold fish	anchovy essence
1 oz (25 g) flour	salt and pepper
1 oz (25 g) butter	egg and bread crumbs
1 gill (150 ml) milk	parsley

(Enough to make eight croquettes)

Remove all skin and bones from the fish, flake finely, make a panada with the butter, flour and milk, add anchovy essence and season nicely, add the fish, turn the mixture on to a wet plate, divide into equal portions and allow it to cool, form into croquettes, cork shape, coat with egg and bread crumbs, fry a golden brown in deep fat, dish on a hot dish with fancy paper, and garnish with fried parsley.

94 KEDGEREE

1 cooked smoked haddock	3 oz (75 g) butter
or any cold fish	salt and pepper
¼ lb (100 g) boiled rice	chopped parsley
2 hard-boiled eggs	curry sauce

(Enough for four people)

Flake the fish, carefully remove all bones and skin, add the butter, 1 egg chopped, salt and pepper, and the rice, get the mixture very hot, pile on a dish, scallop it round with a knife, garnish with chopped parsley and flaked yolk of egg, place a cup of white of egg on the top with a sprig of parsley in it, serve with curry sauce (see No. 635).

95 LOBSTER MOULD AND SAUCE

1 fresh lobster or ½ a tin	1 tablespoonful cream
¾ oz (20 g) butter	lemon juice
¾ oz (20 g) flour	1 white of egg
3 tablespoonfuls milk	salt, pepper—cayenne

(Enough for four or five people)

Make a panada with butter, flour and milk, cook thoroughly, add salt, lemon juice and cayenne, mince the lobster and add to the panada with cream and whipped white of egg, put the mixture into a well-greased tin or mould and steam for three-quarters of an hour covered with greased paper, turn out and serve with the following sauce:

4 tablespoonfuls cream	1 gill (150 ml) milk
½ oz (15 g) flour	½ teaspoonful lemon juice
1 oz (25 g) butter	salt and pepper
yolk of egg	

Cook the flour in the butter, add the milk and boil; mix the cream and the yolk, pour into the saucepan, stir well, cook it but do not allow it to boil, season and serve.

96 LOBSTER AU GRATIN

1 lobster or ½ a tin	1 egg
2 small shallots	1 tablespoonful chopped parsley
1 oz (25 g) butter	little anchovy essence
1 oz (25 g) flour	salt, cayenne
½ pint (300 ml) milk	

(Enough for four people)

Chop lobster into small pieces, lightly fry the chopped shallot in the butter, add the flour and cook, then the milk, simmer for five minutes, put in lobster, parsley, anchovy essence, salt and cayenne, stir till it boils, cool and add the well-beaten egg, grease some scallop shells, fill with the mixture, sprinkle over some bread crumbs and pour over a little melted butter, brown in the oven and serve very hot.

97 HADDOCK À LA ST CLAIR

1 smoked haddock	1 gill (150 ml) milk
1 or 2 tomatoes	2 tablespoonfuls cream
1 oz (25 g) butter	1 yolk of egg (hard boiled)
1 oz (25 g) flour	seasoning

(Enough for four or five people)

Cook the tomato in slices and arrange round a dish, make a sauce with the flour, butter, milk and cream, cook the haddock and flake it, removing skin and bones; add it to the sauce, put it in the centre of the tomato and garnish with yolk of egg rubbed through a sieve.

98 STEWED EELS

1 eel	little lemon juice
1 gill (150 ml) stock	½ oz (15 g) flour
2 tablespoonfuls port wine	1 dessertspoonful mushroom
blade of mace	ketchup
2 cloves	pepper and salt
1 shallot	½ oz (15 g) butter

(Enough for three or four people)

Thoroughly cleanse the eel and cut in pieces three inches long, cook them in a stewpan in the stock and port wine, adding the mace, cloves, chopped shallot and lemon juice, simmer for about an hour, strain and thicken the gravy with the butter and flour, boil up and add ketchup and salt and pepper, dish the eel in a circle and pour the sauce over.

99 SALMON MAYONNAISE

Cold salmon 2 or 3 lb (900 g or	capers, gherkin
1.4 kg)	anchovy fillets
cucumber	aspic jelly
lettuce	mayonnaise sauce (see No. 636)
cress	

(Enough for nine or ten people)

Remove the skin from the salmon, arrange a bed of lettuce on a dish, coat the salmon well with thick mayonnaise sauce with a little liquid aspic added, place it on the salad, garnish tastefully with cucumber slices, little heaps of capers, shredded gherkin, cress and chopped aspic. Lay across two anchovy fillets, or if liked they can be rolled.

100 DRESSED CRAB

1 crab	lemon juice
1½ oz (40 g) bread crumbs	salt and pepper
2 oz (50 g) butter	coraline pepper
chopped parsley	

(Enough for three or four people)

Separate the crab, take meat out carefully from the small claws, mix it with the inside of the crab, add the bread crumbs, lemon juice and seasoning, make it into a paste, wash and dry the shell, put in the mixture, flake the white meat from the large claws finely, pile it on each side, decorate it with chopped parsley and coraline pepper.

101 GRILLED HERRINGS

6 herrings	salad oil

For Sauce

1 oz (25 g) butter	1 teaspoonful made mustard
1 oz (25 g) flour	seasoning
½ pint (300 ml) milk	

(Enough for six people)

Remove the heads, wash and clean thoroughly without breaking, score the fish with a knife and brush with salad oil, put on the grill before a clear fire and cook on both sides. Put on a hot dish with a small piece of butter on each and serve with mustard sauce.

102 RED MULLET

4 mullet	anchovy essence
1 oz (25 g) butter	½ pint (300 ml) white sauce
lemon juice	salt and cayenne
1 glass port or claret	

(Enough for four people)

Wash the fish and dry thoroughly in a cloth, do not open it, only remove the gills and small intestine, which will come out with them, squeeze over some lemon juice, sprinkle with salt and pepper, wrap each fish in thickly-buttered paper, place on a baking tin and bake in a moderate oven for twenty minutes, serve the fish in the paper cases.

Add to the white sauce, some lemon juice, anchovy essence, cayenne, and a glass of port or claret and the liquid which has flowed from the fish, then serve the sauce with the fish.

103 SCALLOPED OYSTERS

2 doz. oysters	1 oz (25 g) butter
½ pint (300 ml) white sauce	bread crumbs

(Enough for six or seven people)

Open the oysters, wash them in their own liquor, put them in a white lined saucepan, strain the liquor over them, slowly heat but do not let them boil, take them out and remove their beards, make the white sauce hot, put in the oysters, strain in the liquor, stand at the side of the fire for a few minutes. Butter some scallop shells, put some of the mixture in each, dividing the oysters equally, sprinkle over the bread crumbs, put on some small pieces of butter, bake in a moderate oven and serve hot.

104 CURRIED PRAWNS

2 or 3 doz. prawns	3 oz (75 g) Patna rice
½ pint (300 ml) curry sauce	lemon and parsley
(see No. 635)	

(Enough for three or four people)

Head, tail and shell prawns, make the curry sauce very hot, put in the prawns and heat them very slowly at the side of the fire. Serve very hot with a border of rice, garnish with cut lemon and parsley.

105 DRESSED COD

1 thick cod steak	1 egg
3 tablespoonfuls bread crumbs	1½ teaspoonfuls parsley
2 oz (50 g) butter	salt and pepper

(Enough for three or four people)

Mix together the bread crumbs, parsley, butter, egg and seasoning; put this stuffing on the cod in a buttered dish, cover with a buttered paper and bake in a moderate oven for three-quarters of an hour. Serve garnished with lemon and parsley.

106 COD PROVENÇALE

2 cod steaks	1 tablespoonful chooped
½ pint (300 ml) white sauce	gherkins
2 yolks of eggs	1 tablespoonful chopped capers
	salt and pepper

(Enough for four people)

Bake the cod in a buttered tin, covered with buttered paper, for twenty minutes, remove to a hot dish, heat the white sauce, add gherkins, capers and egg yolks, season and pour over, garnish with cut lemon and parsley.

107 SALMON CUTLETS

½ lb (225 g) cold salmon	1 teaspoonful chopped parsley
½ lb (225 g) mashed potato	vermicelli
1 oz (25 g) butter	seasoning
2 eggs	lemon juice

(Enough for five or six people)

Melt the butter, mix in with potatoes and finely chopped salmon. When quite hot add 1 yolk of egg, parsley, lemon juice, salt and pepper. Spread the mixture on a plate to cool, form into cutlets, using a little flour, coat with egg and crushed vermicelli or bread crumbs, fry a golden brown in hot fat, serve on a fancy paper either hot or cold.

108 SALMON COQUILLES

½ to ¾ lb (225 to 350 g) cold	½ gill (75 ml) cream
salmon	blade of mace
1 oz (25 g) butter	bread crumbs
¾ oz (20 g) flour	butter
½ pint (300 ml) milk	salt and pepper

(Enough for four or five people)

Remove the skin and bones from the salmon and divide into flakes, make a sauce with the butter, flour and milk, add mace and seasoning and allow to simmer for five minutes, then strain. Butter some scallop shells, add the salmon to the sauce, fill the shells, cover with bread crumbs and put some little bits of butter on the top. Bake a nice brown in a quick oven.

Note. — Any cold fish can be served in this way.

109 BAKED SALMON STEAKS

2 or 3 salmon steaks	lemon juice
chopped parsley	salt and pepper
butter	caper sauce
shallot	

(Enough for four or five people)

Place the steaks in a buttered baking dish, season with chopped parsley, shallot, salt, pepper and lemon juice, cover with buttered paper and cook in a quick oven from ten to fifteen minutes, dish and serve with caper sauce or, if preferred, a rich brown sauce.

110 FILLETS OF SALMON À LA TARTARE

3 or 4 slices of salmon	some chopped tarragon and
½ pint (300 ml) mayonnaise	chervil
1 teaspoonful French mustard	anchovies
1 teaspoonful anchovy essence	olives
	gherkins

(Enough for four people)

Grill the salmon slices and set aside to get cold, add to the mayonnaise sauce the mustard, anchovy essence and chopped tarragon and chervil. Arrange the fish on a dish, pour the sauce over, garnish with stoned olives, filleted anchovies and sliced gherkin. If preferred hot add all the flavourings to some good brown sauce instead of mayonnaise, adding a little tarragon vinegar.

111 SALMON DARIOLES EN BELLE-VUE

½ lb (225 g) cooked salmon	1 gill (150 ml) tomato sauce
aspic jelly	1 tablespoonful anchovy paste
mayonnaise sauce	truffle
2 sheets gelatine	cucumber

(Enough for four or five people)

Line six oval moulds with aspic jelly, decorate with fancy shapes of truffle and cucumber rind. When set pour in a layer of mayonnaise aspic mixed in equal quantities with some cream added. Remove the skin and bone from the salmon and pound, add some mayonnaise cream, anchovy paste and gelatine dissolved in the tomato sauce and seasoning. Fill the moulds with this and put on ice to set. Turn out on a silver dish and garnish with chopped aspic and slices of cucumber.

112 SALMON CREAMS

1 lb (450 g) salmon	1 white of egg
1 oz (25 g) butter	some pounded lobster coral
1 gill (150 ml) white sauce	seasoning
1 gill (150 ml) cream	cardinal sauce (see No. 631)

(Enough for five or six people)

Remove the skin and bone from the salmon and pound in a mortar till quite fine, add the white sauce, seasoning and white of egg, pound well together, rub through a sieve, whip the cream slightly and add. Well butter eight to ten dariole moulds, decorate the bottom with lobster coral. Fill the moulds with the salmon mixture, cover with greased paper and steam from twenty-five to thirty minutes. Turn out on a hot dish, heat the Cardinal sauce and pour round.

113 SOLE GASCOYNE

1 sole	1 tablespoonful Worcester
1 onion	sauce
4 peppercorns	1 gill (150 ml) gravy
6 allspice	salt

(Enough for two people)

Simmer together in a saucepan the gravy, onion, allspice, pepper and Worcester sauce. Skin the sole and lay it in a buttered fireproof dish, cover with a buttered paper and bake in a moderate oven from ten to fifteen minutes, strain the sauce over, garnish and serve hot.

114 SOLE À LA CRÈME

1 filleted sole	½ pint (300 ml) milk
1 oz (25 g) butter	lemon juice
1 oz (25 g) flour	salt and pepper

(Enough for two people)

Wash and dry the fillets, roll up the skinned side inside, cook in the milk till soft, then remove and place on a hot

dish, make a sauce with the butter, flour and flavoured milk, season well and add lemon juice, pour over the sole, garnish with lemon and parsley and serve hot.

115 SOLE AU VIN BLANC

1 sole	salt and pepper
½ pint (300 ml) white wine	

(Enough for two or three people)

Skin the sole, lay in a buttered gratin dish, sprinkle with salt and pepper, pour over the wine and bake very gently for about twenty minutes. Serve in the same dish, garnished with lemon and parsley.

116 SOLE ROUENNAISE

1 sole	½ tin lobster
½ oz (15 g) butter	lemon juice
½ oz (15 g) flour	salt, cayenne
½ gill (75 ml) fish stock or milk	white sauce

(Enough for two or three people)

Skin and fillet the sole. Make a sauce with the butter, flour and fish stock or milk, season with salt and cayenne, chop the lobster finely and add to the sauce with a little lemon juice. Lay some of the mixture on the fillets, fold over in half, place on a greased tin, sprinkle with salt, and lemon juice, cover with greased paper and bake for ten minutes. Place on a hot dish, coat with a well-flavoured white sauce, garnish with cut lemon and parsley.

117 SOLE À LA VENITIENNE

1 large sole	2 chopped truffles
1 small whiting	1 gill (150 ml) cream
2½ oz (65 g) butter	½ lemon
2 oz (50 g) flour	1 pint (600 ml) water
1 yolk of egg	seasoning

(Enough for four people)

Skin and trim the sole, divide down the centre as if for filleting and remove the bone without removing the fillets. Skin and bone the whiting, boil the bones, make a white sauce with 2 oz (50 g) butter, flour and fish stock; pound the flesh of the whiting with the rest of the butter, a little of the sauce, yolk of egg and seasoning. Put the mixture inside the fish, close it up, lay it on a buttered tin, squeeze over some lemon juice; bake about twenty minutes. Heat the sauce, add the cream and truffles. Dish the sole on a hot dish, pour the sauce over and serve immediately.

118 FILLETS OF SOLE À L'AMERICAINE

2 soles	1 shallot
3 tomatoes	½ pint (300 ml) Béchamel sauce
2 oz (50 g) butter	1 gill (150 ml) white wine
1 oz (25 g) bread crumbs	salt and pepper

(Enough for four people)

Make a purée with 1 oz (25 g) of butter and the tomatoes sliced, rub through a sieve. Boil up the béchamel sauce and add the tomato purée, fillet the soles, fold the fillets in half, place in a buttered gratin dish, sprinkle with chopped shallot, pour over the wine, cover with a buttered paper. Cook in a moderate oven from ten to fifteen minutes. Add the liquor from the fish to the prepared sauce, pour over the fillets. Sprinkle the bread crumbs on the top with the butter in small pieces, brown nicely in a quick oven.

119 FILLETS OF WHITING À LA MORNAY

3 large whiting	1 bay leaf
3 oz (75 g) butter	parsley
1 oz (25 g) flour	1 oz (25 g) Gruyère cheese
½ lemon	1½ oz (40 g) Parmesan cheese
1 glass white wine	¾ pint (450 ml) milk
2 shallots	salt and pepper

(Enough for five or six people)

Skin and fillet the fish; boil up the bones with the milk, bay leaf and shallot. Trim the fillets, fold in half and place in a buttered sauté-pan, season, sprinkle with chopped shallot, pour over the wine, cover with greased paper and cook for about fifteen minutes in a moderate oven. Make a sauce with the butter, flour and flavoured milk. Boil for five minutes, add the grated Gruyère cheese and 1 oz (25 g) of the Parmesan, season well. Place the fillets on a hot dish, pour the sauce over, sprinkle over the rest of the Parmesan cheese and brown nicely in a quick oven.

120 FILLETS OF WHITING WITH SHRIMPS

2 or 3 whiting	½ gill (75 ml) cream
½ pint (300 ml) shrimps	½ pint (300 ml) white sauce
½ lemon	salt and pepper
1 oz (25 g) butter	

(Enough for four or five people)

Skin and fillet the whiting, make a fish stock with the bones and trimmings, make a white sauce using the fish stock, pound the shrimp shells in a mortar with 1 oz (25 g) butter and juice of a lemon, pass the shrimp butter through a sieve, add enough to the sauce to flavour and colour it, add the cream. Bake the fillets on a tin. When cooked arrange them round a dish, coat with the sauce, warm the shrimps in a little of the sauce and put in the centre of the fillet and serve.

121 SCALLOPS EN COQUILLES

some scallops	lemon juice
white sauce	bread crumbs
butter	salt and pepper

Trim the scallops, removing the black portion, wash them in vinegar, cut them up, place in some buttered shells mixed with some thick white sauce and some of the bread crumbs. Season and squeeze over some lemon juice, sprinkle over some more bread crumbs, put some small bits of butter on top, brown nicely in a quick oven.

122 FISH OMELET

cold cooked fish	1 oz (25 g) butter
white sauce	little milk
3 eggs	salt and pepper — cayenne

(Enough for two people)

Remove the skin and bone from the fish, flake it and add a little white sauce and season well. Keep it hot. Beat the eggs thoroughly, melt the butter in an omelet pan. When hot pour in the eggs, stir for a moment, then allow them to set. When cooked sufficiently put the pan under the gas or in a quick oven to brown on the top, put in the fish, fold over and serve on a hot dish immediately.

123 HERRING SAUTÉ

2 herrings	salt and pepper
1½ oz (40 g) butter	toast

(*Enough for two people*)

Skin the herrings and cut them in half, remove the bone. Melt the butter in a stew pan, lay in the fish. Cook very gently for ten minutes. Lay on pieces of toast. Season and serve very hot.

124 POTTED PERCH

6 perch	1 doz. peppercorns
4 cloves	salt
1 pint (600 ml) vinegar	

(*Enough for three or four people*)

Wash and clean the fish, lay in a pie-dish with the vinegar, peppercorns, cloves and salt. Bake very gently for 1½ hours and serve.

125 STEAMED FISH PUDDING

1 breakfastcupful cold fish	1 egg
1 teacupful bread crumbs	salt and pepper
1 teaspoonful parsley	white sauce
1 teaspoonful anchovy essence	

(*Enough for three or four people*)

Chop the fish. Add the parsley, bread crumbs, essence and egg. Season well and add a little milk if necessary. Put the mixture into a greased basin or mould. Steam for 1 hour. Turn out and serve coated with white sauce.

126 GRILLED TROUT

trout	salt
butter	

Well clean the fish, sprinkle a little salt inside, wrap it in well-buttered paper and grill over a quick clear fire, turning it occasionally and taking care that the fish does not burn. The time will depend on the size of the fish. Serve very hot.

127 GRILLED MACKEREL

1 mackerel	½ finely chopped shallot
1½ tablespoonfuls oiled butter	salt and pepper
1 teaspoonful chopped parsley	Hollandaise sauce
	(see No. 618 or 619)

(*Enough for two people*)

Wipe, clean and dry the fish well. Score with a sharp knife. Marinade in a deep dish in oiled butter with flavourings. Drain well and grill over a clear fire from twelve to fifteen minutes according to the size.

MEAT DISHES

128 BOILED BEEF

beef (silverside)	dumplings
3 carrots	4 oz (100 g) flour
3 turnips	2 oz (50 g) suet
1 onion	salt and pepper

Well wash the beef to remove the salt, place in tepid water and bring to boiling-point, simmer gently, allowing twenty minutes to the pound (0.5 kg) and twenty minutes over, skim occasionally, prepare the vegetables, cut them up neatly, put them in with the meat; the carrots should go in first; mix the dumplings and cook them with the meat and vegetables about fifteen to twenty minutes, serve the meat on a hot dish with vegetables and dumplings round, some of the liquor in a tureen.

129 ROAST BEEF AND YORKSHIRE PUDDING

sirloin or any roasting piece	horseradish sauce

Wipe the meat, place on a roasting tin, allow a quarter of an hour to the pound (0.5 kg) and a quarter of an hour over. Baste frequently. To make the gravy pour off some of the dripping, brown a little salt in the pan, add water or stock, stir till boiling, pour round the meat, serve with horseradish sauce (see No. 633 or 634) and Yorkshire pudding.

½ lb (225 g) flour	1 oz (25 g) dripping
1 pint (600 ml) milk	salt
2 eggs	

Add the salt to the flour, make a well in the centre and drop in the eggs, add a little milk and mix smoothly, beat until it bubbles, add the remainder of the milk and if possible stand aside for an hour or two. Melt the dripping in the tin, make it quite hot and pour in the batter. Bake in a quick oven, serve on a hot dish, cut in neat sections.

130 STEWED BRISKET OF BEEF

brisket, 5 to 7 lb (2.3 to 3.2 kg)	1 head celery
2 carrots	12 peppercorns
2 onions	6 cloves
1 turnip	bunch of herbs
1 leek	salt

Put the meat into a large stewpan with sufficient water to cover, prepare the vegetables and add them, the cloves stuck in the onions, the peppercorns and herbs tied in muslin. Simmer gently from four to five hours, skimming occasionally. If served hot, take out the meat, thicken some of the liquor and serve as gravy. If to be served cold, take out the bones, press the meat between two boards with a weight on top, strain some of the liquor and reduce it to a glaze, adding a little Liebig's extract. When the meat is cold wipe it with a hot cloth, brush it with the glaze; a drop or two of carmine added improves the colour of the glaze.

131 BEEF STEAK PUDDING

2 lb (900 g) steak	flour
½ lb (225 g) ox kidney	salt and pepper

Pastry

¾ lb (350 g) flour   ½ teaspoonful baking powder
6 oz (175 g) suet   water to mix
(*Enough for seven or eight people*)

Wipe and cut the meat into thin slices, roll a small piece of kidney in each, dip into seasoned flour.

Mix the finely-chopped suet with the flour and baking powder, mix to a stiff dough, knead lightly, place on a board, cut off a piece for the top, roll out and line a greased pudding basin, put in the meat with some stock or water, lay on the top, press the edges together, tie on a scalded and floured cloth and boil for three hours, serve in the basin with a serviette pinned round and send a jug of boiling water to table with it.

132 STEWED STEAK

1 lb (450 g) beef steak   1 oz (25 g) butter
1 onion   1 oz (25 g) flour
1 carrot   ¾ pint (450 ml) stock or water
1 turnip   salt and pepper
bouquet garni
(*Enough for four or five people*)

Wipe and trim the steak, chop the onion, melt the butter in a saucepan, brown the steak, remove it and brown the onion, add the stock, herbs and vegetable trimmings, simmer very gently till tender, from two to two and a half hours. Place the steak on a hot dish. Strain and thicken the gravy with the flour, stir till it boils, season it well and pour it over the meat. Garnish with vegetables, cut in fancy shapes and cooked separately.

133 BEEF STEAK PIE

1 lb (450 g) steak   little flour
¼ lb (100 g) kidney   salt and pepper
stock or water
Flaky Crust
10 oz (275 g) flour   water
6 oz (175 g) butter and lard   salt
(*Enough for six or seven people*)

Cut the steak in thin slices, roll a small piece of kidney in each slice, dip in flour with salt and pepper added, pile in a pie dish, high in centre. Do not pack the dish tightly, but leave enough space to add some stock or water. Make the pastry (for method see No. 514), wet the edges of the dish, line with pastry, egg the edge of pastry and place on the top. Do not touch the cut edges, make some leaves from the trimmings, arrange them round a hole made in the centre, brush over the top with egg, make a rose, place in the centre of the leaves. Bake in a hot oven for two hours. The hole under the rose must be kept open during baking to allow the steam to escape.

134 SEA PIE

½ lb (225 g) lean meat   1 lb (450 g) potatoes
2 or 3 tomatoes   water
2 onions   salt and pepper
Suet Crust
6 oz (175 g) flour   ¼ teaspoonful baking powder
2½ oz (65 g) suet   salt
(*Enough for five or six people*)

Cut up the meat, peel and slice the potatoes, slice tomatoes and onions. Put in layers in a saucepan with a little water for gravy, add salt and pepper, make a suet crust, roll out to the size of the top of the pan, lay it on the meat and cook gently for two hours. To serve either lift out the crust whole and place the stew under or cut into sections and place round the stew.

135 LIVER AND KIDNEY PUDDING

½ lb (225 g) ox kidney   ½ lb (225 g) calf's liver
2 oz (50 g) bacon   2 oz (50 g) dripping
½ pint (300 ml) water or stock   1 oz (25 g) flour
For Pastry
6 oz (175 g) flour   3 oz (75 g) suet
1 oz (25 g) bread crumbs   water
1 oz (25 g) flour   salt and pepper
(*Enough for five or six people*)

Cut the bacon small and fry it in the dripping, cut up the liver and kidney, season with salt and pepper, fry lightly, mix in bacon, flour, and add the stock or water, make a suet crust, line a basin with it, put in the liver and kidney, cover with pastry, steam from one and a half to two hours.

136 TRIPE AND ONIONS

1 lb (450 g) tripe   ½ pint (300 ml) milk
2 onions   salt and pepper
1 oz (25 g) flour
(*Enough for four people*)

Wash the tripe, place it in a stewpan, cover with cold water and bring to the boil, put it on a board, scrape it if necessary, cut into neat pieces, return it to the pan with about three-quarters of a pint (450 ml) water and the onions finely chopped, simmer till the tripe is tender, mix the flour smoothly with the milk, add it, stir till it boils, season well and serve.

137 GRILLED STEAK

1 lb (450 g) rump steak   lemon juice
butter   salt and pepper
1 teaspoonful chopped parsley
(*Enough for three or four people*)

Grease the bars of the griller, brush the steak over with butter, put on the steak and grill over a clear fire from six to eight minutes, according to the thickness, turning every two or three minutes. Serve on a hot dish with a peice of maître d'hôtel butter on the top. This is made by mixing the chopped parsley and lemon juice into the butter on a plate, forming it into a nice shape.

138 VIENNA STEAKS

1 lb (450 g) lean beef (raw)   1 oz (25 g) flour
1 onion or shallot   little stock
1 egg   salt and pepper
(*Enough for three or four people*)

Pass the meat through a mincing machine, add the finely-chopped shallot or onion, season well and bind with well-beaten egg. Divide into small round steaks, using a little flour or bread crumbs, fry in butter or dripping in a frying pan, turning occasionally. When cooked place on a

hot dish, put the flour in the frying pan, allow it to brown, add the stock, boil up, season and pour round the steaks. This dish can be garnished with fried onions if liked.

139 BEEF OLIVES

1 lb (450 g) steak	1½ oz (40 g) butter
1 carrot	1 oz (25 g) flour
1 turnip	¾ pint (450 ml) stock
1 onion	salt and pepper
2 cloves	

Forcemeat

2 oz (50 g) bread crumbs	little grated lemon peel
1 oz (25 g) suet	½ teaspoonful herbs
1 teaspoonful chopped parsley	1 egg
	salt and pepper

(Enough for five or six people)

Cut the beef into thin slices, make a stuffing with the crumbs, suet and seasonings, bind with egg, place a little stuffing on each slice, roll up and secure with a piece of thread or a match, melt the butter, fry the olives brown with the onion stuck with cloves, remove the meat and onion, add the flour and brown it, taking care not to let it burn, add the stock gradually, stir till it boils, add the vegetables and put back the olives, simmer gently till the olives are tender, place them in the centre of a hot dish, removing the thread, strain the gravy round, having carefully seasoned it.

140 STUFFED AND STEWED STEAK

1½ lb (700 g) steak	veal stuffing (see No. 643)
2 oz (50 g) butter or bacon	1 pint (600 ml) stock or water
2 oz (50 g) flour	salt and pepper

(Enough for six or seven people)

Beat the steak well with a rolling pin, spread with veal stuffing, roll up and tie with tape, melt the butter or fat in a stewpan, when hot put in the steak and brown nicely all over, cover with the stock or water and let it simmer gently till quite tender, take out the steak, remove the tape, lay it on a hot dish, thicken the gravy and season it, strain over the steak and serve.

141 STEWED OX KIDNEY

½ lb (225 g) kidney	1 small onion
1 oz (25 g) butter or dripping	1 teaspoonful ketchup
1 oz (25 g) flour	1 teaspoonful Worcester sauce
½ pint (300 ml) stock	salt and pepper

(Enough for four people)

Scald the kidney and cut it in neat slices, melt the butter or dripping and fry the onion, also the kdiney, remove and brown the flour carefully, add the stock gradually. Stir till it boils. Replace the onion and kidney, add the flavourings and seasoning. Simmer very gently for two hours, the kidney will be hardened if it boils, dish with a border of boiled rice or macaroni or mashed potatoes.

142 BOILED OX TONGUE

1 ox tongue	2 sticks celery
1 carrot	bunch of herbs
1 turnip	brown or piquante sauce (see
1 onion	No. 624)

(Enough for eight or nine people)

Wash the tongue in cold water, if it is pickled let it soak for some hours, put it in a saucepan with tepid water to cover, bring it to the boil, remove the scum, add the prepared vegetables and simmer gently from three to four hours. When tender remove the skin, brush over with glaze and put it in the oven for a few minutes, serve with a good brown or piquante sauce. Spinach is a suitable vegetable to serve with the tongue, and can be used to garnish the dish. If the tongue is to be served cold it must be trimmed and fastened on a board in an upright position with skewers. When cold and firm glaze it and decorate with butter, put through a forcing bag with a fancy tube and aspic jelly.

143 BEEF PATTIES

½ lb (225 g) beef	little stock
little flour	salt and pepper

For Pastry

½ lb (225 g) flour	salt
5 oz (150 g) butter and lard	1 egg
water	

(Enough to make six patties)

Make the pastry (see method for flaky pastry, No. 514), roll out a quarter of an inch (0.5 cm) in thickness, cut out the top with a pastry cutter, roll up the pastry again, line the patty tins, put in the meat cut in dice or minced and dipped in seasoned flour, pour over a teaspoonful of stock, egg round the edges, put on the top, press edges together, brush over with egg and make a hole in the top, bake in a hot oven for half an hour.

144 BEEF COLLOPS

½ lb (225 g) beef	1 oz (25 g) butter
1 onion	vegetables for garnish
2 oz (50 g) rice	salt and pepper
½ pint (300 ml) stock	

(Enough for four people)

Mince the beef finely, melt the butter in a stewpan and fry the chopped onion, remove it and fry the beef, add the stock and the rice, which must be washed and previously parboiled, simmer gently till cooked, season well, pile in the centre of a hot dish, garnish with vegetables (carrot and turnip cut in dice or green peas). Serve very hot.

145 MOCK GAME

1 lb (450 g) beef steak	1 wineglass of vinegar
2 or 3 rashers	1 onion
1 oz (25 g) butter	1 teaspoonful red-current jelly
1 oz (25 g) flour	1 teaspoonful capers
½ pint (300 ml) stock	½ teaspoonful lemon rind
salt and pepper	

Cut the meat into thin squares, lay a piece of bacon on each, roll up and secure with thread or a match, dip in seasoned flour, fry in the butter, take out the meat, brown the remainder of the flour, add the stock, stirring till it boils; put in meat, chopped onion, capers, lemon rind, and stew till tender, arrange the meat on a hot dish, add the jelly to the gravy, season it, strain it over the meat, garnish with sippets of fried bread.

146 FILLET OF BEEF À LA POMPADOUR

1 lb (450 g) beef fillet	vegetables for garnish
3 tomatoes	mashed potatoes
½ oz (15 g) butter	½ pint (300 ml) brown or
1 teaspoonful chopped parsley	tomato sauce
	salt and pepper

(Enough for four or five people)

Cut the fillet into neat rounds and fry in butter in a sauté pan, slice the tomatoes and bake on a greased tin with some small pieces of fat of the beef. When cooked dish the fillets on a border of mashed potato with a small piece of fat on each, put on a slice of tomato. Pile a suitable vegetable in the centre, such as peas, beans, spinach, and just before serving pour the brown sauce round and place a small square of maître d'hôtel butter on each fillet.

147 BEEF SCALLOPS À L'ITALIENNE

½ lb (225 g) beef	1 oz (25 g) bread crumbs
2 oz (50 g) butter	salt and pepper
1 oz (25 g) Parmesan cheese	

(Enough for three or four people)

Melt the cheese and butter in a stewpan, mince the beef and add it, season well, put the mixture in some greased scallop shells, sprinkle over the bread crumbs and a little of the grated cheese, serve hot.

148 BEEF GALANTINE

½ lb (225 g) lean beef	1 shallot
½ lb (225 g) raw ham	chopped parsley
½ lb (225 g) sausages	¼ lb (100 g) mushrooms
½ lb (225 g) bread crumbs	salt and pepper
2 or 3 eggs	little glaze

Put the beef and ham through a mincing machine separately, then both together, mix with skinned sausages, bread crumbs, chopped mushrooms, shallot, parsley and plenty of salt and pepper, bind with raw eggs, form the mixture into a smooth roll like a sausage, tie securely in a pudding cloth and boil it gently for two and a half hours; when it is cold brush over with a little glaze made with dissolved gelatine flavoured and coloured with Liebig's extract.

149 FRICANDEAU OF BEEF

2 lb (900 g) fillet or piece of rump	3 cloves
herbs	2 blades mace
larding bacon	salt and pepper
mushrooms	carrot, turnip, onion
tomatoes	wineglass sherry
potatoes	

(Enough for seven or eight people)

Trim the beef and make it a good shape, lard this thickly and neatly with strips of bacon, put a layer of vegetables cut roughly in a stewpan, add the spice, herbs and sherry, and enough stock to barely cover vegetables, place on the meat, cover with a greased paper and cook gently for an hour and a half or till tender. Remove the fillet and crisp it in the oven, place on a hot dish, strain the stock, thicken and season it, pour round the meat, garnish with button mushrooms, small tomatoes and young potatoes.

150 BOILED MUTTON AND BROTH

neck of mutton, (1.4 kg)	2 oz (50 g) barley or rice
about 3 lb	chopped parsley
2 carrots	salt and pepper
2 turnips	caper sauce (see No. 606)
1 onion	

(Enough for seven or eight people)

Wipe the meat, trim the joint and take off chine bone and any superfluous fat, tie it up, place in boiling water, allow it to boil for five minutes, carefully removing the scum, then allow it to simmer very gently for about one and a half hours, wash and blanch the pearl barley and add, also the vegetables, which should be prepared and cut into neat pieces. Place the mutton on a hot dish with carrots and turnips round, coat with caper or parsley sauce, add seasoning and chopped parsley to the broth.

151 SHEEP'S HEAD AND BROTH

1 sheep's head	1 oz (25 g) butter
2 carrots	1 gill (150 ml) milk
2 turnips	3 oz (75 g) rice
1 onion	chopped parsley
1 oz (25 g) flour	salt and pepper

(Enough for five or six people)

Thoroughly cleanse the head, take out the splinters, wash in salt and water, put the head in cold water and bring to the boil, pour away the water, add fresh water and boil, removing the scum, cut up the vegetables and add with the rice, simmer gently for three hours or till the meat will leave the bones. Put the brains into a small piece of muslin and drop into the stewpan about fifteen minutes before the head is done. Cut the meat from the head, place in the centre of a hot dish, put a border of rice and vegetables round, slice the tongue and chop the brains, make a sauce with the butter, flour and milk, adding some of the liquor; season well and add chopped parsley. Coat the head with this sauce and garnish with sliced tongue and chopped brains.

152 STUFFED LOIN OF MUTTON

loin of mutton, 4 lb (1.8 kg)	½ teaspoonful herbs
4 oz (100 g) bread crumbs	little grated lemon peel
2 oz (50 g) suet	1 egg
1 teaspoonful chopped parsley	salt and pepper

(Enough for eight or nine people)

Carefully bone the loin, taking away as little meat as possible, make a seasoning with the bread crumbs, chopped suet and flavourings, season well, bind with egg, place it in the loin where the bone was removed, tie up firmly with tape, roast in the oven, serve as other joints with gravy poured round.

153 ROAST AND STUFFED BREAST OF MUTTON

1 breast of mutton	1 oz (25 g) sage
4 oz (100 g) bread crumbs	little milk
1 oz (25 g) fat	salt and pepper
3 or 4 onions	

(Enough for three or four people)

Remove the bones and some of the superfluous fat, parboil the onions and chop them, add to the bread crumbs, chopped sage, butter or dripping, season and mix with a little milk, lay the stuffing on the breast, roll it up and bind with tape. Bake in the oven and serve with gravy made as for roast joints. Veal stuffing can be used instead of sage and onion stuffing if preferred.

154 ROAST SHEEP'S HEART

1 sheep's heart	1 small onion
2 oz (50 g) bread crumbs	½ teaspoonful herbs
1 oz (25 g) chopped suet	1 egg or little milk
1 teaspoonful parsley	salt and pepper

(Enough for one or two people)

Thoroughly cleanse the heart in salt and water, cut off the muscle, mix the stuffing, fill the heart with it, skewer or sew up the openings. Bake in the oven, basting frequently, dish on a hot dish, pour off the fat, put a little flour in the tin, brown it, add water, boil up, season it and pour round the heart. The heart can be cooked in a saucepan if more convenient.

155 IRISH STEW

1 lb (450 g) neck of mutton	little stock or water
2 lb (900 g) potatoes	salt and pepper
1 lb (450 g) onions	

(Enough for five or six people)

Wipe the meat, chine it and cut into chops, cut the potatoes into slices and chop the onions, put them into a stewpan in layers, adding plenty of salt and pepper. Add a little stock or water, about half a pint (300 ml), simmer the stew gently till cooked.

156 HOT-POT

1½ lb (700 g) mutton (middle neck)	water or stock
3 lb (1.4 kg) potatoes	salt and pepper
½ lb (225 g) onions	

(Enough for seven or eight people)

Cut up the meat into neat joints. It should be rather lean, slice the potatoes and chop the onions, place them in a jar in layers, season highly, add sufficient water or stock to barely cover and cook in the oven for three hours. If possible it should be served in the vessel it is cooked in.

157 HARICOT MUTTON

best end of neck of mutton	1 oz (25 g) butter
1 turnip	1 oz (25 g) flour
1 carrot	½ pint (300 ml) stock
1 onion	salt and pepper
bouquet garni	

(Enough for four or five people)

Cut off the chine bone and the end, divide into chops, remove any superfluous fat, fry the cutlets a nice brown in the butter, remove them and brown the flour well, taking care not to let it burn, add the stock and stir till it boils, put in the meat, herbs and vegetable trimmings and simmer gently for two and a half hours, place the meat on a hot dish, season the gravy and strain it over, garnish with carrot and turnip cut in fancy shapes and cooked separately.

158 SUMMER STEW

2 lb (900 g) neck of lamb	spring onions
6 young potatoes	peas
6 young carrots	water or stock
6 young turnips	salt and pepper

(Enough for four or five people)

Cut the lamb into neat chops, put in a stewpan with enough stock or water to cover, bring to the boil, remove the scum, carefully prepare the vegetables, which should be small and of equal size, put them in the stewpan whole and simmer gently, season and dish up the stew, the meat in the centre and the vegetables arranged nicely round.

Note.—Lamb can be stewed in the same way using old vegetables and served with pea purée (see No. 668).

159 MUTTON CUTLETS

best end of neck of mutton	mashed potatoes
egg and bread crumbs	vegetables for garnish
salt and pepper	brown or tomato sauce (see No. 622 or 628)

(Enough for six or seven people)

Saw off the chine bone carefully and the end of the bones, allowing two inches (5 cm) below the eye of the cutlet, divide the cutlets, trim them, keeping the bone clean, dip in salt and pepper, then egg and bread crumbs, fry in a sauté pan till a nice brown, turning them occasionally, dish in a circle on a border of mashed potatoes, fill the centre with peas, sprouts or any suitable vegetable, strain a good brown or tomato sauce round.

160 MUTTON CUTLETS À LA REFORME

best end of neck of mutton	2 oz (50 g) tongue
1 carrot	mashed potatoes
2 truffles	salt and pepper
2 gherkins	reform sauce (see No. 627)
cooked white of egg	

(Enough for six or seven people)

Cut and trim the cutlets, dip in a mixture of trimmings of truffles, tongue and gherkins seasoned, then coat with egg and bread crumbs, fry a nice brown in a sauté pan, dish on a border of mashed potatoes, make a garnish with shreds of carrot, gherkin, truffles, tongue and white of egg, shake in butter and season, pile it in the centre and pour reform sauce round the cutlets.

161 MUTTON CUTLETS À LA SOUBISE

best end of neck of mutton	4 or 5 onions
1½ oz (40 g) flour	salt and pepper
1 oz (25 g) butter	egg and bread crumbs
¼ pint (150 ml) milk	

(Enough for six or seven people)

Cut the cutlets from the neck of mutton, trim and shape them neatly, cook the onions till tender in milk, pass them through a sieve, cook butter and flour together, add the milk and the purée of onions, cook the mixture thoroughly and well season, allow it to cool. Fry the cutlets a nice brown in a sauté pan, spread on the mixture, set aside to become firm, coat with egg and bread crumbs and fry in hot fat, dish on a border of mashed potato and pour some good gravy round.

162 ROAST FILLET OF VEAL

fillet of veal	1 pint (600 ml) béchamel sauce
veal stuffing (see No. 643)	(see No. 604)
½ lb (225 g) rashers	

Remove the bone from the fillet and stuff with veal stuffing, sew or skewer a piece of fat or skin on each side to keep the stuffing in, tie round firmly, bake in the oven till thoroughly cooked, basting frequently; cut the rashers, roll them and place on a skewer and put them in the oven with the veal for the last ten minutes, dish up the veal, remove string, strain off the fat, pour the pint (600 ml) of béchamel sauce in the dripping pan, place it over the fire, and stir till hot and a nice pale fawn colour. Pour it round the meat and garnish the dish with rolls of bacon.

Note.—A loin of veal is cooked in the same way but is not stuffed.

163 STEWED VEAL AND RICE

knuckle of veal	4 oz (100 g) rice
1 onion	½ pint (300 ml) parsley sauce
1 turnip	(see No. 608)
1 stick celery	salt and pepper
(Enough for five or six people)	

Wash and trim the veal, put in a stewpan with water to cover, with the onion stuck with cloves, turnip and celery. Bring to the boil, remove the scum and simmer gently for two and a half hours, add the washed rice when the veal has been cooking an hour. Take out the knuckle, place on a hot dish, make a border with the rice, pour over the parsley sauce and garnish with lemon and parsley. The broth can be seasoned, chopped parsley added and served.

164 VEAL CUTLETS

1 lb (450 g) fillet of veal	salt and pepper
1 oz (25 g) butter	potatoes
1 yolk of egg	3 or 4 rashers of bacon
1 dessertspoonful chopped	vegetables for a garnish
parsley	good brown or tomato sauce
1 teaspoonful grated lemon	egg and bread crumbs
(Enough for five or six people)	

Cut the meat into neat fillets, dip them into a mixture made with the butter (melted), yolk of egg, lemon peel and parsley, seasoned; drop them into the bread crumbs, then coat again with egg and crumbs, fry them in a sauté pan a nice brown colour, turning them occasionally, mash some potatoes, make a mound in the centre of the dish, leaving a space in the centre, place the fillets round on the potatoes with a roll of bacon on each fillet. A suitable vegetable, such as peas or beans, should be cooked and piled in the centre, and a good brown or tomato sauce strained round.

165 CURRIED VEAL

1 lb (450 g) veal	½ lemon
1 apple	1 teaspoonful curry paste
1 onion	1 teaspoonful chutney
2 oz (50 g) butter	½ pint (300 ml) white stock
1 oz (25 g) flour	little cream
1 oz (25 g) curry powder	pinch sugar and salt
2 oz (50 g) almonds or cocoanut	4 oz (100 g) rice
(Enough for four or five people)	

Chop the apple and onion finely, put the almonds or cocoanut into a basin, pour on about one gill (150 ml) of boiling milk and allow it to infuse. Cut the meat into neat pieces, dip in flour and curry powder mixed, melt the butter in a stewpan, put in apple and onion, cook well without browning it, remove it and cook the meat in the same way, take out the meat and thoroughly cook the curry powder and flour for about fifteen minutes, add the white stock and nut milk, stir till it boils, put back the meat, apple and onion, squeeze in some lemon juice, simmer very gently till the meat is tender—about one and a half hours, add the curry paste, chutney, pinch of sugar and salt, and lastly the cream. Serve in the centre of a hot dish with a border of well-boiled rice, garnish with lemon and parsley.

166 VEAL AND HAM PIE

1 lb (450 g) veal (fillet)	½ teaspoonful herbs
¼ lb (100 g) ham	little grated lemon peel
2 hard-boiled eggs	salt and pepper
1 teaspoonful chopped parsley	stock

For Pastry

10 oz (275 g) flour	water to mix
6 oz (175 g) butter and lard)	egg to glaze
(Enough for five or six people)	

Cook the veal in enough cold water to cover, with an onion stuck with cloves, when cold cut into thin slices, put a pinch of seasoning (parsley, herbs, lemon peel, salt and pepper) on each slice and roll up, pack the rolls in a pie dish not too tightly, with the ham and hard-boiled eggs cut in slices, reduce the stock, add a leaf of gelatine if necessary, pour it into the pie dish. Cover with pastry, decorate with leaves and a rose, brush over with egg, bake for 1½ hours, remove the rose and pour in the remainder of the stock. Rough puff or flaky pastry can be used for this dish (see No. 514 or 515).

167 FRIED LIVER AND BACON

1 lb (450 g) calf's liver	little flour
½ lb (225 g) rashers	salt and pepper
(Enough for five or six people)	

Prepare the rashers and fry lightly, well cleanse the liver, cut it in slices, coat well with flour and fry in the bacon fat, place on a hot dish with the bacon round, put the remainder of flour in the frying pan, brown it carefully, add some stock or water gradually, boil up, season and strain over the liver.

168 STEWED CALF'S LIVER

½ lb (225 g) calf's liver	2 onions
1 oz (25 g) butter or dripping	1 apple
1 oz (25 g) flour	1 potato
½ pint (300 ml) stock or water	salt and pepper
(Enough for three or four people)	

Melt the butter or dripping in a stewpan, dip the liver, cut in small pieces in seasoned flour and fry a nice brown, take out the liver and brown the remainder of the flour, add the stock gradually and stir till it boils, return the liver to the sauce and the vegetables, cut neatly, simmer gently for an hour, season and serve very hot.

169 LIVER À LA FRANÇAISE

1 lb (450 g) calf's or sheep's liver	2 teaspoonfuls ketchup
¼ lb (100 g) bread crumbs	1 teaspoonful Worcester sauce
½ lb (225 g) rashers	¼ teaspoonful herbs
3 or 4 mushrooms	1 teaspoonful chopped parsley
stock or water	salt and pepper

(Enough for five or six people)

Well wash the liver and cut it into neat slices, lay these on a greased baking tin, wash, dry and chop the mushrooms, mix them with the crumbs, parsley, and season nicely, lay a little of this mixture on each slice of liver, cover with a thin slice of bacon, pour round some stock or water, bake in a moderate oven for three-quarters of an hour. Place the liver on a hot dish, add the sauces to the stock, boil up and pour round the liver, serve very hot.

170 MINCED VEAL

½ to ¾ lb (225 to 350 g) veal	1 onion
1 oz (25 g) butter	2 or 3 cloves
1 oz (25 g) flour	blade of mace
1 gill (150 ml) white stock	strip lemon rind
1 gill (150 ml) milk	salt and pepper
little cream	mashed potatoes

(Enough for three or four people)

Cook the veal in the white stock or water with onion, cloves, mace and lemon peel. When tender mince it finely, make a white sauce with the butter and flour, using one gill (150 ml) milk and the liquor the veal was cooked in, add the meat and cream and season well, serve in the centre of a potato border, garnish with cut lemon and parsley. Cold cooked veal can be used for this dish.

171 CALF'S HEAD (BOILED)

half a calf's head or a whole one	vegetables and herbs to flavour
bacon	peppercorns
lemon	parsley sauce
	salt

(Enough for seven or eight people)

Thoroughly wash the head, let it soak in cold water. Put it in a saucepan with enough cold water to cover. When it boils add a little salt and remove the scum as it rises, add the vegetables, herbs and peppercorns, simmer gently from two to three hours till perfectly tender. The brains must be removed and soaked, then tied in muslin and boiled. Take out the head, remove all bones and tongue, place the head on a hot dish, coat well with parsley sauce, garnish with the skinned and sliced tongue, chopped brains, bacon fried and diced, quarters of lemon and parsley.

Another method is to coat the head (boiled and prepared in the same way) with egg sauce (see No. 607), garnished with ham, brains, lemon and parsley, or coat the head and tongue with brown sauce garnished with rolls of ham, the brains formed into balls with bread crumbs and sprinkled with chopped parsley.

172 BLANQUETTE DE VEAU

1 lb (450 g) veal	2 oz (50 g) butter
2 onions	2 oz (50 g) flour
2 cloves	2 yolks eggs
6 peppercorns	¼ pint (150 ml) cream
herbs	white stock or water
juice of 1 lemon	salt and pepper
cooked ham for garnish	

(Enough for four or five people)

Put the veal into a stewpan with the onions, cloves, peppercorns and herbs, cover with stock or water, bring to the boil, skim and simmer gently till tender, strain the liquor, put the meat on a hot dish, cook the butter and flour together, add the liquor gradually, stir till it boils, mix the yolks and cream together and add to the sauce, but do not boil; season and add the lemon juice, pour over the veal, garnish with chopped ham.

Note.—Rabbit and chicken can also be cooked in the same way.

173 GRENADINES OF VEAL

1 lb (450 g) fillet of veal	herbs
some larding bacon	1 oz (25 g) fat
1 carrot	stock
1 turnip	½ pint (300 ml) brown sauce
1 onion	(see No. 623)
2 tomatoes	potatoes for border

(Enough for five or six people)

Cut the veal into neat round fillets, lard them with narrow strips of larding bacon, cut the vegetables into large dice, melt the dripping in a stewpan, cook the vegetables in it for five minutes with the lid on, add enough stock to barely cover, place on the larded fillets, cover with greased paper and braise very slowly, when cooked remove the fillets, crisp them in the oven and brush over with glaze, place them on a potato border, place some suitable vegetable in the centre (peas, beans, sprouts), strain the good brown sauce round.

174 VEAL OR CHICKEN QUENELLES

1 lb (450 g) veal or chicken	salt and cayenne
1 oz (25 g) butter	lemon juice
1 oz (25 g) flour	potatoes for border
1 gill (150 ml) white stock	béchamel sauce (see No. 604)
2 eggs	vegetables for garnish

(Enough for six or seven people)

Pass the meat twice through a mincing machine, make a panada with butter, flour and stock, put it into a mortar with meat and eggs, pound it to a cream, pass it through a sieve, season well, make it into shapes with two dessert spoons dipped in hot water. Place them into a well-greased sauté pan, pour in enough boiling water to nearly cover and poach for fifteen minutes covered with buttered paper, drain on a cloth, dish on a border of mashed potatoes, coat with béchamel sauce, fill the centre with any suitable vegetable, such as peas, beans or tomatoes.

175 VEAL OLIVES AND TOMATO SAUCE

1½ lb (700 g) lean veal	1 turnip
2 oz (50 g) ham	1 onion
3 or 4 mushrooms	1 oz (25 g) butter
1 oz (25 g) bread crumbs	1 glass sherry
1 egg	½ pint (300 ml) tomato sauce
1 carrot	(see No. 628)
	salt and pepper

(Enough for six or seven people)

Cut the veal into thin slices, make a forcemeat with crumbs, chopped ham, mushrooms, seasoning; bind with egg, lay a little on each slice of veal, roll up and secure with thread, prepare the vegetables, melt the butter in a stewpan, brown them lightly. Also allow the olives to brown, add the tomato sauce, and sherry, and cook very gently till the olives are tender, dish on a hot dish, removing the thread, season and strain the sauce over.

176 FRIED SWEETBREADS

2 calf's sweetbreads	little grated lemon peel
1 teaspoonful chopped parsley	salt and pepper
1 dessertspoonful chopped ham	egg and bread crumbs
	little flour

(Enough for three or four people)

Soak the sweetbreads in salted water, put on in cold water and bring it to the boil, throw it away, put on again with fresh water and simmer gently for an hour, drain and press between two plates with a weight on top. When firm dip in seasoned flour, brush over with egg, coat with a mixture of parsley, ham and lemon peel, then again with egg and crumbs, fry a golden brown in hot fat, dish on hot dish with fancy paper, garnish with fried parsley. The sweetbreads can be cut in slices if preferred.

177 STEWED SWEETBREADS

calf's or sheep's sweetbreads	1 oz (25 g) butter
1 shallot	1 oz (25 g) flour
blade of mace	little cream
½ pint (300 ml) milk	salt and pepper

(Enough for three or four people)

Soak the sweetbreads in salted water, put them in a stewpan with cold water, bring to the boil, throw it away, put the sweetbreads on again with the milk, onion and mace and simmer very gently till tender, drain them, press between two plates and trim when firm, make a sauce with the butter, flour and milk the sweetbreads were cooked in, add a little cream, season well, reheat the sweetbreads and serve garnished with cut lemon and parsley.

178 VEAL GATEAU

1½ lb (700 g) lean veal	lemon rind
2 hard-boiled eggs	white stock
½ lb (225 g) cooked lean ham	coraline pepper
chopped parsley	salt and pepper

(Enough for seven or eight people)

Cook the veal in white stock with plenty of flavourings till tender, drain and when cold cut in neat pieces, chop the ham and cut the eggs into rings, arrange them in a pattern in a plain tin mould with the coraline pepper, parsley and chopped ham, fill the mould with veal, ham, and remains of garnish, well season the stock, pour into the mould when nearly cold till quite full. A little gelatine can be added if the stock is not strong enough to jelly. Turn out and serve with salad.

179 ROAST LOIN OF PORK

loin of pork, (2.3 kg) 5 lb	sage and onion stuffing
gravy	(see No. 645)
apple sauce (see No. 629)	salad oil

Choose the pork with thin skin, score it at equal distances with a sharp knife, brush it over with salad oil, bake in the oven, basting frequently; it must be well done; make the gravy in the dripping pan, pour round the meat, serve with apple sauce and baked sage and onion stuffing. If preferred the loin can be stuffed by making an incision under the skin and putting in the stuffing.

180 PORK PIE

1½ lb (700 g) flour	2 lb (900 g) pork
6 oz (175 g) lard	salt and pepper
½ pint (300 ml) water	

Skin the pork and cut into large dice, boil the water and lard together, pour into the centre of the flour and mix to a stiff dough, keeping it as warm as possible; knead it to get it smooth, well grease a pork pie mould, line it with the pastry, keeping one-third for the top, dip the pork in water and pack in neatly, add plenty of seasoning, place on the top, decorate edges and the top with leaves, leaving a hole in the centre. Bake for about five hours.

181 BOILED HAM OR BACON

ham or bacon	brown bread crumbs

Soak a ham for several hours. If dry, all night; if bacon is very salt soak for two hours before cooking. Place in a saucepan with plenty of tepid water, let it come slowly to the boil, remove the scum and simmer gently till cooked, time allowed according to size—twenty minutes to the pound (0.5 kg) and twenty minutes over, take it out, remove the skin and sprinkle over freshly made raspings. When cold lift on to a clean dish. Put a frill round the knuckle if a ham and garnish with parsley.

182 SAUSAGE ROLLS

½ lb (225 g) sausages	lemon juice
½ lb (225 g) flour	salt
6 oz (175 g) butter or butter	water to mix
and lard	1 egg

(Enough to make eight rolls)

Boil the sausages for ten minutes, skin and cut them in half, make the pastry (for method see Rough Puff Pastry, No. 515), roll it into a square shape, divide it into as many squares as there are pieces of sausage, put a piece on each square, brush round the edge with egg, fold over, letting the fold come on top, mark with a knife, brush over with egg, put on a baking sheet and bake in a hot oven for twenty minutes.

183 TOAD IN THE HOLE

½ lb (225 g) sausages   1 egg
¼ lb (100 g) flour   ¼ teaspoonful baking powder
½ pint (300 ml) milk   salt and pepper
(Enough for three people)

Skin the sausages, place in a greased pie dish, mix the flour smoothly with the egg and milk. Beat well, add the baking powder, season, pour over the sausages. Bake in a quick oven for about one hour.

184 SAUSAGES AND POTATOES

1 lb (450 g) sausages   little milk
cooked potatoes   salt and pepper
½ oz (15 g) butter
(Enough for three or four people)

Mash the potatoes, adding the butter, milk, salt and pepper, put them in the centre of a hot dish, prick the sausages, put them into a hot pan with a little dripping, fry till a crisp brown, place them round the potatoes and serve.

185 HARICOT BEANS AND BACON

¼ lb (100 g) haricot beans   pepper
4 or 5 rashers of bacon   chopped parsley
(Enough for four or five people)

Soak the beans for some hours in water with a pinch of carbonate of soda. Boil the beans gently till they are tender. Drain the beans and dry them. The liquor should not be thrown away, but added to the stock pot, fry the bacon, place it round a hot dish, fry the beans lightly in the fat and place in the middle, sprinkle over a little pepper and chopped parsley and serve very hot.

186 BRAWN

1 pig's head   1 teaspoonful mixed spice
1 onion   pepper and salt
6 cloves   1 teaspoonful chopped sage
2 bay leaves   if liked

Well wash the head in salt and water to remove the blood, rub the head with common salt, a little brown sugar, and saltpetre, and leave it for three days, adding a little fresh salt every day. Put it in a stewpan with enough cold water to cover, an onion stuck with cloves and the bay leaves, simmer till quite tender, then remove the bones, cut the meat up roughly, sprinkle over the mixed spice, sage and plenty of pepper and salt, skin the tongue, place some of the head in a brawn tin, lay in the tongue, fill with the rest of the head, pour over some of the liquor in which it was cooked, then put away to get cold. Turn it out of the mould when required for use.

The brawn will be improved if two extra tongues are procured and added.

187 HASH

cold meat, 1½ lb (700 g)   1½ pints (900 ml) stock
2 oz (50 g) butter or dripping   1 dessertspoonful ketchup
2 oz (50 g) flour   salt and pepper
1 onion   toast and parsley
(Enough for six or seven people)

Remove all the fat and gristle from the meat and cut into neat pieces, heat the fat and fry the onion a nice brown, remove it and fry the flour, brown it well, being careful not to burn it, add the stock gradually, stir till it boils, return the meat and onion, add the ketchup and seasoning, thoroughly reheat it, but do not allow it to boil, serve with sippets of toast or fried bread dipped in chopped parsley.

188 MINCE

cold meat, 1 lb (450 g)   ¾ pint (450 ml) stock
1 oz (25 g) butter or dripping   parsley
1 oz (25 g) flour   salt and pepper
1 shallot
(Enough for five or six people)

Mince the meat or chop up finely, make a sauce with the butter, flour and stock, adding finely-chopped shallot or onion, boil well, add the meat and seasoning, serve on a hot dish with a border of mashed potatoes, or sippets of toast or poached eggs, garnish with parsley.

189 DURHAM CUTLETS

¼ lb (100 g) minced meat   ¼ pint (150 ml) stock
1 oz (25 g) butter   1 dessertspoonful Worcester
1 oz (25 g) flour   sauce
3 or 4 tablespoonfuls bread   salt and pepper
crumbs   egg and bread crumbs
(Enough for four or five people)

Make a panada with the butter, flour and stock, mix with the meat and bread crumbs, add flavourings and season well, put the mixture on a wet plate, divide into equal portions and allow it to cool, form each portion into a neat cutlet shape, put an inch (2.5 cm) of raw macaroni into the end of each to represent the bone, coat in egg and bread crumbs, fry in hot fat, arrange in a circle round a high croûton of fried bread on a hot dish with fancy paper, garnish with fried parsley.

190 MEAT CROQUETTES

½ lb (225 g) minced meat   1 gill (150 ml) stock
1 oz (25 g) butter   1 teaspoonful Worcester
1 oz (25 g) flour   sauce
1 egg   1 teaspoonful anchovy sauce
¼ lb (100 g) mashed potatoes   little nutmeg
1 teaspoonful chopped parsley   salt and pepper
egg and bread crumbs
(Enough for four or five people)

Make a panada with the butter, flour and stock, mix with the meat and potatoes, add the flavourings and the raw egg and season well, place on a wet plate, divide in equal portions and allow it to cool, form into cork-shaped pieces, coat with egg and bread crumbs, fry in hot fat, dish on hot dish with fancy paper and garnish with fried parsley.

191 CURRY OF COLD MEAT

1 lb (450 g) cold meat   ¾ pint (450 ml) stock
1 apple   lemon juice
1 onion   salt
1 oz (25 g) flour   ¼ lb (100 g) Patna rice
1 oz (25 g) curry powder   parsley
2 oz (50 g) butter
(Enough for five or six people)

Trim the meat, cut it into neat slices, melt the butter in a stewpan, cook the finely-chopped apple and onion, remove it and cook the flour and curry powder from fifteen to twenty minutes, add the stock gradually, stir till it boils, then allow it to simmer gently with the apple and onion, season well with lemon juice and salt, put in the meat, reheat, but do not boil, serve in the centre of a border of well-cooked rice, garnish with cut lemon and parsley.

192 CORNISH PASTIES

¼ lb (100 g) meat   1 small potato
small piece of onion   pepper and salt

For Pastry

½ lb (225 g) flour   water to mix
1 oz (25 g) fat   pinch of salt
½ teaspoonful baking powder

(Enough to make six pasties)

Put the flour in a basin, rub in the fat, add baking powder and salt, mix to a stiff dough with the water, knead lightly, put on a board, cut into six piecs, roll into rounds, chop the meat, potato and onion into small pieces, season and put some of the mixture on each piece of pastry, moisten the edges, draw them together, pinch into a frill. Bake in a quick oven for three-quarters of an hour.

193 COLD MEAT ROLY-POLY

6 oz (175 g) flour   cold meat
2½ oz (65 g) suet   onion
water   ¼ teaspoonful herbs
salt   salt and pepper

(Enough for four or five people)

Make a suet crust with the flour and chopped suet, roll out to an oblong shape, chop the meat finely, add the onion, finely-chopped herbs and seasoning, mix well and lay it on the suet crust, wet the edges, roll it up, roll it in a scalded and floured cloth, tie it and boil for two hours, serve hot with a good gravy.

194 RISSOLES

¼ lb (100 g) cold meat   ¼ pint (150 ml) stock
4 tablespoonfuls bread crumbs   1 teaspoonful chopped
1 oz (25 g) butter   parsley
1 oz (25 g) flour   ½ teaspoonful anchovy sauce
egg and bread crumbs   salt and pepper

(Enough to make six rissoles)

Mince the meat finely, mix in the bread crumbs, parsley and flavourings, cook the butter and flour together, add the stock, boil well, mix in the anchovy sauce and add to the meat, allow it to cool, form into balls with a little flour, coat with egg and bread crumbs, fry in hot fat. Dish on hot dish with fancy paper, garnish with fried parsley.

195 SHEPHERD'S PIE

½ lb (225 g) cooked meat   ½ oz (15 g) butter or
½ lb (225 g) boiled potatoes   dripping
1 small onion   little milk
stock or gravy   salt and pepper

(Enough for four people)

Mince the meat, season it, put it in a pie dish with some gravy or stock, mash the potatoes, add the butter and milk, cover the meat with the potatoes, smooth the top with a knife, mark round the edge, brush over with milk, bake in a hot oven till a nice brown.

196 MEAT CAKES

½ lb (225 g) minced meat   salt and pepper
½ lb (225 g) cooked potatoes   egg and bread crumbs
little stock   parsley

(Enough to make twelve cakes)

Mash the potatoes smoothly, add the minced meat and a little stock, mix well, season with salt and pepper, form into small flat cakes of even size, coat with egg and bread crumbs, fry a golden brown in hot fat, drain on paper, dish in a circle on a hot dish with a fancy paper, garnish with fried parsley. Serve with a good gravy.

197 PASTRY RISSOLES

minced meat   1 gill (150 ml) stock
½ oz (15 g) butter   salt and pepper
½ oz (15 g) flour   egg and bread crumbs

For Pastry

4 oz (100 g) flour   water to mix
2 oz (50 g) butter or dripping   salt

(Enough to make eight rissoles)

Make the sauce (cold sauce will do, if any), mix with the meat, season well. Rub the butter into the flour, mix stiffly, roll out very thinly, cut into rounds, brush round edges with egg, put a portion of the mixture on each, fold over, cut into half-moon shapes, coat with egg and bread crumbs or egg and crushed vermicelli, fry in hot fat, dish on a hot dish with fancy paper, garnish with fried parsley. These are suitable for picnics when cold.

198 COLD MEAT GATEAU

1 oz (25 g) cooked meat   some gravy
4 oz (100 g) bread crumbs   1 egg
2 hard-boiled eggs   salt and pepper
1 chopped onion   ½ pint (300 ml) brown or
chopped parsley   tomato sauce

(Enough for six or seven people)

Well grease a pie dish, cut the hard-boiled eggs in slices and decorate the dish, mince the meat, add bread crumbs, onion, parsley, salt and pepper, mix with some gravy and well-beaten egg, put the mixture into a pie dish, press it well in. Bake for twenty minutes, turn out on a hot dish and pour brown or tomato sauce round.

199 FILLET OF BEEF À LA VIENNOISE

1 lb (450 g) lean beef   4 oz (100 g) bread crumbs
1 Spanish onion   salt and pepper
1 teaspoonful chopped parsley   Espagnole sauce (see No. 623)
   1 egg

(Enough for four people)

Mince the beef, add the bread crumbs, a little of the onion finely chopped, salt and pepper and egg to bind, shape into neat fillets and fry in butter, divide the Spanish onion into rings, dip them in milk and flour and fry them till cooked.

Make a purée with the rest of the onion finely chopped and cooked in a little of the brown sauce, dish the fillets on a double row of mashed potato, spread the purée on the top of each, pour round the sauce and garnish with the fried onion rings.

200 FILLET OF BEEF À LA BÉARNAISE

1 lb (450 g) beef fillet	1 gill (150 ml) brown sauce
1 oz (25 g) butter	(see No. 623)
1 oz (25 g) glaze	salt and pepper
chopped mushrooms	

(Enough for three or four people)

Cut the beef into neat round fillets, melt the butter, fry the chopped mushroom, then fry the fillets, turning them once or twice, dip each fillet in a little glaze, dish on croûtons of bread same size as the fillets in two straight rows down an entrée dish, pour the brown sauce round and garnish with watercress.

201 RAGOÛT OF BEEF

cold boiled beef	little ketchup
2 onions	½ pint (300 ml) gravy
1 oz (25 g) butter	mustard to taste
1 oz (25 g) flour	salt and pepper
1 tablespoonful vinegar	

(Enough for three or four people)

Slice and fry the onions in the butter, adding the flour, allow to cook till a nice brown, add the gravy and vinegar and boil up, stir well and add some made mustard, ketchup and seasoning. Put in the beef and let the stewpan stand at the side of the stove to cook the meat very gently, serve with a border of boiled haricot beans.

202 GRILLED STEAK À LA RUSSE

1 to 2 lb (450–900 g) rump	salt and pepper
steak	horseradish sauce (No. 633 or
butter	634)

(Enough for four or five people)

Grease the bars of the griller, brush over the steak with butter, put on the steak and grill over a clear fire from six to eight minutes, turning once or twice, serve on a hot dish with horseradish sauce and potato chips.

203 STEAMED CHOP

1 chop	2 oz (50 g) Patna rice
butter	salt and pepper

Trim the chop, sprinkle over a little salt and pepper, place it between two buttered plates over a saucepan of boiling water. Cook the rice as for curry, arrange it on a hot plate. When the chop is cooked place it on the rice, sprinkle over chopped parsley or capers and serve.

204 BEEF STEAK AND TOMATO PIE

2 lb (900 g) steak	stock
tomatoes	Worcester sauce
potatoes	salt and pepper
flour	flaky pastry (see No. 514)

(Enough for seven or eight people)

Cut the steak into thin slices, wrap a small piece of fat in each, dip in seasoned flour and pack loosely in a pie dish,

cover with a layer of small whole tomatoes and slices of parboiled potatoes, pour in a little stock, with a dessert spoonful of Worcester sauce. Cover with pastry, decorate with leaves, brush over with egg, bake for one and a half to two hours.

205 VEAL CUTLETS À LA FRANÇAISE

2 to 3 lb (900g – 1.4 kg) neck	bread crumbs
of veal	mashed potato
1 lemon	salt and pepper
1 egg	brown sauce (see No. 623)

(Enough for four or five people)

Cut and trim the cutlets neatly, season with salt and pepper, rub each side of the cutlets with a cut lemon, coat with egg and bread crumbs, fry them in a sauté pan till a nice golden colour, about eight minutes, drain and dish up on a mound of mashed potatoes with the brown sauce round the dish.

206 CALF'S FEET FRITTERS

3 or 4 calf's feet	tomato sauce (see No. 628)
egg and bread crumbs	

(Enough for four or five people)

Stew the calf's feet till tender, cut open and remove the bones, put the meat aside until cold, then cut it in neat pieces, coat with egg and bread crumbs, fry to a golden brown in hot fat, drain and serve the fritters on a hot dish with tomato sauce.

207 STUFFED SHOULDER OF VEAL

small shoulder of veal	bunch of herbs
2 carrots	veal stuffing (see No. 643)
2 onions	salt and pepper
1 oz (25 g) flour	

(Enough for seven or eight people)

Take out the bone from the veal and fill with veal stuffing, roll up and tie with tape, place in a stewpan with the carrots, onions, herbs and enough water to cover, and stew gently for three hours, remove the meat, thicken the gravy with the flour, season well, strain over the veal, garnish with the chopped vegetables neatly; this joint can be stuffed and roasted, served with good brown gravy and rashers.

208 FRIED CALVES' BRAINS

2 sets of brains	1 tablespoonful vinegar
1 shallot	pepper and salt
chopped parsley	frying batter (see No. 649)
1 tablespoonful salad oil	tomato sauce (see No. 628)

(Enough for three or four people)

Cleanse the brains thoroughly and remove the skin, place in a stewpan with cold water and salt, boil up and simmer for ten minutes, remove the brains, rinse them in cold water and allow them to get cold, and then cut into neat pieces, soak the brains for an hour in a deep dish with the oil, vinegar, chopped parsley and shallot, take the brains out, dry them, dip in flour lightly and then in frying batter, and fry a golden brown in deep fat, drain carefully and dish on a fancy paper or folded serviette, garnish with fried parsley and serve with tomato sauce.

209 VEAL CREAM

cold veal	pistachio nuts
½ pint (300 ml) cream	coraline pepper
5 sheets gelatine	salad
truffle	

(Enough for four or five people)

Mince, pound and sieve the veal, there should be about a breakfast cupful, whip the cream, add veal, chopped truffle, seasoning, and dissolved gelatine, decorate a mould with chopped pistachio nuts or parsley and coraline pepper, pour in the mixture, turn out when set and dish on a bed of salad.

210 VEAL CUTLETS À LA MILANAISE

1 lb (450 g) veal cutlet	2 eggs
12 small mushrooms	bread crumbs
1 shallot	salt and pepper
1 tablespoonful chopped	Milanaise sauce
parsley	tomato sauce (see No. 628)
1 gill (150 ml) white sauce	

(Enough for four people)

Chop the mushrooms and shallot very finely, put into a saucepan with the white sauce, chopped parsley, salt and pepper. Stir till it is quite thick, then spread on a plate to cool, cut the fillet into thin cutlets, lay some of the mixture on one side, coat with egg and crumbs, fry in deep fat for three or four minutes.

For the Milanaise Sauce

Boil some macaroni, cut into short lengths, beat in some white sauce with cheese and seasoning, arrange the cutlets on a border of potatoes, put the Milanaise sauce in the centre and pour tomato sauce round.

211 VEAL À LA REINE

2 lb (900 g) veal cutlet	4 cloves
1 onion	2 eggs
1 stick celery	1 gill (150 ml) milk or cream
bunch herbs	white stock
1 oz (25 g) butter	lemon juice
1 oz (25 g) flour	salt and pepper

(Enough for five or six people)

Trim the fillet, bind into a good shape and place in a stewpan with the onions, celery, cloves, herbs and enough water or stock to cover, boil and skim carefully, make a sauce with the butter and flour, adding some of the veal liquor, lemon juice and seasonings, add slowly the beaten yolks of eggs and a little milk or cream, stir till it thickens, but do not let it boil, put the veal on a hot dish, pour over the sauce, garnish with rolls of fried bacon and pieces of boiled cauliflower.

212 MUTTON CUTLETS À LA NELSON

8 mutton cutlets	truffles
lean ham	1 gill (150 ml) white sauce
2 oz (50 g) butter	salt and pepper
3 oz (75 g) bread crumbs	egg and bread crumbs
3 oz (75 g) macaroni	

(Enough for four people)

Trim the cutlets neatly, chop the ham and truffles finely, cover one side of the cutlets with ham and the other with truffle, dip in egg and coat with bread crumbs, put the butter in a sauté pan when hot, cook the cutlets for about eight to ten minutes, drain them, dish in a circle, fill the centre with the cooked macaroni cut in short lengths with strips of truffle and heated in white sauce, pour some espagnole or good brown sauce round the dish and serve.

213 COLD LAMB WITH GREEN PEA SALAD

cold lamb	peas
mint sauce	pickled beetroot and gherkin
1 lettuce	mayonnaise (see No. 636)
1 pint (600 ml) cooked green	salt and pepper

(Enough for three or four people)

Cut the lamb into neat slices, place it on a dish on a bed of lettuce, sprinkle over a little mint sauce, drain the peas, add the mayonnaise sauce, arrange these round the slices of meat and garnish with fancy shapes of beetroot and gherkin and serve.

214 MUTTON OLIVES

slices of cold mutton	salt and pepper
veal stuffing (see No. 643)	mashed potato
allspice	red-currant jelly
gravy	

Take as many slices of cold mutton as required, of equal size, season with salt, pepper and a little allspice, place on each slice a little veal stuffing, roll up and secure with thread, place in a baking dish, pour over some good gravy, cover with greased paper and cook for thirty minutes. Serve with mashed potato and red-currant jelly.

215 MUTTON COLLOPS AND TOMATO SAUCE

1 lb (450 g) cold mutton	mashed potato
salad oil	tomato sauce (see No. 628)
salt and pepper	

(Enough for four people)

Cut the mutton in neat, rather thick, slices, season well with salt and pepper. Steep them in salad oil, then broil them over a clear fire. Serve on a mound of mashed potato with tomato sauce.

216 LAMB OR MUTTON FRITTERS

cold lamb or mutton	1 gill (150 ml) tepid water
white sauce	thin slices of bacon
4 oz (100 g) flour	1 egg
1 oz (25 g) melted butter	salt and pepper

(Enough for three or four people)

Mince the meat finely, moisten it with some white sauce and season well, make the frying batter with the flour, oiled butter, tepid water and white of egg, allow it to stand. Place some of the minced lamb on the thin slices of bacon, roll up, dip in flour 1and then in the batter. Fry a golden brown in hot fat, dish on a fancy paper or folded serviette, garnish with lemon and fried parsley.

217 PORK CUTLETS AND TOMATO SAUCE

1 lb (450 g) cold pork	little flour
½ pint (300 ml) tomato sauce	salt and pepper
½ oz (15 g) butter	mashed potatoes

(Enough for four people)

Heat the potatoes, mash them and make a mound in the centre of a dish, cut the pork into cutlets, brush over with melted butter and broil over a clear fire, thicken some tomato purée with the butter and flour, dish the cutlets on the potatoes and pour the tomato sauce round. This is a useful way of serving up cold pork.

218 CASSEROLE OF COLD MEAT

1 lb (450 g) cooked meat	½ pint (300 ml) good gravy
2 oz (50 g) macaroni	salt and pepper
cold potatoes	1 egg

(Enough for four people)

Sieve the potatoes, season and mix with egg, line a well-buttered mould with the mixture and bake for half an hour in a moderate oven, remove and place on a hot dish, boil the macaroni till tender, cut into small pieces, chop or mince the meat, add the gravy, season, make hot and put in the centre of the potato and serve hot.

219 DRESDEN PATTIES

thick slices of bread	gravy
cold meat	salt and pepper

Cut the thick slices of bread into small rounds, mark with a small cutter and hollow out the centre; fry the cases in hot fat, also a small round for a top. Mince the cold meat, add some good gravy or brown sauce, season well, make hot, fill the bread cases, put on the top and serve on a fancy paper, garnish with fried parsley.

POULTRY AND GAME

220 ROAST FOWL

fowl	bread sauce (see No. 638)
veal stuffing (see No. 643)	bacon

(Enough for four people)

Draw the fowl, make some veal stuffing, put it in the breast where the crop was, remove the gall from the liver and the bag from the gizzard, put them into the skin of the wings and turn the tips over on the back. Pass a threaded trussing needle through the lower points of wings and upper part of legs, taking a stitch to secure the flap to keep in stuffing, tie on the back, place the legs together, fasten them to the body. Wrap in buttered paper and roast, basting frequently. When nearly done remove the paper, dredge with flour and froth★ and brown it nicely. Trim the bacon, roll up, thread the rolls on a skewer, cook in the oven with fowl from ten to fifteen minutes. Dish up the fowl, remove the string, place on a hot dish, make the gravy as for roast meat. Pour a little round the fowl, place round the rolls of bacon, garnish with watercress. Serve with bread sauce and the rest of the gravy.

221 BOILED FOWL

1 fowl	1 hard-boiled egg
stock to cover	chopped parsley
1 pint (600 ml) béchamel sauce	salt and pepper
(see No. 604)	boiled bacon or ham
lemon	

Draw and truss the fowl, taking care to loosen the skin of the legs and to push them well up inside the body. Put it into hot stock, having first wrapped it in buttered paper with two slices of lemon on the breast. Simmer gently till tender. When cooked lift out on to a hot plate, drain and remove string and paper, place on a hot dish, coat with béchamel sauce, decorate with yolk of egg put through a sieve and chopped parsley, garnish the dish with lemon and parsley and the cups of white of hard-boiled egg filled with vegetables. Serve with boiled ham or bacon.

222 CHICKEN CROQUETTES

½ lb (225 g) cooked chicken	1 teaspoonful chopped parsley
2 oz (50 g) ham	little lemon juice
1 oz (25 g) butter	salt and pepper
1 oz (25 g) flour	egg and bread crumbs
1 gill (150 ml) white stock	

(Enough to make six croquettes)

Mince or chop the chicken finely, add the chopped ham and parsley, cook the flour in the butter, add the white stock and cook till it thickens, add to the chicken and ham, season well with salt and pepper and a squeeze of lemon juice, place on a wet plate, divide into equal portions, set aside to cool, form into cork shapes, using a little flour or bread crumbs, coat with egg and bread crumbs, fry in hot fat. Serve on a hot dish with a fancy paper, garnish with fried parsley.

223 FRICASSÉE OF CHICKEN

1 chicken	2 oz (50 g) butter
1 onion stuffed with cloves	2 oz (50 g) flour
1 blade of mace	½ pint (300 ml) white stock
bunch of herbs	½ pint (300 ml) milk
1 lemon	salt and pepper

(Enough for six or seven people)

Cut the chicken into neat joints, place in a stewpan with onion, mace, herbs and strip of lemon peel, add the white stock and simmer very gently till tender, cook the flour in the butter, add the stock the chicken was cooked in and the milk, stir till it boils, season well with salt and pepper and lemon juice, put back the joints of chicken, serve with a rose border of mashed potato, garnish with cut lemon and parsley. Cold boiled fowl can be served in this way, using the liquor it was boiled in.

224 POULET À LA SEFTON

remains of cold fowl	little butter
2 tablespoonfuls Harvey sauce	2 tablespoonfuls mustard
1 tablespoonful mushroom	1 tablespoonful Bengal
ketchup	chutney
	1 tablespoonful curry powder

Cut up fowl into neat joints — remains of a plainly-boiled fowl are best — mix all the ingredients well together, brush over each joint, put in the oven for a few minutes to

★ 'Froth': dust with flour and baste to give a crisp skin.

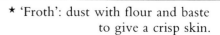

set, then grill over a clear fire for ten minutes. Just before serving brush over with butter, and serve hot with mustard sauce if liked.

225 POULET À LA MARENGO

1 chicken	1 glass white wine (Sauterne)
1 oz (25 g) butter	mushrooms
1 tablespoonful olive oil	1 gill (150 ml) tomato purée
1 shallot	½ pint (300 ml) brown sauce
bunch of herbs	salt and pepper

(Enough for six or seven people)

Cut the chicken up in neat joints, fry them a nice brown in the oil and butter in a stewpan, pour away the oil and add the wine, shallot and herbs, allow this to cook a little, then add the brown sauce and tomato purée and mushrooms, simmer very gently for about forty minutes or till chicken is tender. Arrange the joints neatly on a croûte of fried bread, season the sauce and pour it over, garnish with small croûtons of fried bread and serve. Rabbit can be cooked in the same manner.

226 GALANTINE OF CHICKEN

1 chicken	12 pistachio nuts
1 lb (450 g) sausage meat	3 truffles
¼ lb (100 g) tongue	1 teaspoonful chopped parsley
¼ lb (100 g) ham	salt and pepper
2 hard-boiled eggs	aspic jelly (see No. 647)

(Enough for nine or ten people)

Bone the fowl, cut the egg into slices, the ham and tongue in strips, place in half of the sausage meat, then the tongue, ham, slices of egg, blanched pistachio nuts, chopped truffles and seasoning in layers, then the rest of the sausage meat. Roll in a cloth and tie tightly for boiling, simmer gently in well-flavoured stock from two to two and a half hours. Take it out, untie the cloth and roll it up again firmly, place it between two dishes with a weight on top. When cold take off the cloth, wipe the galantine with a hot cloth, glaze with aspic and serve with salad, and garnish with chopped aspic jelly.

227 CHAUDFROID OF CHICKEN

1 boiled chicken	aspic jelly
1 pint (600 ml) béchamel sauce	salad
(see No. 604)	ham
truffles	

(Enough for six or seven people)

Cut the chicken into neat joints, remove the skin and trim them, place on a cake rack with a dish underneath, warm the béchamel sauce, add about two tablespoonfuls of liquid aspic, coat the joints with it, decorate the joints with little fancy shapes of truffle and coat again with aspic. When cold and set arrange round a high croûte of fried bread, using fancy skewers to keep them in place; place some dressed salad round the dish and garnish with chopped aspic and chopped ham.

228 ROAST DUCK

1 duck	watercress
sage and onion stuffing	gravy
(see No. 645)	apple sauce (see No. 629)

(Enough for four or five people)

Draw the duck, cut off the legs at the first joint, wipe and put in the sage and onion stuffing, take off the wings at the first joint, truss it firmly, roast in the oven from one and a half to one and three-quarter hours according to age and size, basting well, dredge with flour and froth and brown it well before dishing.

Put the duck's giblets in a saucepan with a sage leaf, onion and some stock, simmer them, using the stock for gravy, which can be made as for roast meat or thickened if preferred. Put the duck on a hot dish, remove the string, garnish with watercress, and serve it with the gravy in a tureen and apple sauce. If a couple of ducks are cooked it is advisable to stuff one only.

229 ROAST TURKEY

1 turkey	sausages
forcemeat	bread sauce
gravy	bacon or ham

Draw, singe and wipe the inside of the turkey with a clean wet cloth, cut off the feet and draw the sinews from the thighs, put the liver and gizzard in the wings, stuff the breast where the crop was with forcemeat, either veal stuffing with sausage meat added or chestnut stuffing (see No. 644), truss for roasting, place in a baking tin with some dripping, put in hot oven. After the first fifteen minutes cook very gently, basting frequently. When nearly cooked dredge with flour, put it back in the oven and baste well till brown and frothy. Remove the skewers and string, put it on a hot dish, make the gravy as for a joint of roast meat, using the stock the giblets (neck, heart, liver, gizzard and feet) have been boiled in, strain some round the turkey, garnish with the sausages previously fried, serve with bread sauce and boiled ham or bacon and the rest of the gravy in a tureen.

230 BOILED TURKEY

1 turkey	celery or oyster sauce (see
stock	No. 614 or 611)
boiled ham or tongue	

Draw, singe and truss as a fowl for boiling, wrap in greased paper with slices of lemon on the breast. Place the turkey in enough hot stock to cover, simmer very gently, allowing fifteen minutes to the pound (0.5 kg) and fifteen minutes over. Put on a hot dish, remove paper, skewers and string, coat with celery or oyster sauce, serve with boiled tongue or ham and the rest of the sauce in a tureen; if liked the turkey can be stuffed with oyster stuffing and served with egg sauce.

231 ROAST PIGEONS

pigeons	butter
larding bacon	bread sauce (see No. 638)
toast	gravy

Draw, singe and truss the pigeons, lard the breasts, roast in a hot oven, basting frequently from twenty to thirty minutes, serve on squares of toast with bread sauce and gravy. A plain French salad of lettuce dressed with oil and vinegar can also be served.

232 PIGEON PIE

3 or 4 pigeons	2 oz (50 g) ham
1 lb (450 g) beef steak	stock
3 hard-boiled eggs	salt and pepper
flour	flaky or puff-pastry (see No. 514 or 516)

(Enough for seven or eight people)

Prepare, singe and draw the pigeons, cut them in halves or quarters. Cut the steak in small pieces, dip them into seasoned flour, put the steak, pigeons, ham and slices of hard-boiled eggs in a pie dish in layers, pour over enough good gravy or stock to half fill the dish, cover with pastry, trim edges, glaze and decorate in the usual way. Bake from two to two and a half hours, scald and skin the feet and put in the centre when the pie is cooked, to show what the pie is made of. If the pie is to be eaten cold, when it is cooked pour in some more good gravy or stock to which some gelatine has been added.

233 ROAST PHEASANT

1 brace of pheasants	bread sauce (see No. 638)
fat bacon	fried bread crumbs
little butter	watercress
gravy	

Pluck, singe and draw the pheasants, scald and skin the legs, removing the claws, wipe with a damp cloth, put a small piece of butter with pepper inside, truss for roasting, tie some pieces of fat bacon over the breasts, cook for about one hour, basting frequently, remove the bacon, dredge with flour and cook again till brown and frothy. Remove the string, place on a hot dish, garnish with watercress. Serve with bread sauce, fried bread crumbs and some good gravy.

For the Fried Bread Crumbs—Melt some butter in an enamelled frying pan, put in some white bread crumbs, stir them carefully over the fire until they are nicely browned, drain them on paper, place in the oven for a few minutes. Serve on a lace paper.

234 SALMI OF PHEASANT

remains of pheasant	pinch of herbs
1 oz (25 g) butter	1 teaspoonful red-currant jelly
½ oz (15 g) flour	½ pint (300 ml) stock made
1 shallot	from pheasant bones
1 bay leaf	salt and pepper
glass of port wine	

(Enough for three or four people)

Remove the bones from the pheasant, cook them in stock, cut the meat into neat pieces, melt the butter in a stewpan, brown the flour, add the stock, stir the mixture till it boils, add the chopped shallot, herbs, jelly, wine and bay leaf, simmer slowly for twenty minutes, strain and put in pieces of pheasant, season and reheat, garnish with triangles of fried bread.

235 ROAST PARTRIDGE

1 brace of partridges	watercress
a little fat bacon	fried crumbs
gravy	croûtons of toast
bread sauce	

(Enough for three or four people)

Pluck, singe and draw the birds, truss firmly, making them look plump, roast for thirty minutes, basting frequently. A slice of fat bacon can be tied on the breast to keep them moist; remove it and flour and froth them well a few minutes before dishing. Dish on croûton of toast, garnish with watercress, serve with bread sauce and fried bread crumbs (see Roast Pheasant).

236 ROAST HARE

1 hare	flour
veal forcemeat	½ pint (300 ml) brown sauce
butter	red-currant jelly
½ pint (300 ml) milk	glass of port wine

(Enough for eight or nine people)

Choose a young hare for roasting and hang it for a few days without paunching it. When required skin it, leaving on the ears. Wipe it well inside and out if necessary, soak it to remove the blood, make a veal stuffing, add the parboiled and chopped liver, put it in the hare, sew it up and truss. Place it in a meat tin with a little milk, roast in the oven, basting constantly. Flour the hare well and baste with butter to froth the outside. The time allowed will depend on the size of the hare. Place on a hot dish, remove the string, pour the fat off from the tin, sprinkle in a little flour and brown it over the fire, pour in the brown sauce, add the wine, boil for a few minutes and strain it, garnish the hare with some little balls of forcemeat fried, serve with red-currant jelly and the gravy in a tureen.

237 JUGGED HARE

1 hare	3 oz (75 g) butter
1½ lb (700 g) beef steak	3 oz (75 g) flour
2 onions	2 glasses of port wine
2 or 3 cloves	red-currant jelly
bunch of herbs	salt and pepper
strip of lemon rind	forcemeat balls
stock or water	

(Enough for nine or ten people)

Skin the hare, do not wash it, let the blood from the upper part of the body run into a basin and put it aside, then wipe it carefully. Cut into neat joints, dip them in well-seasoned flour and fry a nice brown in butter, put the joints into a large stewing jar with the steak cut in pieces, herbs, onions, cloves, lemon rind. Cover with stock or water, cover the jar closely, cook gently in the oven for three or four hours. When ready to serve take out the joints, onion and herbs, mix the flour with some water. Add it to the gravy and boil, then add the wine and forcemeat balls, lastly the seasoning and blood. Do not boil after the blood is added. Put back the joints to reheat. Dish with joints piled in centre, gravy poured round, garnish with forcemeat balls and serve with red-currant jelly.

To make Forcemeat Balls.—To some veal stuffing well seasoned add the parboiled and chopped liver of hare, fry in butter.

238 ROAST GROUSE

grouse	gravy
butter	bread sauce
fat bacon	browned bread crumbs

Pluck, singe and draw the grouse, wiping well with a damp cloth (game should never be washed), put a small piece of butter with a little pepper and lemon juice inside the birds, truss for roasting. A slice of fat bacon and a vine leaf or two should be wrapped over the breast of each bird. Roast in the oven or before the fire, baste frequently, remove the bacon and froth just before dishing. Place on a hot dish on a croûton of toast, which should be made and put under the grouse in the dripping pan, garnish with watercress and serve the dish with bread sauce and browned bread crumbs.

239 ROAST WILD DUCK

1 wild duck	juice of 1 lemon
lemon	juice of 1 orange
watercress	1 shallot
1 gill (150 ml) brown sauce	1 glass port wine

(Enough for three or four people)

Carefully draw the duck, singe and truss it, put in a baking tin with some dripping, dredge over some flour and roast till a nice brown, rather underdone than otherwise. Dish, remove the string, place on hot dish, garnish with watercress and cut lemon. Add the juice of lemon and orange to the brown sauce, also the port wine; boil up and strain, serve in a tureen. Orange salad is also served with wild duck if liked.

240 BOILED RABBIT

1 rabbit	chopped parsley
1 pint (600 ml) white sauce	bacon or pork

(Enough for four or five people)

Skin and cleanse the rabbit, slit the thighs so as to be able to draw the legs forward, turn the head to the right side, pass a skewer through the legs, shoulders and out through the head, keeping the rabbit as flat as possible. Boil gently for about an hour. When tender place on a hot dish, remove the skewers and string, coat with parsley sauce, garnish with the liver boiled and finely chopped. Onion sauce can be used instead of parsley sauce if liked. Serve with boiled bacon or pork.

241 ROAST RABBIT

1 rabbit	gravy
veal forcemeat (see No. 643)	slice of bacon

(Enough for four or five people)

Skin and wash the rabbit, make some veal stuffing, parboil the liver, chop it and add to the stuffing, fill the body and sew it up, truss as a roast hare, bringing the legs forward and the head back on the body, bind with tape, roast for one and a half to two hours, baste frequently. A slice of fat bacon can be laid on the back. Flour well at the end to make it brown. Dish on a hot dish, remove skewers and tape, serve with gravy made as for roast meat and bread sauce or with piquante sauce (see No. 624).

242 STEWED RABBIT

1 rabbit	1 pint (600 ml) stock
1 onion	bunch of herbs
2 oz (50 g) butter or dripping	salt and pepper
2 oz (50 g) flour	

(Enough for five or six people)

Skin and wash the rabbit, cut into neat joints, melt the butter or dripping in a stewpan, fry the chopped onion a nice brown, remove it, dip the rabbit into flour and fry, take out the joints and brown the flour, taking care it does not burn, add the stock, stir till it boils, put back rabbit, onion, add the herbs, simmer gently for three hours, season well, place joints in centre of a hot dish, strain the gravy over.

243 RABBIT PIE

1 rabbit	stock
1 small onion	pinch of herbs
¼ lb (100 g) ham or bacon	salt and pepper
2 hard-boiled eggs	flaky or rough puff pastry
little flour	

(Enough for four or five people)

Skin and wash the rabbit, cut into neat joints, dip them in flour seasoned with salt and pepper and fry them in butter or dripping. Place them in a pie dish with the ham, slices of hard-boiled eggs; sprinkle over a pinch of sweet herbs, season with salt and pepper, add enough stock to half fill the dish, cover with pastry, decorate and glaze in the usual way, bake for two hours, when cooled add more stock. A hole should be left to allow the steam to escape during cooking.

244 RABBIT CROQUETTES

¼ lb (100 g) cooked rabbit	grated lemon rind
¼ lb (100 g) ham or bacon	salt and pepper
1 or 2 eggs	egg and bread crumbs
chopped parsley	

(Enough for four people)

Mince the rabbit and the ham or bacon, add the chopped parsley and grated lemon rind, season well with salt and pepper, mix with beaten egg, form into cork shapes, using a little flour, coat with egg and bread crumbs, fry in hot fat, dish on a hot dish with a fancy paper, garnish with fried parsley.

245 CHICKEN MOUSSE

½ lb (225 g) cold chicken	3 eggs
1 gill (150 ml) thick white sauce	1 gill (150 ml) cream
	salt and pepper

(Enough for three or four people)

Pound the chicken and pass through a sieve, add the whipped cream and seasoning and the yolks of eggs, whip the whites very stiffly, fold in lightly to the mixture, put it in a well-buttered mould, steam for one hour, turn out and serve coated with the white sauce.

246 VOL AU VENT OF CHICKEN

½ lb (225 g) puff pastry	white sauce
(see No. 516)	ham
cold chicken	salt and pepper

(Enough for three or four people)

Make an oval vol au vent case with the puff pastry, bake it and scrape out the soft paste in the centre, make a savoury mixture with the minced chicken and sauce, chopped ham and seasoning, fill the centre and serve at once.

247 CHICKEN À LA CIMIEZ

1 chicken	6 peppercorns
1 onion	blade of mace
1 carrot	white sauce
slices of ham	salt
green peas	lemon juice
asparagus heads	truffle

(Enough for four people)

Truss the chicken as for boiling, pour three pints (1.7 litres) of water in a stewpan with the vegetables, peppercorns, two slices of ham, salt and lemon juice, boil for fifteen minutes, then add the chicken and simmer gently for three-quarters of an hour, cut it into neat joints, skin it, place on a hot dish, pour over a white sauce, garnish with cooked green peas and asparagus heads, chopped ham and truffle.

248 CHICKEN PATTIES

some cold cooked chicken	salt and pepper
white sauce	puff pastry (see No. 516)
ham	

Make the pastry, cut into rounds, mark with a cutter two sizes smaller and cut out some rounds with this cutter for the tops, brush over with egg, taking care not to brush the cut edges as this prevents the pastry from rising, place the pastry on a tin, let it stand twenty minutes, then bake in a hot oven from fifteen to twenty minutes, when cool hollow out the centre, put in a mixture of minced chicken, ham and white sauce well seasoned, place on the top, reheat and serve.

Note.—Lobster and oyster patties can be made in the same way.

249 DEVILLED CHICKEN

1 chicken	1 teaspoonful chopped parsley
2 oz (50 g) butter	1 dessertspoonful mustard
3 tablespoonfuls brown	salt and pepper
bread crumbs	

(Enough for four or five people)

Roast the chicken for three-quarters of an hour, cut into neat joints, place in a fireproof dish, cover with seasoning, bread crumbs and parsley, put the butter on top and bake in the oven for twenty minutes and serve in the same dish.

250 CHICKEN PIE

1 chicken	chicken stock
½ lb (225 g) ham	salt and pepper
2 hard-boiled eggs	puff pastry (see No. 516)
veal stuffing	

(Enough for seven or eight people)

Boil the chicken, remove and cut into neat joints, reduce the broth, season well and add a leaf or two of gelatine, make the veal forcemeat, parboil the liver and add, form into balls, lay the chicken in a pie dish with the ham cut in strips, the eggs in slices and the forcemeat in balls, strain over the stock, cover with pastry, decorate with leaves, brush over with egg and bake in a hot oven from one and a quarter to one and a half hours; before serving pour in some more stock.

251 BRAISED DUCK WITH TURNIPS

1 duck	stock
3 turnips	1 glass white wine
1 carrot	2 oz (50 g) butter
1 onion	salt and pepper
½ pint (300 ml) brown sauce	croûtons of bread

(Enough for four or five people)

Truss the duck as for roasting, place in a baking tin with the butter and partially roast it, allow it to cool and cut into neat joints, put the brown sauce in a stew pan, add the carrot and onion sliced, the wine and seasoning and simmer gently for thirty minutes, dish on a hot dish, strain the sauce over, garnish with fried croûtons of bread and the turnips cut into quarters, boiled, drained and fried.

252 MINCED DUCK AND TOMATOES

½ lb (225 g) cold duck	salt and pepper
4 or 5 tomatoes	rice
some good brown sauce	

(Enough for three or four people)

Peel the tomatoes, cook for ten minutes in the brown sauce, then add the duck minced finely, season and reheat, serve with a border of boiled rice.

253 DUCK AU GRATIN

remains of duck	1 teaspoonful herbs
2 oz (50 g) butter	1 teaspoonful parsley
2 oz (50 g) bread crumbs	salt and pepper
pinch mushroom powder	

(Enough for two or three people)

Mix all the dry ingredients together, put half in the bottom of a gratin dish, cut the duck into neat pieces and lay in the dish, put on the remainder of the crumbs, then the butter, bake for fifteen minutes.

254 COMPÔTE OF PIGEONS

3 pigeons	1 turnip
2 oz (50 g) lean ham	1 oz (25 g) flour
3 oz (75 g) butter	1 pint (600 ml) stock
6 mushrooms	½ gill (75 ml) sherry
2 shallots	salt and pepper
1 carrot	

(Enough for four or five people)

Clean the pigeons and truss neatly, drawing the legs inside the skin, cut the ham into strips and fry in butter, remove and fry the shallots, mushrooms and a little carrot and turnips cut small, fry the pigeons brown, add the stock, flour, sherry and seasoning and simmer gently till tender,

remove the trussing strings, arrange the pigeons on a mound of potato or spinach, strain the gravy round and garnish with vegetables.

255 PHEASANT EN COCOTTE

1 pheasant	6 potatoes
2 oz (50 g) lean ham	½ pint (300 ml) stock
2 carrots	pepper and salt
1 onion	

Draw and prepare the pheasant, cut into joints, cut the ham and vegetables into small pieces, place half in an earthenware jar, then put in the pheasant, the remainder of the vegetables, and the stock, cook gently in the oven for one and a half to two hours, season and serve in the jar.

256 GRILLED PHEASANT

joints of pheasant	salt and pepper
slices of bacon	toast

Score the flesh of the joints to the bone, sprinkle in a little seasoning, wrap each joint in a thin slice of bacon, grill over a clear fire from fifteen to twenty minutes, turning it frequently, serve on buttered toast.

257 STEWED PARTRIDGES

2 partridges	beans
onions	2 oz (50 g) butter
carrots	gravy browning
turnips	sherry
chopped parsley	salt and pepper
bunch of herbs	

(Enough for four people)

Prepare the partridges, cut in halves, place in a stewpan with the butter and seasoning and prepared vegetables, cover and cook over a moderate fire for five or six minutes, then place the stewpan in the oven and leave it there for three-quarters of an hour, dish the partridges on a hot dish with the vegetables round, add some gravy browning to the liquid, boil up, season, add chopped parsley, pour over the partridges and serve with potato chips.

258 GROUSE PIE

2 or 3 grouse	hard-boiled eggs
1 lb (450 g) beef steak	butter
mushrooms	gravy
2 shallots	salt and pepper
mace	puff pastry (see No. 516)

Pluck, singe and draw the grouse, cut each neatly into four pieces, fry till half cooked in butter seasoned with salt, pepper and mace, cut the beef into pieces and fry with some mushrooms and shallots chopped, arrange both neatly in a pie dish with some hard-boiled eggs cut in quarters and some good gravy, cover the dish with puff pastry, decorate with leaves, brush over with egg and cook from one and a half to two hours in a quick oven; more gravy should be added when the pie is taken from the oven.

259 GAME PIE

1 pheasant or partridge	1 doz. almonds
4 oz (100 g) lean ham	6 pistachio nuts
2 hard-boiled eggs	4 sheets gelatine
1 pint (600 ml) stock	salt and pepper

(Enough for four or five people)

Bone the game, boil the bones in the stock, cut the flesh and the ham into small pieces, arrange in layers in a game pie dish with egg in slices, nuts, pepper and salt, add the gelatine to the stock, when dissolved strain the stock over the game, bake in a moderate oven one and a half hours, serve when cold.

260 RAISED GAME PIE

1½ lb (700 g) flour	2 lb (900 g) game
6 oz (175 g) lard	salt and pepper
½ pint (300 ml) water	1 egg

(Enough for four or five people)

Cut the game into small pieces, season well with salt and pepper, boil water and lard together, pour into the centre of the flour, mix to a stiff dough, knead well, set aside to cool a little, mould into shape, put the game in the centre, cover with pastry, decorate the lid, brush over with egg, make a hole in the centre and bake in a steady oven for one and a half hours.

261 ZEPHIRES OF GAME

½ lb (225 g) cooked game	1 tablespoonful white sauce
2 oz (50 g) cooked ham	½ pint (300 ml) aspic jelly
2 truffles	seasoning
2 yolks of hard-boiled eggs	salad
2 tablespoonfuls cream	

(Enough for five or six people)

Line six or seven dariole moulds with aspic jelly, decorate with truffle cut in fancy shapes, mix nearly a gill (150 ml) of aspic with the cream, line the mould with it and put on ice to set. Pound the game in a mortar with the yolks of eggs, sauce, chopped truffle and seasoning, and a little melted aspic, fill the moulds with this and allow to set, turn out when required on to a silver entrée dish with some dressed salad and garnish with chopped aspic.

262 ROAST HAUNCH OF VENISON

haunch of venison	gravy
flour, about 3 lb (1.4 kg)	red-currant jelly
water	

Cover the haunch with a paste made of flour and water, wrap in greased paper and roast in a moderate oven for three to four hours, baste frequently; within half an hour of serving remove the paper and paste, dredge lightly with flour and baste with butter until a good colour, serve quickly with a rich brown gravy and red-currant jelly.

109

VEGETABLES AND SALADS

263 NEW POTATOES

2 lb (900 g) new potatoes	1 oz (25 g) butter
sprig of mint	chopped parsley
salt	boiling water

Scrape the potatoes gently, putting them at once into cold water, put them into a saucepan of boiling water with the salt and mint, cook gently from twenty to thirty minutes, drain off the water, add the butter, shake gently to coat them, turn into a hot vegetable dish and sprinkle over some finely chopped parsley.

264 OLD POTATOES

2 lb (900 g) potatoes	cold water
salt	

Peel the potatoes thinly, put them in a saucepan with cold water, add the salt, cook very gently with the lid on till tender, test with a skewer, pour off the water, put them back on the stove with the lid half on the pan to dry, place a folded clean cloth over them, dish in a hot vegetable dish.

265 POTATO CROQUETTES

cold potatoes	chopped parsley
½ oz (15 g) butter	salt and pepper
little milk	egg and breadcrumbs

Put the potatoes through a sive or potato masher, make them hot and add the butter, little milk, chopped parsley and season well with salt and pepper, divide into equal portions, form into balls, coat *twice* with egg and bread crumbs, fry a golden brown in hot fat, put a small piece of parsley stalk in each, dish on a hot vegetable dish on a folded serviette or a fancy paper.

266 POTATO CHIPS

potatoes	salt

Peel the potatoes thinly and cut into thin slices, dry well in a folded cloth, keep covered with the cloth till wanted. Put the slices a few at a time in a frying basket and plunge them in hot fat for a few minutes to cook, drain them and put them in another pan of smoking hot fat to crisp, drain well on paper, sprinkle with salt and serve at once on a folded serviette or fancy paper. If one pan of frying fat only is available, it must be left to get several degrees hotter for the second cooking. Straws can be cooked in the same way, and should be cut in even lengths about a quarter of an inch (0.5 cm) thick.

267 SAUTÉ POTATOES

1 lb (450 g) potatoes.	2 oz (50 g) butter
salt	chopped parsley

Cut the potatoes into neat shapes, parboil them with a little salt, melt the butter and let it get hot, add the potatoes, toss them over the fire until they are a nice golden colour, sprinkle with chopped parsley and serve at once. Cold potatoes can be sautéed in the same way, cut into slices.

268 FRIED POTATOES

potatoes	salt and pepper
butter or dripping	

Parboil the potatoes—they can be fried whole or in slices—make the dripping hot in a frying pan, put in the potatoes, brown them well all over, drain on paper and serve hot on fancy paper. Cold potatoes can be mashed, seasoned well and fried in the same way, and turned out into a hot vegetable dish.

269 POTATOES À LA MAÎTRE D'HÔTEL

potatoes	½ pint (300 ml) maître d'hôtel
salt	sauce (see No. 616)

Cook the potatoes. If old cut them in slices and place them in a hot vegetable dish, make the sauce, season well and pour over the potatoes and serve.

270 CARROTS

young carrots	chopped parsley
butter	salt and pepper

Prepare the carrots, boil them in water with salt or in stock till tender with the lid on the pan, drain well, melt the butter in the saucepan, toss the carrots in it. When thoroughly hot sprinkle with chopped parsley and serve them standing upright in a vegetable dish.

271 MASHED TURNIPS

turnips	cream
1 oz (25 g) butter	salt and pepper

Peel the turnip thickly, put into boiling water with salt, cook gently with lid on the pan, skim. When tender drain them well, and mash them, add butter, cream, salt and pepper, serve in a hot vegetable dish. If very moist shake in a little flour and cook. This also improves the colour.

272 BOILED CABBAGE

1 or 2 cabbages	salt
pinch carbonate of soda	

Remove the outside leaves, cut in half and across the stalk, soak in salt and water for an hour. Put into a saucepan with boiling water to which has been added salt and the pinch of carbonate of soda. Boil rapidly uncovered, skim occasionally. When tender drain in a colander, press out all the water, put in a hot vegetable dish and cut across in squares.

To prevent the smell rising when the cabbage is boiling put in a crust of bread.

273 BRUSSEL SPROUTS

sprouts	carbonate of soda
salt	

Take off the outside leaves of the sprouts and cut across the stalk, leave to soak in salted water. Place them in boiling water with salt and a pinch of carbonate of soda and cook gently uncovered till tender, drain well in a colander, arrange neatly in a hot vegetable dish.

274 BOILED ONIONS

Spanish onions   ½ pint (300 ml) white sauce
salt

Skin the onions, put them into boiling water with salt and cook for two or three hours, according to the size. Drain them, place them in a hot dish and pour the white sauce over and serve. Another method is to put about an ounce of butter in the pan when the water is poured off, allow it to get quite hot, season with salt and pepper and serve in a hot vegetable dish.

275 STEWED ONIONS

6 Spanish onions   flour
stock   salt and pepper

Peel the onions carefully, cutting off as little of root and top as possible, otherwise they will fall to pieces in cooking, place them in a stewpan, cover with stock and cook for two or three hours according to size. When tender thicken and brown the liquor, season well, dish the onions and pour the sauce over. The onions can be stewed in butter only if preferred. In this case it would be better to cook them well covered in the oven and very slowly.

276 STUFFED ONIONS

4 or 6 onions   brown sauce
minced meat   salt and pepper

Choose large onions, peel very carefully, cut off a slice at the top, scoop out as much as possible from the inside, fill with minced meat well seasoned and mixed with a little sauce. Replace the top, and stew very slowly for as long as possible. Serve with brown sauce. The onions can be parboiled, the inside removed and stuffed in the same way and baked in the oven, basting them well. Serve with brown sauce. Any cold meat, game or poultry will be suitable for the stuffing.

277 GREEN PEAS (BOILED)

peas   a little sugar
salt   butter
sprig of mint

Shell the peas, wash them, put them into a saucepan of boiling water with a little salt, a sprig of mint and a lump of sugar, bring to the boil, remove the scum, cook very gently uncovered for fifteen to twenty minutes, drain them, remove the mint, put back in the pan with a lump of butter. Serve in a hot vegetable dish.

278 BROAD BEANS

beans   parsley sauce (see No. 608)
salt

Shell the beans, put in boiling water with salt, boil quickly uncovered till beans are tender, drain well, place in a hot vegetable dish, coat with parsley sauce.

279 FRENCH BEANS

beans   carbonate of soda
salt   butter

String the beans and slice them thinly in a slanting direction, put them in salted water till required. When ready put them in a pan of boiling water with salt and pinch of carbonate soda, let them boil quickly uncovered until tender, drain them, serve in a hot vegetable dish with a lump of butter.

280 HARICOT BEANS

1 pint (600 ml) haricots   chopped parsley
1½ oz (40 g) butter   pepper and salt
carbonate of soda

Soak the beans for twelve hours in cold water with a pinch of carbonate of soda. Put them into a saucepan, cover with cold water and boil gently for about two hours. When tender drain in a colander (the water should be saved for the stock pot). Melt the butter in the saucepan, add the beans, parsley (one dessertspoonful), pepper and salt, toss them over the fire till hot. Serve in a vegetable dish.

281 PARSNIPS

parsnips   little butter
salt

Peel the parsnips, cut into quarters, place in boiling water with salt, cook till tender, drain them and dish in a hot vegetable dish with a little butter. Parsnips can be served with boiled meat and salt cod.

282 BOILED ARTICHOKES

artichokes (Jerusalem)   ½ pint (300 ml) white sauce
salt

Wash, peel and shape the artichokes in oval or pyramid shapes, put at once into cold water with a little lemon juice or vinegar. Put them in boiling water with salt and lemon juice, boil gently from thirty to forty minutes. When tender drain well, put them in a hot vegetable dish and pour over the white sauce.

283 BOILED SALSIFY

salsify   lemon juice
salt   ½ pint (300 ml) white sauce

Wash and peel the salsify roots, keeping them under water as much as possible during the process, place them at once into cold water with salt and lemon juice to prevent them from becoming discoloured. Put them into boiling water with salt and lemon juice and boil till quite tender, drain them. Dish in a hot vegetable dish and pour the white sauce over and serve.

284 SCALLOPED SALSIFY

some cooked salsify   grated cheese
½ pint (300 ml) white sauce   butter
bread crumbs   salt and pepper

Cut the cooked salsify into neat pieces, warm in the white sauce, which must be well seasoned with salt, cayenne and a little lemon juice. Place in some well-buttered scallop shells. Sprinkle over some fresh bread crumbs, then a little grated cheese and a few small pieces of butter on top, brown in a hot oven and serve.

Note.—Artichokes can be cooked in the same way.

285 BOILED LEEKS

leeks   ½ pint (300 ml) white sauce
salt   toast

Wash the leeks thoroughly, trim into even lengths, tie them into bundles, put them into boiling water with salt and boil till quite tender, drain them, dish on a slice of toast in a hot vegetable dish, remove the tape, pour the white sauce over and serve.

286 VEGETABLE MARROW (BOILED)

1 marrow   ½ pint (300 ml) white sauce
salt   toast

Peel the marrow, cut in half and remove the seeds, then cut in neat pieces, place in a saucepan of boiling water with a little salt, cook gently till tender—from fifteen to thirty-five minutes, drain very well, place on a slice of toast in a hot vegetable dish and pour over the white sauce.

287 VEGETABLE MARROW (STUFFED)

1 marrow   herbs
minced meat   1 small onion
bread crumbs   little brown sauce
chopped parsley   salt and pepper

Peel the marrow, cut in half lengthways, scoop out the seeds. Boil in salted water till half cooked, drain it, make a stuffing with the minced meat, bread crumbs, finely-chopped onion, parsley and herbs, moisten with a little brown sauce, season well, place in the marrow, bind together, place on a greased baking tin, cover with greased paper and bake for half an hour. Sprinkle with brown bread crumbs and serve with brown or tomato sauce.

288 SEA-KALE

sea-kale   ½ pint (300 ml) white sauce
salt   toast

Well wash, trim and tie the sea-kale in bundles, put into boiling salted water and boil from twenty to thirty minutes. When tender drain it, dish on a slice of toast and pour the white sauce over and serve.

289 STEWED CELERY

3 or 4 heads celery   ½ pint (300 ml) white sauce
salt   toast

Well wash and trim the celery, split each head into four lengthways, tie firmly into bundles, cut in equal lengths, place in a stewpan with enough boiling water to cover and a little salt. Boil till tender (about an hour), drain it carefully, dish in a hot vegetable dish on a slice of toast and pour the white sauce over. Celery can also be boiled in a nice brown stock and a sauce to coat it made of 1 oz (25 g) butter, 1 oz (25 g) flour (browned), and ½ pint (300 ml) of the stock the celery was boiled in. Seasoned and served in the same way.

290 SPINACH

spinach   hard-boiled egg
salt   croûtons of fried bread
soda   salt and pepper
butter

Pick the spinach over and remove the stalks and mid ribs of the leaves, wash thoroughly in several waters to remove the grit, put in a saucepan with no water except that which adheres to the leaves, add a little salt and pinch of carbonate of soda, stir occasionally. When tender drain it and pass it through a sieve, return to the pan, add a little butter or cream, season it, dish in a pyramid shape in a hot vegetable dish, garnish with quarters of hard-boiled egg and triangles of fried bread.

291 BOILED CAULIFLOWER

1 cauliflower   soda
salt   ½ pint (300 ml) white sauce

Remove the rough outside leaves, cut across the stalk and soak for an hour in salt and water. Put in boiling water with salt and soda, cook very gently uncovered, skim occasionally. When tender lift out carefully with a slice and drain in a colander. Serve in a hot vegetable dish coated with the white sauce.

292 CAULIFLOWER AU GRATIN

1 cauliflower   ½ pint (300 ml) white sauce
salt and soda   2 oz (50 g) grated cheese
½ oz (15 g) butter   few bread crumbs

Boil the cauliflower, put into a hot dish, mix 1 oz (25 g) of the grated cheese with the white sauce and pour it over the cauliflower. Sprinkle over a few bread crumbs, next the rest of the cheese and then a few little pieces of butter. Brown nicely in a quick oven and serve at once. This dish can be browned under a gas griller or with a salamander.

293 CAULIFLOWER IN BATTER

1 cauliflower   1 tablespoonful oil or butter
salt and soda   1 white of egg
3 oz (75 g) flour   salt and pepper
2 tablespoonfuls tepid water

Boil the cauliflower and divide the flower into neat pieces, dry them and dip in a batter made with the above ingredients, and fry in deep fat, drain on kitchen paper, pile on a hot dish and serve.

294 ASPARAGUS

asparagus   butter
toast   salt and soda

Wash and scrape the white part of the asparagus, tie in bundles with tape, cut the stalks an even length. Put them in a saucepan of boiling water (stand the bundles up if possible) with salt and a pinch of carbonate of soda, boil very gently for about twenty to thirty minutes, taking care not to break the heads. Lift out the bundles, drain, untie them and place on a slice of toast in a hot vegetable dish. Serve the butter melted in a tureen. Hollandaise sauce is sometimes served.

295 STEWED MUSHROOMS

½ lb (225 g) mushrooms   1 gill (150 ml) brown sauce
1 oz (25 g) butter   salt and pepper
chopped parsley

Peel and well wash the mushrooms, then remove the stalks, melt the butter in a stewpan, put in the mushrooms and fry for a few minutes, add the brown sauce (see No. 622) and simmer gently for fifteen to twenty minutes till tender, season with salt and pepper, serve sprinkled with chopped parsley.

296 SAUTÉ TOMATOES

1 lb (450 g) tomatoes	chopped parsley
2 oz (50 g) butter	salt and pepper

Cut the tomatoes in slices and fry in butter, put in a hot dish, season and sprinkle with chopped parsley. Tomatoes cooked in this way are suitable to serve with bacon as a breakfast dish.

297 STUFFED TOMATOES

4 or 6 tomatoes	little butter
2 tablespoonfuls bread crumbs	chopped parsley
1 tablespoonful cheese	salt and pepper

Choose tomatoes of equal size, make a small hole in the top, scoop out the pulp, mix the stuffing, moisten with the pulp and season, refill the tomatoes, sprinkle on a few crumbs and place a small piece of butter on each. Put on a greased baking tin, bake in a moderate oven for about twenty minutes. Serve on croûtons of toast or fried bread and garnish with parsley.

298 TOMATOES À LA BRESLAU

3 tomatoes	little lemon juice
1 oz (25 g) butter	6 croûtons of fried bread
1 teaspoonful chopped parsley	

Cut the tomatoes in halves, bake in a moderate oven on a greased tin, mix the butter with parsley and lemon juice into six small pats. Place each piece of tomato on a hot croûton of fried bread and place a pat of butter on the tomato. Serve on a fancy paper, garnish with parsley.

299 BOILED CHESTNUTS

chestnuts	brown sauce (see No. 622)
salt	

Slit the nuts and blanch to remove the shells. When peeled put into boiling salted water and cook very gently for three-quarters hour. Strain and serve with brown sauce.

300 BOILED CUCUMBER

1 or 2 cucumbers	white sauce (see No. 603)
salt	

(Enough for three or four people)

Peel the cucumbers thinly. Cut in three-inch (7.5 cm) lengths and remove the seeds from the centre. Boil gently in salted water for three-quarters hour, drain well, dish, and coat with white sauce.

301 STUFFED CABBAGE

1 large cabbage	½ gill (75 ml) brown sauce
3 oz (75 g) cold meat	salt and pepper

(Enough for three or four people)

Mince the meat, mix with the brown sauce, season well, wash the cabbage thoroughly, split open, remove the centre, stuff with the mince, tie up with tape, boil in gravy for one hour and serve.

302 BRAISED CUCUMBER

1 or 2 cucumbers	some sausage meat
1 turnip	½ pint (300 ml) stock
1 carrot	little glaze
1 onion	salt and pepper

(Enough for three or four people)

Peel cucumber thinly, cut into pieces two inches (5 cm) long, remove the seeds with a round vegetable cutter, fill the centre with seasoned sausage meat, put into a stewpan with vegetables and stock, simmer gently for one hour, add the glaze, season and strain the gravy over the cucumber.

303 BEAN CROQUETTES

½ pint (300 ml) haricot beans	egg and bread crumbs
½ gill (75 ml) white sauce	salt and pepper

(Enough for three or four people)

Soak the beans for twelve hours and cook till tender, mash them and mix with the white sauce and season well, form into croquettes, using a little flour, coat with egg and bread crumbs and fry in hot fat till a golden brown. Drain and serve on a fancy paper, garnish with fried parsley.

304 STEWED LENTILS

½ pint (300 ml) lentils	1 pint (600 ml) stock or water
1 oz (25 g) butter	1 teaspoonful chopped parsley
1 onion	salt and pepper

(Enough for three or four people)

Soak the lentils twenty-four hours, put them in a saucepan with cold water or stock, chopped onion, salt and pepper, and simmer very gently for three or four hours. Mix in the parsley and serve hot.

305 CURRIED LENTILS

½ pint (300 ml) lentils	½ pint (300 ml) stock
1 oz (25 g) fat	1 oz (25 g) curry powder
1 onion	lemon juice
1 apple	salt

(Enough for four or five people)

Soak and wash the lentils, make the curry sauce in the usual way with fat, curry powder, apple, onion, stock, salt and lemon juice. Put in the lentils, simmer very gently for 2½ to 3 hours. Serve with a border of boiled rice, garnish with lemon and parsley.

306 GRILLED MUSHROOMS

6 mushrooms	salt and pepper
2 oz (50 g) butter	6 rounds of toast

(Enough for four or five people)

Choose good-sized mushrooms, peel and remove stalks, place on a tin, sprinkle over salt and pepper and a grate of nutmeg if liked, put a piece of butter on each mushroom, grill for about ten minutes, place on the rounds of toast and serve very hot.

307 SAVOURY VEGETABLE MARROW

a marrow	salt and pepper
2 oz (50 g) butter	nutmeg
2 oz (50 g) grated cheese	croûtons of fried bread
garlic or shallot	

(Enough for five or six people)

Peel and quarter a marrow, remove the seeds and cut into small neat pieces, rub the frying pan with shallot, melt the butter and fry the marrow in it till tender, add salt and pepper and a little grated nutmeg and lastly stir in the grated cheese. Turn out on a hot dish, garnish with croûtons of fried bread and serve hot.

308 SAVOURY CABBAGE

cabbage	4 oz (100 g) grated cheese
1½ oz (40 g) butter	salt and pepper

(Enough for four people)

Choose a cabbage with a good firm heart, boil in the usual way till tender, drain thoroughly, chop it finely, season well, place in a gratin dish, put the butter on in small pieces, sprinkle over a good layer of grated cheese, bake in a quick oven for ten minutes and serve hot.

309 CELERY À L'ITALIENNE

2 heads of celery	1 egg
2 oz (50 g) butter	bread crumbs
½ pint (300 ml) milk	salt and pepper

(Enough for four people)

Boil the celery when well cleansed for ten minutes, drain and place in a stewpan with some of the butter, salt and pepper. Stew gently until the celery is tender, allow to cool, add the well-beaten egg, pour the celery into a buttered fire-proof dish, cover with bread crumbs, put on the remainder of the butter in small pieces. Bake until a nice brown.

310 LYONNAISE POTATOES

cold boiled potatoes	juice of ½ lemon
2 small onions	1 tablespoonful chopped
3 oz (75 g) butter	parsley
	salt and pepper

(Enough for four people)

Heat the butter in a sauté pan, slice the onions and toss them in the butter, add the cold potatoes cut in slices and cook both till a nice brown colour, then add the parsley, salt, pepper and lemon juice, mix well and serve hot.

311 DUCHESS POTATOES

2 lb (900 g) potatoes	1 tablespoonful cream
3 yolks of eggs	nutmeg
2 oz (50 g) butter	salt and pepper

(Enough for five people)

Prepare potatoes and boil till tender, rub through a sieve while warm, add the butter, yolks of eggs, cream and seasoning. Lay the mixture on a floured board and divide into about ten small pieces, shape into squares, mark with a knife, brush with egg, place on a greased tin and bake in a quick oven about fifteen minutes.

312 POTATO SOUFFLÉ

1½ oz (40 g) butter	4 eggs
1½ oz (40 g) flour	1 teacupful sieved potato
1 gill (150 ml) milk	salt and pepper

(Enough for three or four people)

Melt the butter in a stewpan, add the flour, stir in the milk, boil for a minute or two, add the sieved potato, well-beaten yolks of eggs with salt and pepper. Whisk the whites stiffly and fold in lightly to the mixture, pour into a prepared tin, steam gently for about forty-five minutes.

313 SPINACH SOUFFLÉ

1 breakfastcupful cooked	2 eggs
spinach	salt and pepper
½ gill (75 ml) white sauce	

(Enough for three or four people)

Add spinach and seasoning to white sauce, then the well-beaten yolks of eggs. Whip the whites very stiffly and fold into the mixture lightly. Pour into a prepared soufflé dish and bake for thirty minutes.

314 VEGETABLE PIE

short or flaky crust	2 carrots
2 oz (50 g) butter	2 turnips
2 onions	parsley
1 head celery	salt and pepper
boiled haricot beans	

(Enough for five or six people)

Melt the butter in a stewpan, add the vegetables, cut in small pieces and cook till tender, season and add the chopped parsley. When cool put in a pie dish, cover with a nice light pastry and bake in a quick oven, serve hot with a rich brown sauce.

315 SALAD DRESSING NO. 1

1 teaspoonful salt	3 tablespoonfuls salad oil
¼ teaspoonful pepper	1 tablespoonful vinegar
1 teaspoonful mustard	pinch of sugar

Put the salt, pepper, sugar and mustard in a basin, add the oil (always in the proportion of three parts oil to one part vinegar), stir in the vinegar slowly with a wooden spoon until all the ingredients are thoroughly mixed. Use dressing as directed.

316 SALAD DRESSING NO. 2

1 raw egg	1 gill (150 ml) vinegar
1 dessertspoonful sugar	½ gill (75 ml) cream
1 teaspoonful mixed mustard	salt and pepper

Put the salt, mustard, pepper and sugar in a basin, add the beaten egg, vinegar and cream. Use as directed.

317 MAYONNAISE DRESSING

2 yolks of eggs	1 tablespoonful tarragon
1 gill (150 ml) salad oil	vinegar
½ teaspoonful mustard	1 tablespoonful cream
1 tablespoonful vinegar	salt and cayenne.

Place two yolks in a basin, add salt and mustard, stir in the oil drop by drop to prevent curdling. When all the oil is in stir in the vinegar in the same way, add the cream last of all. This sauce will keep for some time if kept air-tight and in a cool place.

318 FRENCH LETTUCE SALAD

lettuce	tarragon
watercress	1 hard-boiled egg
parsley	beetroot
chervil	salad dressing No. 1

Wash the lettuce and cress thoroughly, break the lettuce leaves into small pieces, drain in a clean dry cloth or in a salad basket. Place in a salad bowl, mix the dressing, add the chopped parsley, tarragon and chervil, pour over the lettuce and cress just before serving, garnish with quarters of hard-boiled egg and slices or dice of beetroot.

319 TOMATO SALAD

tomatoes	shallot
parsley	tarragon
3 tablespoonfuls salad oil	salt and pepper
1 tablespoonful vinegar	1 teaspoonful mustard

Place the tomatoes in boiling water for a minute or so, drain them and remove the skin, cut them in slices and place in a salad bowl, mix the dressing, put the salt and pepper in a basin with the mixed mustard, pour in the oil, stir in the vinegar thoroughly with a wooden spoon, pour over the tomatoes and sprinkle over the finely-chopped shallot, parsley and tarragon.

320 POTATO SALAD

cooked potatoes	chervil
shallot	tarragon
parsley	salad dressing No. 1

The potatoes should not be overcooked, cut them into neat slices, mix the dressing, pour it over the potatoes, sprinkle over some finely-chopped shallot, parsley, chervil and tarragon.

321 BEETROOT SALAD

1 beetroot	watercress
white of egg	dressing No. 1

Scrub the beetroot, do not cut it, boil gently till tender. When cold peel and slice it, place the slices in a salad bowl, pour over the salad dressing, garnish with cress and the white of egg finely chopped or rubbed through a sieve.

322 GREEN PEA SALAD

1 pint (600 ml) peas	2 tomatoes
2 lettuces	mayonnaise dressing (see No. 636)

Boil the peas with a sprig of mint and salt and sugar. When cold mix them with the mayonnaise sauce, wash and well dry the lettuces, tear them into pieces. Arrange in a salad bowl, in a border; pile the peas in the centre, decorate with the tomatoes skinned and cut into quarters.

323 CAULIFLOWER SALAD

1 cauliflower	mayonnaise dressing (see No. 636)
shallot	
little parsley, chervil, and tarragon	1 or 2 tomatoes

Boil the cauliflower in the usual way, divide into pieces, place in a salad bowl. Just before serving pour over the mayonnaise sauce, sprinkle with a little finely-chopped shallot, parsley, chervil and tarragon, garnish if liked with tomato cut in pieces.

324 CELERY AND BEETROOT SALAD

celery	chopped parsley
beetroot	mayonnaise dressing (see
shallot	No. 636)

Carefully prepare about two heads of celery, soak and wash it well, cut the best parts into shreds and put into a salad bowl with some thin slices of boiled beetroot, sprinkle over a little finely-chopped shallot and parsley. Just before serving pour over the mayonnaise sauce, garnish with the tops of the heads of celery. Either of the plainer dressings can be used for this salad.

325 WINTER SALAD

¼ lb (100 g) Brussel sprouts	1 head celery
2 carrots	mustard and cress
1 beetroot	1 shallot
¼ lb (100 g) potatoes	mayonnaise dressing (see No. 636)

Cook all the vegetables carefully. They must not be *over*cooked. Cut into fancy shapes with a vegetable cutter. Chop the trimmings roughly, mix with mayonnaise sauce, pile in the centre of a salad bowl, arrange the fancy shapes of the vegetables round in layers, garnish with mustard and cress and celery tops, pour over a little more mayonnaise sauce.

326 EGG SALAD

6 hard-boiled eggs	coraline pepper
aspic jelly (see No. 647)	green salad
chopped parsley	mayonnaise dressing (see No. 636)

Boil the eggs until quite hard, cut into slices, rinse out on a border mould with cold water, pour in a little liquid aspic, decorate the bottom of the mould alternately with chopped parsley, coraline pepper and yolk of egg passed through a sieve, pour in a little more aspic and allow it to set on ice, fill the mould with layers of hard-boiled egg and aspic. When set turn out on a bed of green salad, fill the centre with chopped egg mixed with mayonnaise, decorate with cress and chopped aspic.

327 CUCUMBER SALAD

cucumber	vinegar
oil	salt and pepper

Peel and slice the cucumber very thinly, place on a dish, sprinkle with salt and let them remain from ten to fifteen minutes, pour off the liquid, mix the dressing, using one part of oil to two parts of vinegar, season with salt and pepper, pour over the cucumber. This salad is served with cold salmon.

328 CHICKEN SALAD

cold boiled fowl	boiled green peas
lettuce	beetroot or tomato
cucumber	hard-boiled egg
watercress	mayonnaise dressing (see No. 636)

Cut the meat from the bones of the fowl, wsh, tear into pieces and thoroughly dry the lettuce, arrange in a salad bowl with slices of cucumber, a few cooked green peas, slices of beetroot or tomato and the chicken cut into neat pieces. Just before serving pour over some good mayonnaise sauce, garnish with quarters of hard-boiled egg and watercress.

329 FISH SALAD

cold white fish	gherkin
lettuce	a few shrimps
hard-boiled egg	aspic jelly
capers	mayonnaise dressing (see No. 636)

Flake the cooked fish, taking great care to remove all bones, mix in a bowl with the picked shrimps, chopped white of egg, a few capers, shreds of gherkin, pour over some mayonnaise sauce. Make a border of lettuce (torn into pieces and well dried) on a dish, place the fish salad in the centre, garnish with watercress, chopped aspic, and yolk of egg passed through a sieve.

330 LOBSTER SALAD

1 lobster	hard-boiled egg
lettuce	chopped parsley
watercress	aspic jelly (see No. 647)
mayonnaise sauce	

Split the lobster lengthways and remove the meat from the shell and claws. Rinse out a border mould with cold water, pour in a little liquid aspic and allow it to set, decorate the bottom of the mould with the meat from the claws, chopped parsley, etc., pour over a little more aspic and allow it to set, then fill the mould with lobster and aspic. turn out when cold on a bed of lettuce, mix the remainder of the lobster and egg with mayonnaise sauce and place in the centre, garnish with chopped aspic and cress.

331 NUT SALAD

some walnuts	chopped chervil and tarragon
2 heads celery	mayonnaise dressing

Well wash and trim the celery, shred finely and put into a salad bowl, shell and skin the walnuts and cut into shreds, mix with the celery, pour over some good mayonnaise sauce, sprinkle with finely-chopped chervil and tarragon.

332 SALAD FOR COLD MEAT

1 head of celery	cream
1 beetroot	vinegar
some capers	salt and cayenne
hard-boiled egg	

Wash and trim the celery, cut into fine shreds, chop the beetroot into small dice, mix together with about a tablespoonful of capers and the chopped white of the egg, whip the cream, flavour carefully with a little vinegar, salt and cayenne, mix with the other ingredients just before serving and sprinkle over finely-grated yolk of egg.

333 ORANGE SALAD

2 or 3 oranges	1 tablespoonful vinegar
1 teaspoonful castor sugar	little tarragon vinegar
1 tablespoonful salad oil	salt and pepper

Skin and remove all the white pith from the oranges, cut into slices and arrange in a bowl, sprinkle with salt, sugar and pepper and let it stand for an hour, mix the oil and the vinegars, pour over the oranges, garnish with cress.

334 SAHARA SALAD

cold potatoes	chopped parsley
cold cooked salsify	chopped chervil
2 bananas	salad dressing No. 1
1 or 2 truffles	

Cut the cold new potatoes into dice and the salsify into shreds, slice the bananas and truffles, mix all together in a salad bowl, pour over the dressing, sprinkle over the chopped chervil and parsley and serve.

335 RUSSIAN SALAD

aspic jelly (see No. 647)	filleted anchovies
cold boiled vegetables	chervil and tarragon
truffles	little shallot
capers	lettuce and cucumber
gherkins	mayonnaise sauce (see No. 636)
stoned olives	
shrimps	

Fill a border mould with aspic jelly, decorating it with fancy shapes of boiled carrot, green peas and the red part of some radishes. Cut all the cold boiled vegetables into dice or fancy shapes, add the capers, shreds of gherkins, sliced truffles, stoned olives, picked shrimps, filleted anchovies, a tablespoonful of chopped chervil, tarragon and shallot, mix all well together and stir in some mayonnaise sauce. Arrange some lettuce, washed, dried and shredded, on a flat dish, turn out the border of aspic jelly on to it, garnish round the mould with slices of cucumber or beetroot and place the mayonnaise mixture in the centre. Much trouble can be saved by using a bottle of vegetable macédoine, which should be drained well and used as above.

336 HAM AND EGG SALAD

6 hard-boiled eggs	cucumber
4 oz (100 g) cooked ham	seasoning
lettuce	salad dressing No. 2

(Enough for three or four people)

Cut the hard-boiled eggs into slices, chop the ham, slice and chop the cucumber, mix together and add some shredded lettuce, pour over a thick salad dressing, garnish and serve. A very little chopped shallot could also be added if liked.

SAVOURY DISHES

337 MACARONI CHEESE

2 oz (50 g) macaroni	2 oz (50 g) cheese
1½ oz (40 g) butter	few bread crumbs
1 oz (25 g) flour	salt and cayenne
½ pint (300 ml) milk	

(Enough for three or four people)

Cook the macaroni in fast-boiling water with some salt for twenty to thirty minutes. Drain it and cut in inch (2.5 cm) lengths, make a sauce, using the ounce (25 g) of butter, flour and the milk, add 1½ ounces (40 g) of grated cheese, season well, add the macaroni and place in a greased dish, sprinkle over a few bread crumbs, the remainder of the cheese, and put some small pieces of butter on top. Brown nicely in the oven.

338 RICE AND CHEESE

4 oz (100 g) rice	2 oz (50 g) grated cheese
milk	salt and cayenne

(Enough for three or four people)

Boil the rice in milk or milk and water till well cooked, add the grated cheese, keeping back a little, season well with salt and cayenne, put it into a greased pie dish, sprinkle over the remainder of the cheese and brown in the oven. This is a good way of using up dry pieces of cheese.

339 CHEESE STRAWS

2 oz (50 g) flour	½ teaspoonful mustard
2 oz (50 g) grated cheese	yolk of an egg
2 oz (50 g) butter	salt and cayenne.

(Enough for three or four people)

Sift the flour into a basin, add the mustard, salt, cayenne and grated cheese, rub in the butter, mix to a paste with yolk of egg and a little water if necessary, knead slightly, roll out on a pastry board till about an eighth of an inch (0.3 cm) thick, cut into narrow strips about three inches (7.5 cm) long, place on a greased baking tin and bake in a quick oven.

340 CHEESE PUDDING

4 oz (100 g) bread crumbs	1 pint (600 ml) milk
3 oz (75 g) grated cheese	2 eggs
1 oz (25 g) butter	salt and pepper

(Enough for three or four people)

Pour the boiling milk on the bread crumbs, add the grated cheese, butter, salt and pepper, mix well, beat the two eggs well and add them, pour the mixture into a buttered pie dish and bake in a moderate oven about half an hour.

341 CHEESE BALLS

3 oz (75 g) cheese	¼ pint (150 ml) tepid water
2 oz (50 g) flour	1 teaspoonful mustard
½ oz (15 g) butter	salt and cayenne
1 egg	

(Enough for five or six people)

Mix the flour and mustard, salt and cayenne, separate the yolk from the white of the egg, mix it to the flour with the butter (melted), add the grated cheese a little at a time and the whipped white of egg, mix all to a smooth batter, drop a teaspoonful of the mixture into hot fat and fry. Half of this quantity makes a good dish.

342 CHEESE AIGRETTES

½ pint (300 ml) water	2 oz (50 g) Parmesan cheese
3 oz (75 g) Vienna flour	2 whole eggs
1 oz (25 g) butter	salt and cayenne

(Enough for six or seven people)

Boil the water and butter together, sift the flour and put it in all at once, cook till it balls in the saucepan, allow it to cool, add the eggs one at a time, beating well. One extra yolk may be used if necessary. Then add the grated cheese, season well, drop small rough heaps into hot fat, fry a good golden brown, drain, serve very hot, sprinkled with grated Parmesan.

343 CHEESE SOUFFLÉ

3 oz (75 g) flour	yolks of 3 eggs
3 oz (75 g) butter	whites of 4 eggs
6 oz (175 g) cheese (Parmesan)	brown bread crumbs
¼ pint (150 ml) milk	salt and cayenne

(Enough for four or five people)

Cook the flour in the butter, add the milk, stir till it boils and thickens. When it cools add the yolks and beat well, then the grated cheese, salt and cayenne and lastly the stiffly-beaten whites of eggs, pour into a well-buttered pie dish, sprinkle over some brown crumbs. Bake in a quick oven and serve immediately.

344 CHEESE PYRAMIDS

2 oz (50 g) flour	1 yolk of egg
1 oz (25 g) butter	cream
1 oz (25 g) grated cheese	salt and cayenne
some Cheddar cheese	

(Enough to make ten or twelve pyramids)

Add the grated cheese to the flour with salt and cayenne, rub in the butter, mix to a dough with yolk of egg, knead slightly, roll out and cut into rounds with a pastry cutter (about 1½ inches (4 cm) in diameter), bake in a hot oven on a greased tin. On each biscuit when cold place three small squares of Cheddar cheese, whip and season the cream, put it in a forcing bag and pipe it between the squares of cheese. Serve on a fancy paper.

345 CHEESE OMELET

4 eggs	2 tablespoonfuls cheese
2 oz (50 g) butter	salt and pepper
1 tablespoonful cream or milk	

Beat the eggs in a basin, add the milk or cream, grated cheese (Parmesan or Gruyère) and seasoning, melt the butter in an omelet pan. When quite hot pour in the mixture, stir until it begins to thicken, cook until a golden brown, put the pan in the oven for a minute or so to brown, fold over, turn on to a hot dish, sprinkle with grated cheese and serve immediately.

346 WELSH RAREBIT

3 oz (75 g) cheese	2 tablespoonfuls milk
1 oz (25 g) butter	salt and pepper
½ teaspoonful mustard	buttered toast

Put the butter, milk, grated cheese, mustard, salt and pepper into a saucepan, stir over the fire until quite smooth. Pour over rounds of buttered toast and serve hot.

347 SAVOURY SEMOLINA

2 oz (50 g) semolina	little mustard
½ pint (300 ml) milk	salt and cayenne
2 oz (50 g) grated cheese	egg and breadcrumbs

(Enough for four or five people)

Cook the semolina in the milk till transparent, add the mustard, grated cheese, salt and cayenne, mix well together, allow it to cool, form into small squares, coat with egg and bread crumbs, fry a golden brown in hot fat, arrange neatly on a hot dish with fancy paper, sprinkle over some grated cheese and serve hot. Half this quantity is sufficient for a small dish.

348 MACARONI À LA MILANAISE

6 oz (175 g) macaroni	3 oz (75 g) cheese (Gruyère
½ oz (15 g) butter	or Parmesan)
1 shallot	tomato sauce (see No. 621)
2 tablespoonfuls cream	salt and pepper

(Enough for four or five people)

Boil the macaroni in water with the butter, salt and shallot. When quite tender drain and cut into pieces, put the cheese, seasoning and cream into a clean stewpan and stir over a slow fire from three to five minutes, add the cooked macaroni and reheat. Arrange in the shape of a dome on a hot dish and pour a thick tomato sauce over and serve the dish at once.

349 SAVOURY MACARONI

¼ lb (100 g) small macaroni	½ pint (300 ml) tomato sauce
¼ lb (100 g) cooked ham	(see No. 628)
or tongue	brown bread crumbs
1 oz (25 g) butter	salt and pepper

(Enough for three or four people)

Boil the macaroni till tender in water with salt, drain and cut into inch (2.5 cm) lengths, melt the butter in a stewpan, add the ham or tongue cut into shreds, pour in the tomato sauce and put in the macaroni, season well, put the mixture in a buttered fireproof dish, sprinkle over a few brown bread crumbs, bake for ten minutes in a hot oven and serve hot.

350 MACARONI CUTLETS

2 oz (50 g) macaroni	1 oz (25 g) flour
1 oz (25 g) cooked ham	¼ pint (150 ml) milk
2 oz (50 g) grated cheese	salt and cayenne
1 oz (25 g) butter	egg and bread crumbs

(Enough to make six small cutlets)

Cook the macaroni in salted water till tender, drain and cut in short pieces, mix with the chopped ham, make a panada with the butter, flour and milk, add the macaroni and ham and grated cheese, season well with salt and cayenne, put on a wet plate, divide into equal portions, set aside to cool. Form into cutlet shapes, coat well with egg and crumbs, fry a golden brown in hot fat. Stick a piece of parsley stalk in the end of each cutlet and dish them in a circle on dish with a fancy paper and garnish with fried parsley.

351 ANCHOVY EGGS

2 eggs	anchovy essence or paste
butter	cayenne
chopped parsley	croûtons of bread

(Enough for four people)

Boil the eggs hard, put into cold water for a few minutes, remove the shells and cut the eggs in half, pound the yolks with a little butter, anchovy essence, cayenne, cut some bread into neat rounds, either fry them a golden brown or toast and butter them, cut a little off the cups of white of egg, stand on the croûtons, put in the mixture with a forcing bag and fancy tube, sprinkle over chopped parsley, serve on a dish with cress.

352 SCALLOPED EGGS

3 or 4 hard-boiled eggs	bread crumbs
½ pint (300 ml) white sauce	grated cheese
½ oz (15 g) butter	salt and pepper

(Enough for three or four people)

Cut the hard-boiled eggs in dice, add to the white sauce, season well with salt and pepper, well butter some scallop shells, place some of the mixture in each, sprinkle over some fresh bread crumbs, then a little grated cheese and lastly some small pieces of butter. Brown in the oven and serve hot.

353 ŒUFS AU FROMAGE

4 hard-boiled eggs	mashed potato
½ pint (300 ml) white sauce	salt and cayenne
3 oz (75 g) grated cheese	

(Enough for three or four people)

Cut the hard-boiled eggs into quarters lengthways, place them round a fireproof dish, leaving a space in the centre, grate the cheese (Parmesan or Gruyère should be used if possible), add half to the white sauce and place the rest in the centre of the dish. Coat the eggs with the white sauce nicely seasoned with cayenne. Put the potato in a forcing bag with a rose tube and decorate the dish with it, brown in a hot oven or under griller and serve at once.

354 EGG CROQUETTES

3 hard-boiled eggs	1 gill (150 ml) milk
1 oz (25 g) butter	salt and pepper
1 oz (25 g) flour	egg and bread crumbs

(Enough to make eight croquettes)

Chop the hard-boiled eggs, make a panada with the butter, flour and milk, add the eggs, season with salt and pepper, mix well, place on a wet plate, divide into equal portions, set aside to cool, form into cork shapes, coat with egg and bread crumbs, fry a golden brown in hot fat. Serve on a hot dish on a fancy paper, garnish with fried parsley.

355 POACHED EGGS

2 or 3 eggs	buttered toast
salt	

Break the eggs one at a time in a cup, pour gently into a shallow saucepan or frying pan of boiling water with a little salt, cook very gently. When just set take out the eggs, place them on a round of buttered toast, trimming them so that they are the same size as the toast, serve immediately.

356 SCRAMBLED EGGS

3 eggs	little milk or cream
1 oz (25 g) butter	salt and pepper
little chopped parsley	buttered toast

(Enough for two people)

Put the butter into a saucepan, well beat the eggs, season with salt and pepper, add the chopped parsley and cream or milk. When the butter has melted pour in the eggs, stir over the fire until the mixture begins to thicken. Put it on to the hot buttered toast and serve at once.

357 SCOTCH EGGS

2 eggs	salt and pepper
½ lb (225 g) sausage meat	egg and bread crumbs
1 or 2 tomatoes	croûtons of bread

(Enough for four people)

Hard boil the eggs, put them in cold water for a few minutes, remove the shells, dry them well with flour, coat with sausage meat, then with egg and crumbs, rolling them into a nice shape, fry well in hot fat, allowing time for the sausage meat to be well cooked, cut off a little of each end of the egg, then cut in half, stand each half on a croûton of fried bread on which is placed a round of tomato, serve on a fancy paper, garnish with parsley.

358 CURRIED EGGS

3 or 4 hard-boiled eggs	½ pint (300 ml) milk
1 small onion	lemon juice
1 small apple	salt
½ oz (15 g) curry powder	croûtons of fried bread
½ oz (15 g) flour	

(Enough for three or four people)

Fry the finely-chopped apple and onion in the butter, add the curry powder and flour, cook for ten minutes, add the milk and simmer for another ten minutes, season with lemon juice and salt and a pinch of castor sugar. Cut the eggs in halves, put each half on a croûton, round side up, coat carefully with the curry sauce, garnish with white of egg cut in fancy shapes.

359 SWISS EGGS

4 eggs	½ oz (15 g) butter
1 gill (150 ml) cream	1 teaspoonful parsley
2 oz (50 g) grated cheese	salt and pepper
few bread crumbs	

(Enough for two or three people)

Break the eggs one by one, slide gently into a well-buttered fireproof dish, whip the cream slightly, well season it with salt and pepper, pour over the eggs, sprinkle over the chopped parsley and grated cheese a few bread crumbs and lastly small pieces of butter. Cook in a slow oven till the eggs are set but not hard and serve hot.

360 EGGS BAKED IN TOMATOES

3 or 4 eggs	chopped parsley
3 or 4 tomatoes	salt and pepper
butter	buttered toast

(Enough for three or four people)

Choose rather large tomatoes of equal size, cut a piece off the top of the tomatoes, scoop out the pulp carefully, sprinkle on a little salt and pepper, break an egg into a cup and pour it into the hollow of the tomato, place on a greased baking tin and cook slowly until the egg is set, basting with a little butter. Serve on rounds of buttered toast with a little parsley sprinkled over the top of each.

361 LOBSTER AU GRATIN

½ tin lobster	1 shallot
1 oz (25 g) butter	1 egg
1 oz (25 g) flour	anchovy sauce
½ pint (300 ml) milk	salt and cayenne

(Enough for four people)

Cut the lobster into small pieces, melt the butter in a saucepan and lightly brown the chopped shallot, add the flour and cook, then the milk and simmer for five minutes, put in lobster, parsley, anchovy essence, salt and cayenne, stir till it boils, allow it to cool and add the well-beaten egg. Butter some scallop shells, put in the mixture, sprinkle over some bread crumbs, pour on a little melted butter, put in oven for twenty minutes, serve hot.

362 DEVILLED KIDNEYS

4 kidneys	chutney
devil paste (see No. 646)	buttered toast

(Enough for four people)

Skin the kidneys, cut them open, spread with the devil paste and grill them over a clear fire, put them on rounds of buttered toast spread with chutney, serve very hot.

363 FRIED COD'S ROE

1 lb (450 g) cod's roe	salt and pepper
flour	egg and bread crumbs

Wash the roe in salt and water, cook gently for thirty minutes, drain, cut into slices, dip in seasoned flour, coat with egg and bread crumbs, fry a golden brown, drain on kitchen paper. Dish on a hot dish on a fancy paper, garnish with fried parsley. If for a luncheon dish serve a piquante sauce with it.

364 RISSOLES À LA POMPADOUR

4 tablespoonfuls minced chicken, rabbit or veal	¼ pint (150 ml) stock
	3 mushrooms
4 tablespoonfuls ham or tongue	¼ lb (100 g) short crust
	salt and pepper
½ oz (15 g) flour	egg and bread crumbs
½ oz (15 g) butter	

(Enough to make eight rissoles)

Make a panada with the butter, flour and stock, cook well, add the minced chicken, mushrooms, ham and seasoning,

allow it to cool, make the pastry, roll out very thin and cut into rounds, put a little of the mixture on one round and cover with another, pinch the edges together, coat with egg and bread crumbs and fry a golden brown in hot fat, dish in a circle with fried parsley in the centre.

365 PRINCESS CUTLETS

some cold game, chicken, or pigeon	1 yolk of egg
¼ pint (150 ml) milk	1 tablespoonful ham or tongue
blade of mace	1 truffle
1 small shallot	2 mushrooms
1 oz (25 g) butter	salt and cayenne
1 oz (25 g) flour	egg and bread crumbs

(Enough to make eight or ten cutlets)

Boil milk with shallot and mace, strain, make a panada with the butter, flour and flavoured milk, boil and then add raw yolk of egg and recook but do not boil, mix in the chopped chicken or game with the ham, seasoning, minced mushrooms and sliced truffles, put mixture on a plate to cool, form into tiny cutlets, using a little flour; coat with egg and crumbs, fry in hot fat, dish in a circle, serve a rich brown sauce.

366 CHICKEN KROMESKIES

4 oz (100 g) cooked chicken	1 gill (150 ml) white sauce
2 oz (50 g) cooked ham	1 yolk of egg
1 or 2 mushrooms	salt and pepper
6 rashers of bacon	frying batter (see No. 649)

(Enough to make twelve kromeskies)

Remove all skin, gristle and bone from the chicken, chop the meat finely, add to it the ham and mushrooms chopped. Heat the white sauce, stir in the chicken and ham, etc., season well, add the yolk of egg, allow it to get thoroughly hot, put the mixture on a plate and set aside to cool, form up into small rolls. Wrap each in a very thin rasher of bacon, dip in frying batter and fry a golden brown, drain well, serve on a hot dish with fancy paper.

367 SAVOURY OMELET

3 eggs	pinch of herbs
1 teaspoonful parsley	garlic or shallot
¾ oz (20 g) butter	salt and pepper

Well whisk the eggs, add the chopped parsley, herbs, salt and pepper, rub the omelet pan with a head of garlic or a piece of shallot, melt the butter in the pan. When hot pour in the eggs, stir till the mixture begins to set. When cooked sufficiently (it should be of a creamy consistency inside) fold over into an oval shape and serve immediately.

368 HAM OMELET

3 eggs	1 oz (25 g) butter
1½ oz (40 g) cooked ham	salt and pepper

Beat the eggs well, add the finely-chopped ham and the seasoning, melt the butter in an omelet pan. When hot pour in the eggs, stir till the mixture begins to set, fold over and serve on a hot dish immediately.

369 KIDNEY OMELET

4 eggs	1 shallot
1½ oz (40 g) butter	1 teaspoonful parsley
1 kidney	salt and pepper

Skin the kidney and chop finely, put half an ounce (15 g) of butter into a small saucepan, add the finely-chopped shallot and fry for a few minutes, then add the kidney and cook for three or four minutes, season well with salt and pepper. Beat the eggs, melt the remainder of the butter in an omelet pan, pour in the eggs and stir till the mixture begins to set. When cooked sufficiently put the kidney in the centre and fold over in the usual way, serve on a hot dish with a little gravy poured round if liked.

370 KIDNEY TOAST

3 kidneys	1 tablespoonful Worcester
1 teaspoonful chopped parsley	sauce
¼ oz (10 g) flour	salt and pepper
	buttered toast

(Enough for three people)

Mince the kidney finely, cook the chopped shallot in the butter for five minutes, add the flour and Worcester sauce, boil for two minutes, put in the minced kidney, season with salt and pepper. Put on the buttered toast, sprinkle with bread crumbs, bake in a quick oven for seven or eight minutes and serve hot.

371 BOMBAY TOAST

1 oz (25 g) butter	few chopped capers
2 eggs	salt and cayenne
1 teaspoonful anchovy essence	buttered toast

(Enough for two or three people)

Put the butter in a double saucepan. When melted stir in the eggs and other ingredients, stir till the mixture begins to set, then spread on rounds of buttered toast and serve very hot.

372 CHUTNEY TOAST

1 oz (25 g) Bengal chutney	1 oz (25 g) grated cheese
2 oz (50 g) ham	salt and cayenne
2 tablespoonfuls cream	croûtons of fried bread or toast

(Enough for three or four people)

Mince the ham finely, mix it with the cream, season well, spread it on the rounds of toast or fried bread, put a layer of chutney over and spread thickly with grated cheese. Brown in a quick oven and serve hot.

373 HAM TOAST

3 eggs	pinch of sweet herbs
3 oz (75 g) ham	salt and cayenne
1½ oz (40 g) butter	buttered toast
½ teaspoonful parsley	

(Enough for two or three people)

Melt the butter in a saucepan, well beat the eggs, add the finely-chopped ham, parsley, herbs and seasoning, pour into the butter and cook until it thickens, cut the buttered toast into rounds, put some of the mixture on each and serve at once.

374 SARDINES ON TOAST

6 or 8 sardines   buttered toast
salt and cayenne
(Enough for six or eight people)

Cut the buttered toast in long pieces, same length as the sardines, remove the centre bone and skin from the sardines, place one on each piece of toast, season with little salt and cayenne and serve very hot.

375 SARDINE PYRAMIDS

6 sardines   salt and cayenne
1 oz (25 g) butter   lemon juice
chopped parsley   buttered toast
(Enough for six or seven people)

Take the skin and bones from the sardines, pound them in a mortar with the butter, season well with salt, cayenne and a squeeze of lemon juice, cut the toast into fingers, put the mixture on pyramid shape, sprinkle over a little chopped parsley and coraline pepper, serve with watercress as a garnish.

376 SARDINES À LA ROYAL

6 or 8 sardines   gherkin
lettuce   beetroot
salad oil   hard-boiled egg
vinegar (tarragon)
(Enough for six or eight people)

Skin the fish and remove the bones, close up again, wash, dry and shred the lettuce, season with oil and a few drops of tarragon vinegar, place on a dish and arrange sardines on the lettuce, decorate the sardines with strips of gherkin and white of egg, crossways, finely-chopped beetroot down the sides. Serve as hors d'œuvre or savoury.

377 CURRIED POTATOES

3 or 4 boiled potatoes   little stock
1 teaspoonful curry powder   dripping
lemon juice   salt and pepper
1 onion

Fry the onion and slices of potato in a little dripping, shake over the curry powder, add the stock, a little lemon juice and salt and stew gently for fifteen minutes.

378 RIZ AU CHOU

1 spring cabbage   little cream
2 oz (50 g) rice   chopped parsley
1 oz (25 g) butter   anchovy paste
1 small shallot   coraline pepper
2 tablespoonfuls of cheese   salt and pepper

Cook the cabbage and rice separately, dry the rice when cooked, drain and mince the cabbage, melt butter in a stewpan, lightly fry the chopped shallot, add the cabbage and rice, allow it to get quite hot, then add the grated cheese and cream, season well, pile in a dish, decorate with small croûtons of fried bread or toast spread with anchovy paste and sprinkled with parsley and coraline pepper.

379 RISOTTO À L'ITALIENNE

2 oz (50 g) butter   ½ pint (150 ml) tomato sauce
½ lb (225 g) rice   2 oz (50 g) Parmesan cheese
1 shallot   little nutmeg
1 pint (600 ml) stock   salt and pepper

Chop the shallot finely and cook in the butter, wash, drain and dry the rice and fry lightly, add the stock by degrees as the rice swells, stir in the tomato sauce (see No. 628), season well, add a grate of nutmeg. When rice is tender add the grated cheese, serve very hot.

380 CROÛTES À L'ITALIENNE

1 beetroot   4 or 6 anchovy fillets
1 hard-boiled egg   croûtons of fried bread
4 or 6 olives
(Enough for four or six people)

Place a thin slice of beetroot on a small fried croûton of bread, then a thin slice of hard-boiled egg, white and yolk, turn the olive—that is, remove the stone without altering the shape, place it in the centre of the egg with an anchovy fillet curled round it.

381 TOMATOES WITH CHEESE CREAM

3 or 4 tomatoes   2 tablespoonfuls aspic
1 gill (150 ml) cream   salt and pepper
1½ oz (40 g) grated cheese   cress
(Parmesan and Gruyère)   cheese buscuits

Cut the tomatoes in half, remove seeds and drain them, whip the cream stiffly, season with salt and pepper, whisk in the aspic jelly liquid but cool, add the grated cheese, put the mixture into a forcing bag with a small rose pipe, place each piece of tomato on a cheese biscuit (made of cheese pastry; see No. 402), fill the cheese cream and pipe a pretty border, garnish with small cress and stick a tiny sprig into the middle of the cream.

382 TIMBALES OF HADDOCK À LA GENOISE

¼ lb (100 g) dried haddock   lemon juice
(cooked)   yolk of hard-boiled egg
½ gill (75 ml) white sauce   coraline pepper
½ gill (75 ml) whipped cream   chopped parsley
aspic jelly (see No. 647)   salt and pepper
salad
(Enough to fill six dariole moulds)

Remove skin and bones from haddock and flake finely, mix with the white sauce and cream, add a little liquid aspic. Decorate some dariole moulds with chopped parsley, coraline pepper and flaked yolk of egg (two moulds of each), set with aspic. When firm put in some of the fish mixture, about three-quarters full, put a spoonful of liquid aspic to quite fill the mould, turn out when set, serve on a bed of salad garnished with chopped aspic.

383 CROÛTES DE COBURG

smoked haddock   2 or 3 pickled walnuts
white sauce   croûtons of fried bread
2 tomatoes
(Enough for five or six people)

Remove skin and bone from some cooked smoked haddock, mix with a little white sauce, spread on small

croûtons of fried bread, place on a slice of tomato, then a round of pickled walnut, serve on a fancy paper as hors d'œuvre or savoury.

384 ANCHOVY FRITTERS

6 rounds of bread	few drops lemon juice
1 teaspoonful anchovy essence	cayenne
1 teaspoonful anchovy paste	

(Enough for three or four people)

Cut the bread into small rounds, mix the anchovy essence with an equal quantity of water, sprinkle on bread, dip in flour, fry in hot fat, spread with anchovy paste, decorate and serve hot.

385 FOIE-GRAS IN PASTRY

puff pastry (see No. 516)	egg
foie-gras	

Roll out the pastry into small thin rounds, put a piece of foie-gras in the centre, fold over, brush with egg and bake in a very hot oven for fifteen minutes; serve hot.

386 DEVILLED SHRIMPS

1 gill (150 ml) picked shrimps	1 tablespoonful chopped
1 tablespoonful chutney	gherkins
1 oz (25 g) butter	1 tablespoonful Worcester
6 rounds of toast	sauce
	salt and cayenne

(Enough for three people)

Mix chutney, gherkins, salt, cayenne and Worcester sauce together, add the shrimps, warm thoroughly in the butter, place on rounds of buttered toast and serve hot.

387 EGGS AND TOMATOES

3 eggs	2 oz (50 g) butter
3 tomatoes	salt and pepper

(Enough for two or three people)

Butter a gratin dish, cut the tomatoes in slices, lay in the dish, sprinkle with salt and pepper, break in the eggs carefully, sprinkle again with seasoning and bake in a moderate oven about eight minutes.

388 WATER LILY SAVOURY

6 cheese biscuits (see No. 339)	sieved yolk of egg
1 gill (150 ml) cream	salt and pepper
1 oz (25 g) grate cheese	watercress

(Enough for three or four people)

Whip the cream, add the grated cheese, salt and pepper, place in a forcing bag and pipe a rose of the mixture on each biscuit, put a little portion of sieved yolk of egg in the centre and arrange tiny leaves of watercress round the edge to give the appearance of a flower, serve on a lace paper.

389 CANAPES FUMÉS

1 small finnan haddock	1 oz (25 g) butter
1 tablespoonful white sauce	6 croûtons of bread
1 egg	salt and pepper

(Enough for four people)

Cook the haddock in water till done, fry the croûtons a golden brown, melt the butter in a saucepan, add the sauce, beaten egg, haddock finely flaked and seasoning, cook till the egg thickens—this will be in about seven minutes—pile the mixture on the croûtons, garnish with coraline pepper and serve very hot.

390 CHEESE CUSTARD

2 eggs	mustard
½ pint (300 ml) milk	salt and pepper
2 oz (50 g) grated cheese	

(Enough for two or three people)

Beat the eggs well, add cheese, mustard to taste, salt and pepper, bake in a buttered pie dish very gently for half an hour till set, serve hot.

391 FARCED OLIVES

6 olives	6 rounds of toast
6 anchovies	1 teaspoonful anchovy essence
1 oz (25 g) butter	

(Enough for five or six people)

Stone the olives, mix the essence with the butter and fill the olives, stand them on the rounds of toast, bone the anchovies and twine them round the olives, serve cold.

392 CHEESE FRITTERS

1 oz (25 g) butter	1½ gills (225 ml) milk
1 oz (25 g) flour	salt and cayenne
2 oz (50 g) Parmesan cheese	egg and bread crumbs

(Enough for three or four people)

Melt butter in a saucepan, add flour, cook together, add milk and stir till it boils, mix in grated cheese, salt and cayenne, put on a plate to cool, form into flat cakes, coat with egg and bread crumbs and fry a golden brown in hot fat, serve on a fancy paper sprinkled with grated cheese.

393 ANCHOVY STRAWS

2 oz (50 g) flour	pepper
1 oz (25 g) butter	cayenne
1 yolk of egg	carmine colouring

(Enough for three or four people)

Rub the butter into the flour, mix with yolk of egg and about two teaspoonfuls of anchovy essence to a stiff paste, colour with a little carmine if required, roll out thinly, cut into thin strips about three inches (7.5 cm) long, bake in a moderate oven from five to seven minutes; this mixture can be cut into rounds and called anchovy biscuits.

394 EGGS AND LUXETTE

2 or 3 hard-boiled eggs	1½ oz (40 g) butter
1 tablespoonful luxette	seasoning

(Enough for four people)

Divide the hard-boiled eggs in half, remove the yolks and mix smoothly with butter and luxette, rub through a sieve, then pipe into the egg, stand each cup on a slice of cooked beetroot or tomato, garnish with cress and serve.

395 SARDINE CIGARETTES

3 or 4 sardines	egg
short pastry	bread crumbs

(Enough for two or three people)

Remove skin and bones from sardines, roll out pastry *very thinly*, cut into small squares, lay a sardine on each fold up, dip in egg and bread crumbs, fry about eight minutes in hot fat, dish on a fancy paper and serve hot.

396 CHEESE CREAMS

2 oz (50 g) grated cheese	4 leaves gelatine
½ gill (75 ml) milk	mustard
1 gill (150 ml) cream	salt and pepper

(Enough for three four people)

Dissolve cheese and gelatine in the milk, whip cream very stiffly, add to the dissolved cheese, etc., with the seasoning, pour into prepared dariole moulds, when set turn out and garnish with coraline pepper and chopped parsley or pistachio nuts.

397 EGGS AU GRATIN

4 eggs	brown crumbs
2 oz (50 g) butter	salt and pepper
1 tablespoonful parsley	

(Enough for two or three people)

Sprinkle the bottom of a gratin dish with brown crumbs, salt, pepper, some parsley and a little butter, drop in the eggs whole, sprinkle the top with the remainder of the crumbs, parsley and butter, bake in a moderate oven about five minutes and serve hot.

398 ROSETTES OF ANCHOVY

6 anchovies	cayenne
2 oz (50 g) butter	6 rounds of toast
anchovy paste	salt

(Enough for five or six people)

Fillet the anchovies, spread the rounds of toast with anchovy paste, cream the butter with salt and pepper, colour half green and leave half plain, curl two anchovy fillets on each round of toast, force a rose of plain butter in the centre of the anchovies and pipe small roses of green round the edge of the toast, serve on a fancy paper.

399 SPINACH AND CHEESE

1 breakfastcupful cooked spinach	2 oz (50 g) grated cheese
	salt and pepper
½ gill (75 ml) cream	

(Enough for two or three people)

Mix half the grated cheese with the spinach, cream and seasoning, put in a buttered soufflé dish, sprinkle over the remainder of the cheese and bake for twenty minutes.

400 SPROUTS AND CHEESE

1 lb (450 g) sprouts	¾ pint (450 ml) milk
1 oz (25 g) butter	2 oz (50 g) grated cheese
1 oz (25 g) flour	salt and cayenne

(Enough for three or four people)

Boil the sprouts in water with salt and soda, drain well, melt butter, add flour, cook together, add milk, stir till it boils, season and add grated cheese, dish the sprouts in a hot dish, pour over the sauce, sprinkle a little cheese on the top and serve hot.

401 SARDINE CANAPES

4 or 5 sardines	salt and pepper
1 oz (25 g) grated cheese	6 rounds of toast
1 oz (25 g) butter	

(Enough for five or six people)

Rub the sardines through a sieve, mix with the butter, grated cheese, salt and pepper, pile some of the mixture on the rounds of toast, sprinkle with grated cheese, put under the grill to heat and brown the cheese and serve hot.

402 CHEESE BISCUITS

2 oz (50 g) flour	1 yolk of egg
¾ oz (20 g) butter	salt and cayenne
1½ oz (40 g) grated cheese	

(Enough for three or four people)

Rub butter into flour, add cheese and seasoning, mix with the yolk of egg, roll out thinly, cut in small rounds and bake till pale brown, about eight to ten minutes.

403 SPANISH RICE

4 oz (100 g) rice	2 tablespoonfuls grated cheese
2 large tomatoes	salt and pepper
1 oz (25 g) butter	

(Enough for three or four people)

Boil the rice as for curry, drain it well, heat the butter and fry until lightly browned, bake the tomatoes in slices, stir them into the rice, add the grated cheese, salt and pepper, pile neatly on a dish and serve very hot.

404 EGGS À LA NORFOLK

3 or 4 eggs	egg and bread crumbs
little flour	piquante sauce (see No. 624)

(Enough for four people)

Hard boil three or four fresh eggs, cut them into half lengthways, dip them lightly in flour, coat with egg and bread crumbs, fry a golden brown in hot fat, drain and serve with piquante sauce.

405 ŒUFS À LA NORWEGIENNE

4 hard-boiled eggs	1 tablespoonful salad oil
small pot caviare	1 tablespoonful tarragon
3 tomatoes	vinegar
½ chopped shallot	salt and cayenne
½ lemon	mustard and cress

(Enough for four or five people)

Hard boil the eggs, remove the shells and place in cold water, cut the eggs in half, scoop out the centre of the yolk carefully, skin the tomatoes and slice them, pour the oil and vinegar over them, mix the caviare with the lemon juice, shallot and seasoning with a plated knife or spoon, fill the centre of the eggs with the mixture, dish on the slices of tomato and garnish with mustard and cress.

406 MEAT AND EGG TOAST

2 eggs   1 oz (25 g) butter
2 tablespoonfuls minced meat   salt and pepper
or ham   4 rounds of toast
(*Enough for four people*)

Put the butter, eggs, meat and seasoning into a saucepan and stir till the eggs become thick, pile on the rounds of toast, decorate and serve hot.

407 CHEESE ECLAIRS

choux pastry (see No. 519)   whipped cream
grated cheese   salt and pepper

Make the choux pastry, put into a forcing bag and force into small eclairs one and a half inches (4 cm) long, bake in a hot oven; when cold fill the centre with a well-seasoned mixture of grated cheese and whipped cream.

408 HERRING ROES ON TOAST

2 bloaters (soft roes)   1 tablespoonful white sauce
2 yolks of eggs   salt and cayenne
1 oz (25 g) butter   croûtons of fried bread
little cream
(*Enough for three or four people*)

Fillet the bloaters, putting aside the roes, pound the flesh with the butter, yolk of eggs, sauce and seasoning, rub through a sieve and add about one tablespoonful of cream, fry the croûtons, pile the bloater mixture on them in small heaps, lay a little piece of roe on each and warm in a quick oven, serve very hot.

409 SARDINES À LA SUISSE

8 sardines   some thin brown bread and
frying batter (see No. 649)   butter
(*Enough for four people*)

Remove the bones and wipe off the skin of the sardines, cut the bread and butter into fingers a little larger than the sardines, lay a sardine between two slices, press together, dip in frying batter, fry a golden brown in deep fat, drain and dish on a fancy paper and serve very hot.

410 ANGELS ON HORSEBACK

6 oysters   cayenne
6 rounds of toast   lemon juice
6 thin slices of bacon   watercress
(*Enough for three people*)

Beard and trim the oysters, sprinkle each one with lemon juice and cayenne, roll it in the bacon, lay on a round of buttered toast, put in a hot oven to cook the bacon, serve very hot, dish on watercress.

411 BEIGNETS À LA TURQUE

slices of thin brown bread   ¼ lb (100 g) cooked ham
and butter   parsley
chutney   frying batter (see No. 649)
(*Enough for three or four people*)

Cut the thin bread and butter into rounds, cut as many half rounds of ham the same size, spread some chutney on the bread and butter, lay a half round of ham on the top, fold over and press them together, dip into frying batter, fry a golden brown in hot fat, drain and serve on a fancy paper garnished with fried parsley.

412 RICE FRITTERS

4 oz (100 g) rice   butter
1 shallot   chopped parsley
1 egg   salt and pepper
(*Enough for six or seven people*)

Boil the rice till tender in stock, drain and leave at the side of the stove to dry, chop the shallot and fry lightly in butter, mix to the rice with parsley, beaten egg, salt and pepper, heat some butter in a sauté pan, fry the rice in small cakes a nice golden brown, serve with Hollandaise or tartare sauce.

413 CHEESE D'ARTOIS

4 oz (100 g) puff pastry (see   2 oz (50 g) grated Parmesan
No. 516)   cheese
4 yolks and 2 whites of eggs   nutmeg
2 oz (50 g) fresh butter   salt and pepper
(*Enough for seven or eight people*)

Beat three yolks and one white of egg in a basin, melt the butter and add it gradually, stir in the cheese and season well, roll out half the pastry very thinly, spread with the cheese mixture, roll out the remainder, lay it over the cheese and press it down well, beat up the remaining egg and brush over the top of the pastry, cut into small rounds with a cutter, place on a greased tin, bake about ten minutes in a quick oven, serve hot.

414 CHEESE RAMAKINS

2 oz (50 g) crumb of bread   2 yolks and 3 whites of eggs
2 oz (50 g) grated Parmesan   1½ gill (225 ml) milk
cheese   salt and cayenne
1 oz (25 g) butter
(*Enough for five or six people*)

Put the bread into a stewpan with the milk, let it simmer until the bread is soaked, but do not let it boil, drain off the milk, beat it smooth with a fork, add the butter, grated cheese, yolks of eggs and seasoning, whip the whites to a very stiff froth, stir in lightly, put the mixture in small paper soufflé cases slightly oiled, bake in a quick oven about ten minutes and serve immediately.

415 CROÛTES DE CHAMPIGNONS

8 mushrooms   ½ lemon
2 tomatoes   salt and cayenne
soft roe of 2 bloaters   croûtons of fried bread
1½ oz (40 g) butter
(*Enough for five or six people*)

Wash the mushrooms, dry and place them on a greased tin, sprinkle over some lemon juice and seasoning, cut the tomatoes into eight even slices and put on the tin, cut the roes into eight pieces, season with lemon juice, salt and cayenne, place on the tin and bake altogether in a moderate oven. When cooked place a mushroom on each croûton, lay on a slice of tomato and a piece of roe on the tomato, garnish with fried parsley and serve very hot.

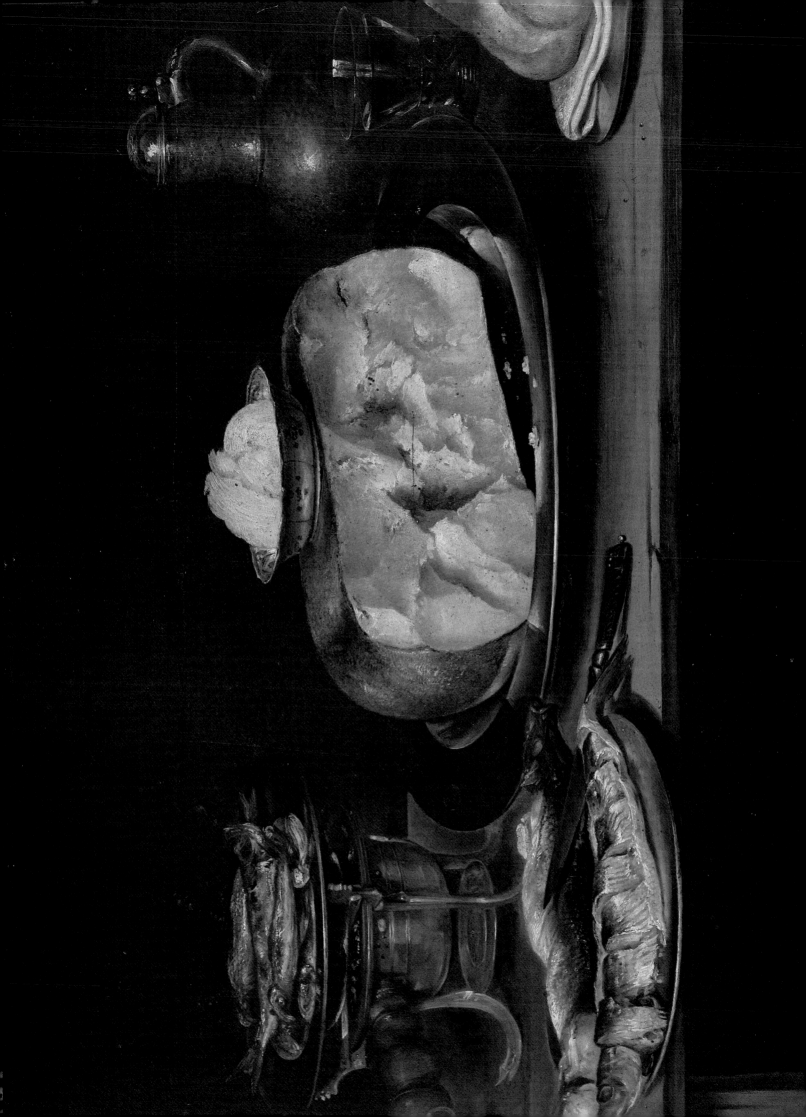

416 MARROW TOAST

rounds of toast	salt and pepper
butter	cayenne
beef marrow	

Butter some neat rounds of toast, put the marrow into a small stewpan with cold water and salt, bring to the boil, drain and spread on the toast, season with salt, cayenne and black pepper, make quite hot and serve.

417 CHEESE GONDOLES

3 oz (75 g) short crust	½ pint (300 ml) aspic jelly
1½ oz (40 g) grated Parmesan cheese	1 gill (150 ml) cream
	salt, cayenne
1 oz (25 g) grated Gruyére cheese	raw rice
2 tablespoonfuls béchamel sauce	

(Enough for five or six people)

Roll out the pastry thinly and line boat-shaped moulds evenly, fill with raw rice and bake. When cooked remove the rice, turn out and let them get cold, reduce the aspic jelly to half the quantity, stir in the sauce and the whipped cream, when setting add the grated cheeses and season well, put into a forcing bag with a rose pipe, fill the cases, sprinkle over some Parmesan cheese and serve.

418 CHEESE CROÛTONS

2 oz (50 g) grated cheese	chopped parsley
1 tablespoonful cream	salt and cayenne
1 egg	croûtons of bread
½ oz (15 g) butter	

(Enough for three or four people)

Mix together the grated cheese, cream, oiled butter, salt and cayenne to taste, fry some small round croûtons, put some mixture between two croûtons and press them together, sprinkle some grated cheese, yolk of egg and parsley on each, make hot and serve on a fancy paper.

419 MACARONI À L'ITALIENNE

macaroni	grated cheese
tomato purée	salt and pepper

Boil the macaroni in salted water till tender, cut in short lengths, place in tomato purée, add two heaped tablespoonfuls grated cheese and seasoning, serve very hot.

420 HAM CROÛTES À L'ITALIENNE

3 or 4 slices ham	bread
2 oz (50 g) butter	salt and cayenne
2 oz (50 g) grated cheese	

(Enough for six people)

Cut out about twelve small rounds of bread with a cutter, they must be thin and even, melt the butter, dip in the rounds of bread, sprinkle with cayenne and dip into the grated cheese, put a slice of ham between two rounds of bread, place on a tin and bake from eight to ten minutes in a quick oven and serve hot.

421 CHEESE AND CELERY SAVOURIES

cheese pastry (see No. 339)	celery
1 gill (150 ml) cream	salt, cayenne
2 oz (50 g) grated cheese	coraline pepper

(Enough for four or five people)

Make the cheese pastry, cut the pastry into small rounds with a cutter and bake in a quick oven, and allow to get cold. Whip the cream, add the grated cheese and finely chopped celery, season well, pile the mixture on the biscuits, using a fork, decorate the savouries with coraline pepper and serve on a lace paper.

SWEET DISHES

422 BOILED FRUIT PUDDING

½ lb (225 g) suet crust	water
(see No. 513)	sugar
any fruit	

(Enough for six people)

Well grease a pudding basin with butter or dripping, line with suet crust, put in some fruit, add the sugar and a little water, put in the rest of the fruit, cover with the rest of the pastry, tie on a scalded and floured cloth, boil the fruit for two hours.

423 TREACLE PUDDING NO 1

½ lb (225 g) flour	3 tablespoonfuls treacle
3 oz (75 g) suet	1 dessertspoonful ground ginger
½ oz (15 g) candied peel	½ teaspoonful carbonate of soda
1 gill (150 ml) milk	

(Enough for six or seven people)

Put flour into a basin, shred and chop the suet, add all the dry ingredients, dissolve the soda in some of the milk, add with the treacle and the rest of the milk, mix thoroughly, put into a greased basin, boil for two hours and serve with following sauce.

Sauce

½ oz (15 g) butter	1 gill (150 ml) milk
½ oz (15 g) flour	little lemon juice
little sugar	

424 TREACLE PUDDING NO 2

½ lb (225 g) flour	2 eggs
6 oz (175 g) suet	1 gill (150 ml) milk
4 tablespoonfuls treacle or golden syrup	juice and rind of lemon

(Enough for six or seven people)

Chop the suet finely, add to the flour with grated rind of lemon and a pinch of salt. Beat the eggs, add to the treacle, stir into dry ingredients, add the milk, mix thoroughly, boil in a greased basin for three or four hours. Serve with syrup sauce (see No. 652).

425 JAM ROLY-POLY

½ lb (225 g) suet crust	jam
(see No. 513)	

(Enough for six or seven people)

Make the pastry, roll out to an oblong shape, spread with jam, moisten the edges, roll up, fold in a scalded and floured cloth, tie up the ends with string. Boil for one and a half hours, turn out carefully.

A treacle roll can be made in the same way as a jam roly-poly, by simply using golden syrup, some bread crumbs and lemon juice instead of jam.

426 PLAIN PLUM PUDDING

½ lb (225 g) flour	2 tablespoonfuls golden syrup
3 oz (75 g) suet	½ teaspoonful carbonate of soda
1 oz (25 g) raisins	pinch of salt
1 oz (25 g) currants	water to mix

(Enough for six or seven people)

Chop the suet and mix with the flour, stone and chop the raisins, clean the currants, dissolve the soda in a little water, mix in with the syrup, make into a light dough with water, steam in a prepared basin covered with a greased paper for one and a half to two hours. This mixture can be cooked in the oven in a pie dish.

427 LIVERPOOL PUDDING

4 oz (100 g) bread crumbs	2 eggs
4 oz (100 g) suet	little milk
4 oz (100 g) flour	rind and juice of 1 lemon
2 oz (50 g) sugar	1 teaspoonful baking powder
2 oz (50 g) currants	nutmeg
	pinch of salt

(Enough for six or seven people)

Mix all the dry ingredients together, beat up the eggs, add the treacle, mix with the dry ingredients, add lemon juice, and a little milk if too stiff, pour into a greased basin or mould, cover with greased paper and steam for two hours. Serve with treacle sauce (see No. 652).

428 MARMALADE PUDDING

4 oz (100 g) flour	4 tablespoonfuls marmalade
4 oz (100 g) bread crumbs	2 eggs and little milk
4 oz (100 g) suet	½ teaspoonful baking powder
2 oz (50 g) sugar	

(Enough for six or seven people)

Chop suet finely, mix all dry ingredients together, mix marmalade with beaten eggs and add, using a little milk if necessary, put into a greased basin or mould, cover with greased paper and steam for two and a half hours, serve with sauce.

Marmalade Sauce

2 tablespoonfuls marmalade	2 tablespoonfuls water
juice of ½ lemon	

Boil together and strain.

429 GINGER PUDDING

4 oz (100 g) flour	2 tablespoonfuls treacle
4 oz (100 g) bread crumbs	2 eggs
4 oz (100 g) suet	1 dessertspoonful ground ginger
2 oz (50 g) sugar	1 teaspoonful baking powder
pinch of salt	

(Enough for six or seven people)

Mix all the dry ingredients together, stir in the beaten eggs and treacle—if too stiff add a little milk; pour into a greased mould, cover with greased paper, steam for two and a half hours. Serve with treacle sauce (see No. 652).

430 PLUM DUFF

8 oz (225 g) flour	6 oz (175 g) raisins
4 oz (100 g) suet	1 egg

1 oz (25 g) sugar	little milk
pinch of salt	½ teaspoonful baking powder

(Enough for six or seven)

Add the choped suet and stoned raisins to the flour, with sugar, salt and baking powder, mix with the egg and milk, tie in a cloth and boil for two or three hours. Serve with Demerara sugar.

431 RAISIN PUDDING

¾ lb (350 g) flour, or ½ lb	¾ lb (350 g) raisins
(225 g) flour and 4 oz (100 g)	3 oz (75 g) sugar
bread crumbs	½ pint (300 ml) milk
6 oz (175 g) suet	pinch salt

(Enough for six or seven people)

Chop suet finely, stone and divide raisins, mix all ingredients together with the milk, put mixture into a well-greased basin, tie securely with prepared cloth, boil three or four hours. Sift sugar over when turned out.

Note—Dates or figs may be used instead of raisins.

432 FIG PUDDING NO 1

4 oz (100 g) flour	½ lb (225 g) figs
4 oz (100 g) bread crumbs	2 eggs
6 oz (175 g) suet	½ pint (300 ml) milk
4 oz (100 g) sugar	a little nutmeg
pinch of salt	

(Enough for six or seven people)

Chop the suet and figs finely, mix with the dry ingredients, add the eggs well beaten and the milk, mix all thoroughly together, put into a greased basin, cover with prepared cloth and boil for three or four hours.

Note—Dates may be used instead of figs.

433 FIG PUDDING NO 2

4 oz (100 g) chopped figs	2 tablespoonfuls ground
4 oz (100 g) flour	almonds
4 oz (100 g) suet	little milk, 1 gill (150 ml)
4 oz (100 g) sugar	1 teaspoonful baking powder
4 oz (100 g) bread crumbs	pinch of salt
4 eggs	noyeau, or any flavouring

(Enough for six or seven people)

Chop the suet and figs finely, warm the milk and pour over the bread crumbs, add the sugar and yolks of eggs and beat well. Mix the baking powder with the flour and add to the mixture with the ground almonds, figs and suet. Stir in lightly the whipped white of eggs, put in a well-greased mould and steam for three hours.

434 ORANGE ROLL

½ lb (225 g) flour	2 tablespoonfuls orange
4 oz (100 g) suet	marmalade
salt	breadcrumbs
water	Demerara sugar
	lemon juice

(Enough for five or six people)

Make suet crust with the flour and chopped suet mixed to a stiff dough with water, roll out to an oblong shape, spread over a thin layer of marmalade, on this spread a layer of slices of orange, free from skin and pips. Sprinkle over with fresh bread crumbs and a little Demerara sugar, squeeze

over some lemon juice, roll up, tie in a floured cloth, boil for two and a half hours. Serve with marmalade sauce (see No. 654).

435 CHRISTMAS PUDDING NO 1

1 lb (450 g) raisins	¼ lb (100 g) almonds
1 lb (450 g) currants	½ lb (225 g) sugar
½ lb (225 g) sultanas	10 eggs
1 lb (450 g) suet	1 pint (600 ml) milk
1 lb (450 g) bread crumbs	1 gill (150 ml) brandy
¾ lb (350 g) mixed peel	½ teacupful treacle
1 small nutmeg	pinch of salt
¼ teaspoonful cinnamon	

Prepare all the ingredients carefully, mix well together, put into buttered basins, cover with greased paper, tie on cloths. Boil from nine to twelve hours.

436 CHRISTMAS PUDDING NO 2

1 lb (450 g) flour	1 nutmeg
1 lb (450 g) bread crumbs	¼ lb (100 g) almonds
2 lb (900 g) suet	½ lz (15 g) mixed spice
2 lb (900 g) currants	¼ teaspoonful salt
2 lb (900 g) raisins	1 gill (150 ml) brandy
1 lb (450 g) sugar	1 gill (150 ml) porter
½ lb (225 g) candied peel	8 to 10 eggs
juice and rind of 2 lemons	milk if required
1 lb (450 g) sultanas	

Prepare all ingredients carefully, mix thoroughly, put into buttered basins and boil for nine hours.

437 CHRISTMAS PUDDING NO 3

1 lb (450 g) potatoes	¾ lb (350 g) sugar
½ lb (225 g) boiled and mashed	2 oz (50 g) mixed peel
carrots	1 grated apple
½ lb (225 g) flour	1 teaspoonful spice
½ lb (225 g) bread crumbs	2 tablespoonfuls treacle
1 lb (450 g) raisins	2 or 3 eggs
1 lb (450 g) currants	milk
½ lb (225 g) suet	salt

Prepare ingredients and mix all thoroughly with eggs and as much milk as required, boil in well-greased basins for twelve hours.

438 BOILED BATTER PUDDING

½ lb (225 g) flour	pinch of salt
1 pint (600 ml) milk	marmalade
2 eggs	

(Enough for four or five people)

Add the salt to the flour, make a well in the centre, drop in the eggs, mix smoothly with a little of the milk, beat till it bubbles, add the remainder of the milk and if possible allow the batter to stand, well grease the mould or basin, line with marmalade, pour in the batter. Boil for two hours, serve with marmalade sauce (see No. 654).

Note—Currants may be used instead of marmalade, they sink and form a black cap—called Black Cap Pudding. Serve with a sweet sauce.

439 HALF-PAY PUDDING

½ lb (225 g) flour	2 oz (50 g) candied peel
½ lb (225 g) suet	1 teaspoonful spice
½ lb (225 g) raisins	pinch of salt
½ lb (225 g) currants	½ a cup of treacle
½ lb (225 g) bread crumbs	1 cup of milk

(Enough for eight or ten people)

Chop the suet finely, stone and chop raisins, mix all the ingredients well together and boil for at least four hours.

440 CHELMSFORD PUDDING

1 oz (25 g) sago	½ oz (15 g) flour
1 gill (150 ml) milk	1 oz (25 g) sugar
3 oz (75 g) bread crumbs	2 eggs
2 oz (50 g) suet	a few stoned raisins

(Enough for four or five people)

Cook the sago in some water till tender and nearly dry, beat the eggs with the milk, add the bread crumbs, sugar, chopped suet and flour to the sago and mix with the egg and milk, well butter a mould or basin, line it with stoned raisins, put in the mixture carefully, boil for one hour and serve with a sweet sauce.

441 RICE PUDDING

2 oz (50 g) rice	1 teaspoonful chopped suet
1 pint (600 ml) milk	nutmeg
sugar to taste	

(Enough for two or three people)

Wash the rice, put into a pie dish with the sugar and milk, sprinkle over the finely-chopped suet and grate with nutmeg. Bake in a slow oven for two hours.

Note—Sago and tapioca can be cooked in the same way, using same quantities.

442 SCRAP BREAD PUDDING

½ lb (100 g) stale bread	1 gill (150 ml) milk
1 oz (25 g) suet or dripping	1 egg
currants	nutmeg
½ oz (15 g) sugar	pinch of salt

(Enough for two or three people)

Soak the bread in cold water, squeeze it dry, put a layer into a greased pie dish, then a little chopped suet and some sugar and a few currants, repeat this until the dish is nearly full, grate on a little nutmeg, beat the egg, mix with the milk, add a pinch of salt, pour over the bread, bake in the oven for about three-quarters of an hour.

443 QUEEN OF PUDDINGS

1 pint (600 ml) milk	lemon flavouring
5 oz (150 g) bread crumbs	2 oz (50 g) sugar
2 eggs	jam
1 oz (25 g) butter	

(Enough for three or four people)

Boil the milk with some strips of lemon peel, strain it over the bread crumbs and cook them for a few minutes, allow the mixture to cool slightly, add the butter, sugar and yolks of eggs, pour it into a buttered pie dish, bake in the oven for about half an hour, spread the jam over, make a meringue with the stiffly-beaten whites and some sugar, pile it on the top of the pudding and bake till crisp.

444 LEMON RICE

3 oz (75 g) rice   1 lemon
2 eggs   little apricot jam
1 pint (600 ml) milk   1 oz (25 g) sugar
(Enough for three or four people)

Cook the rice in the milk with the grated lemon rind. When quite tender add the well-beaten yolks of eggs, sugar and lemon juice, put it in a buttered pie dish, cook in the oven till firm, spread over a thin layer of apricot jam. Make a meringue with the whipped white of egg, pile on the top and crisp in the oven.

445 MONKS' PUDDING

some stale sponge cakes   2 oz (50 g) butter
apricot jam   1 oz (25 g) sugar
3 eggs   1 gill (150 ml) sherry
(Enough for three or four people)

Place the sponge cakes in a buttered pie dish, pour over the sherry and allow them to soak. Spread over a thin layer of apricot jam, melt the butter, add to well-beaten eggs and sugar, pour over the sponge cakes. Bake slowly in a moderate oven, serve hot or cold.

446 SEMOLINA PUDDING

½ oz (15 g) semolina   1 teaspoonful sugar
½ pint (300 ml) milk   1 egg
(Enough for one or two people)

Boil the milk, shake in the semolina, cook till transparent, add the sugar, remove from the fire, add the beaten yolk of egg, beat the white to a stiff froth with a pinch of salt, stir the white in lightly, flavour with vanilla or lemon, put into a greased pie dish, bake in a moderately quick oven, serve hot or cold.

447 SAGO PUDDING

2 oz (50 g) sago   ½ oz (15 g) sugar
1 pint (600 ml) milk   any flavouring
(Enough for two or three people)

Wash the sago, put into a saucepan with the milk, cook till transparent, add the sugar and flavouring, put in a greased pie dish, bake in a quick oven. Serve hot or cold.
Note—Rice and tapioca can be cooked as above.

448 MACARONI PUDDING

2 oz (50 g) macaroni   1 egg
1 pint (600 ml) milk   flavouring
1 oz (25 g) sugar   nutmeg
(Enough for two or three people)

Break the macaroni into short lengths and soak in the milk for some time. Put it in a saucepan and cook till tender, add the sugar, beaten egg and flavouring, put into a greased pie dish, grate over a little nutmeg, bake for about twenty minutes.

449 BREAD AND BUTTER PUDDING

slices of bread and butter   sugar
3 eggs   sultanas or currants
1½ pints (900 ml) milk   nutmeg
(Enough for four or five people)

Well grease a pie dish, put some sultanas or currants at the bottom, place in some slices of bread and butter (cut neatly and crust removed), butter side downwards, sprinkle over some sugar, a few more sultanas, more bread and butter, until the dish is three-quarters full, beat up the eggs, add the milk, strain over the bread and butter, allow it to stand an hour to soak, grate over with nutmeg. Bake for an hour in a slow oven.
Note—This pudding can be made in a mould and steamed. Serve with jam sauce.

450 CORNFLOUR MOULD

2 oz (50 g) cornflour   1 oz (25 g) sugar
1 pint (600 ml) milk   flavouring
(Enough for three or four people)

Mix the cornflour with a little cold milk, add to the milk when boiling, stir until it thickens, then boil for five minutes, stirring well all the time, add sugar and flavouring, pour into a wet mould, turn out when set.
Note—Ground rice mould can be made as above, using 2½ oz (65 g) ground rice to one pint (600 ml) milk.

451 RHUBARB AND SAGO MOULD

1 lb (450 g) rhubarb   ¼ lb (100 g) sugar
3 oz (75 g) fine sago   strip of lemon rind
½ pint (300 ml) water   a little carmine colouring
(Enough for three or four people)

Wash the sago, put it in a white lined pan with the rhubarb, cut in short lengths, sugar, water and strip of lemon rind, boil gently for half an hour, remove the lemon rind, add a few drops of colouring, turn into a wet mould, turn out when cold and serve with custard sauce (see No. 657 or 658).

452 RICE MOULD

3 oz (75 g) rice   2 oz (50 g) sugar
1 pint (600 ml) milk   flavouring
(Enough for three or four people)

Wash the rice, allow it to soak in the milk for some time, put into a saucepan and cook till tender and the milk is taken up, add the sugar and flavouring, pour the rice into a wet mould, turn out when cold and serve with stewed fruit or jam.

453 CHOCOLATE MOULD

3 oz (75 g) cornflour   vanilla essence
2 oz (50 g) chocolate powder   custard sauce (see No 657 or
1 oz (25 g) sugar   658)
1½ pints (900 ml) milk

Mix the cornflour and chocolate powder with cold milk, put on remainder of milk to boil, pour on to cornflour and powder and return to the saucepan, cook thoroughly, add sugar and vanilla essence to taste, pour into a wet mould, turn out when set and serve with custard sauce.

454 AMBROSIA

2 oz (50 g) cornflour   1 pint (600 ml) milk
2 oz (50 g) butter   1 wineglass sherry
2 oz (50 g) sugar
(Enough for four or five people)

Mix the cornflour with a little of the milk, put the remainder on to boil with the butter. When boiling pour on to the cornflour and return it to the saucepan and cook thoroughly, add the sherry and sugar, pour into a wet mould, turn out when set.

455 COFFEE MOULD

¾ pint (450 ml) milk   2 tablespoonfuls coffee essence
½ oz (15 g) gelatine   2 tablespoonfuls sugar
(*Enough for three or four people*)

Soak the gelatine in a little cold milk, when dissolved add it to the remainder of the milk and coffee essence and boil, add the sugar, pour into a wet mould, turn out when set. Strong coffee can be used instead of essence, but it must be very carefully strained.

456 COCOANUT CREAM

3 oz (75 g) cornflour   1½ oz (40 g) cocoanut
1½ pints (900 ml) milk   1 oz (25 g) sugar
1½ oz (40 g) butter   little carmine colouring
(*Enough for five or six people*)

Mix the cornflour with a little of the milk, put the remainder on to boil. When boiling add the cornflour and cook thoroughly, stir in the butter and cocoanut, leaving out a little, add the sugar and colour with carmine, pour into a wet mould, turn out when set and sprinkle over the rest of the cocoanut.

Note—Ground rice may be used instead of cornflour.

457 CRYSTAL PALACE PUDDING

8 sponge cakes   2 eggs
1½ pints (900 ml) milk   flavouring
½ oz (15 g) gelatine   glacé cherries
sugar to taste   cream
(*Enough for five or six people*)

Cut the sponge cakes into dice. Dissolve the gelatine in the milk, strain on to the beaten eggs, add sugar to taste and flavouring (essence of vanilla or almonds), cook till it thickens. Put the sponge cakes in a mould decorated with the glacé cherries, pour over the custard. When set turn out and serve with cream.

458 LEMON SAGO

4 oz (100 g) sago   grated rind and juice of 2 lemons
1 pint (600 ml) water   custard sauce (see No 657 or 658)
4 tablespoonfuls golden syrup
(*Enough for five or six people*)

Boil the sago with the water till quite clear, add the syrup and lemon rind and juice, boil all together for a few minutes and pour into a wet mould. Turn out when set and serve with custard sauce.

459 APPLE SNOW

¾ lb (350 g) apples   rind of 1 lemon
½ oz (15 g; gelatine   juice of ½ lemon
4 oz (100 g) castor sugar   whites of 2 eggs
½ gill (75 ml) water   custard sauce (see No 657 or 658)
(*Enough for four or five people*)

Peel, core and slice the apples, stew them with the sugar, dissolve the gelatine in the water and add with the grated rind and juice of lemon. Whip the whites to a stiff froth and stir in lightly. Put into a mould. Turn out when set and serve with custard sauce.

460 RHENISH CREAM

6 yolks of eggs   1 oz (25 g) gelatine
½ pint (300 ml) sherry   rind and juice of 2 lemons
1 pint (600 ml) boiling water   sugar to taste
(*Enough for five or six people*)

Dissolve the gelatine in the boiling water, allow it to cool, add to the beaten yolks, cook in a double saucepan until it thickens, add the grated lemon rind, juice, sherry and sugar to taste. Pour into a wet mould.

461 LEMON SPONGE

1 pint (600 ml) water   rind and juice of 3 lemons
1 oz (25 g) gelatine   3 whites of eggs
¼ lb (100 g) loaf sugar
(*Enough for five or six people*)

Peel the lemons thinly and put into a saucepan with lemon juice, sugar and gelatine, boil gently for fifteen minutes. Allow to get cool, beat up the whites very stiffly, add the gelatine and water, etc., whisk well till it begins to stiffen, pour into a wet mould and turn out when set.

462 PRUNE MOULD

1 lb (450 g) prunes   rind and juice of 1 lemon
1 pint (600 ml) water   1 wineglass claret
3 oz (75 g) sugar   carmine to colour
1 oz (25 g) gelatine
(*Enough for five or six people*)

Soak the prunes in a pint (600 ml) of water, then put them in a stewpan in the same liquid with sugar, lemon rind and cook till tender. Remove the stones, rub through a sieve, add the dissolved gelatine, claret, colour with carmine, pour into a wet mould, turn out when set and serve in a glass dish.

463 HONEY COMB MOULD

3 eggs   2 oz (50 g) castor sugar
1 pint (600 ml) milk   lemon or vanilla flavouring
½ oz (15 g) gelatine
(*Enough for five or six people*)

Dissolve the gelatine in the milk, beat the yolks of eggs, pour over the hot milk, return to the saucepan and stir till it thickens, add the sugar and flavouring, whip the whites stiffly, stir them lightly to the mixture, pour into a wet mould and leave till set.

464 VIENNOISE PUDDING

5 oz (150 g) stale bread   grated rind of lemon
3 oz (75 g) sultanas   ¾ pint (450 ml) milk
3 oz (75 g) castor sugar   1 gill (150 ml) sherry
3 eggs   1 oz (25 g) loaf sugar
1 oz (25 g) peel   German sauce (see No 660)
(*Enough for five or six people*)

Cut the bread into small dice and soak in the sherry, put the loaf sugar in a saucepan with a little water and two teaspoonfuls of lemon juice and boil together till a rich brown, add the milk gradually, beat the eggs and strain the milk into them, mix the fruit with the bread, pour over the milk and eggs, turn into a well-buttered and decorated mould. Steam slowly for 1½ to 2 hours. Serve with German sauce.

465 CABINET PUDDING

4 sponge cakes	1 oz (25 g) sugar
some ratafias	1 oz (25 g) glacé cherries
1 pint (600 ml) milk	1 oz (25 g) sultanas
3 eggs	1 oz (25 g) peel
essence of almond or vanilla	jam sauce (see No 650)

(Enough for five or six people)

Well grease a mould, decorate with cherries, cut the sponge cakes into dice, put in the mould in layers with chopped peel, sultanas and ratafias, boil the milk, pour on to the well-beaten eggs, add the sugar and flavouring, pour in the mould, allow it to soak, place over a greased paper and steam from 1 to 1½ hours. Let it stand for a few minutes before turning out. Serve with jam sauce.

466 ORLEANS PUDDING

3½ oz (90 g) butter	2 eggs
3½ oz (90 g) flour	1 tablespoonful milk
1½ oz (40 g) sugar	½ teaspoonful carbonate of soda
4 oz (100 g) marmalade	pinch of salt

(Enough for five or six people)

Cream the butter and the sugar, add eggs and flour alternately, beat well, add marmalade and last the carbonate of soda dissolved in the milk. Put in a well-greased mould and steam for 1½ hours. Serve with marmalade sauce (see No 654).

467 BERESFORD PUDDING

2 eggs	2 tablespoonfuls bread crumbs
their weight in butter	grated rind of 2 oranges
sugar	½ teaspoonful baking powder
flour	pinch of salt

(Enough for five or six people)

Cream the butter and sugar, sift the flour and add with the eggs alternately, beat well, add bread crumbs and orange rind and lastly the baking powder. Put into a well-greased mould, cover with greased paper and steam 1½ hours.

Sauce

1 gill (150 ml) water	½ oz (15 g) sugar
1 teaspoonful cornflour	juice of 2 oranges
rind and juice of 1 lemon	

468 PRESERVED GINGER PUDDING

2 eggs	3 oz (75 g) preserved ginger
their weight in butter	½ teaspoonful baking powder
sugar	pinch of salt
flour	

(Enough for five or six people)

Cream the butter and sugar, add the sifted flour and eggs alternately, beating well between each addition, add the finely-chopped ginger and lastly the baking powder. Put in

a well-greased mould, cover with greased paper, and steam for two hours.

Sauce

1 gill (150 ml) water	1 tablespoonful brandy
1 stick ginger	2 oz (50 g) sugar
juice of 1 lemon	1 glass sherry
strip of lemon rind	

Boil and strain.

469 RASPBERRY PUDDING

2 eggs	2 tablespoonfuls raspberry jam
their weight in butter	½ teaspoonful baking powder
sugar	pinch of salt
flour	carmine colouring

Cream the butter and sugar, add the sifted flour and eggs alternately, beating well between each, add jam and lastly the baking powder and a drop or two of colouring if required. Put in a well-greased mould, cover with greased paper, steam for two hours.

Sauce

3 tablespoonfuls raspberry jam	lemon juice
1 gill (150 ml) water	colouring

Boil for six minutes and strain.

470 CHOCOLATE PUDDING

2 eggs	2 bars of grated chocolate
their weight in butter	½ teaspoonful baking powder
sugar	vanilla essence
flour	pinch of salt

(Enough for five or six people)

Cream the butter and sugar, add the sifted flour and eggs alternately, beat well, add grated chocolate and vanilla essence and lastly the baking powder. Decorate the mould with blanched almonds or cherries and angelica. Steam for two hours.

Sauce

2 oz (50 g) chocolate	½ oz (15 g) crème de riz
½ pint (300 ml) water	vanilla essence
sugar	little brandy

Dissolve chocolate in the water, thicken with crème de riz, boil and add flavourings.

471 LEMON PUDDING

6 oz (175 g) bread crumbs	3 oz (75 g) suet
3 oz (75 g) brown sugar	2 lemons
3 oz (75 g) flour	1 teaspoonful baking powder
1 egg and a little milk	pinch of salt

(Enough for six or seven people)

Chop the suet finely, mix with the flour, crumbs, sugar, grated lemon rind, salt and baking powder, beat the egg and add with enough milk to make into a stiff mixture, add the juice of the two lemons, steam in a greased mould covered with greased paper for 1½ hours.

Sauce

½ pint (300 ml) milk	½ oz (15 g) castor sugar
1 dessertspoonful cornflour	rind of ½ and juice of 1 lemon

Boil the milk with lemon rind, pour it on the cornflour smoothly mixed, cook the mixture for ten minutes, add lemon juice and sugar.

472 BROWN BREAD PUDDING

4 oz (100 g) brown bread crumbs	3 eggs
2 oz (50 g) brown sugar	1 teaspoonful baking powder
2 oz (50 g) butter	pinch of salt
2 oz (50 g) glacé cherries	jam sauce (see No 650)
2 oz (50 g) peel	

(Enough for five or six people)

Cream the butter and the sugar, add the brown bread crumbs and eggs alternately and beat well, cut the cherries in half and add with the baking powder, and stir in lightly the stiffly-whipped whites of eggs, well grease and decorate a mould, put in the mixture, cover with greased paper and steam for an hour. Serve with jam sauce.

473 MADEIRA PUDDING

2 eggs	1 oz (25 g) peel
their weight in butter	essence of lemon
sugar	½ teaspoonful baking powder
flour	pinch of salt

(Enough for five or six people)

Cream the butter and sugar, add the sifted flour and eggs alternately and beat well, add the sultanas and chopped peel, flavouring and baking powder, put in a well-greased mould, cover with greased paper, steam for 1½ hours. Serve with jam sauce (see No 650).

474 ORANGE PUDDING

3 oz (75 g) butter	pinch of salt
4 oz (100 g) sugar	grated rind of 2 oranges
4 oz (100 g) flour	juice of 1 orange
2 eggs	½ teaspoonful baking powder

(Enough for five or six people)

Cream the butter and sugar together, add the eggs and flour alternately, beating well between each, add grated orange rind, juice and lastly baking powder. Well butter a mould, decorate with quarters of orange, pour in the mixture, cover with buttered paper, steam for 1½ to 2 hours. Serve with orange sauce (see No 653).

475 CANARY PUDDING

2 eggs	grated rind of 2 lemons
their weight in butter	½ teaspoonful baking powder
sugar	pinch of salt
flour	

(Enough for five or six people)

Cream the butter and sugar together, add the sifted flour and eggs alternately, beating well, add the grated lemon rind and lastly the baking powder. Put mixture into a well-greased mould, steam for 1½ hours. Serve with lemon sauce (see No 651).

476 BACHELOR'S PUDDING

2 oz (50 g) bread crumbs	½ teaspoonful ground ginger
2 oz (50 g) flour	1 egg and little milk
2 oz (50 g) suet	½ teaspoonful baking powder
2 oz (50 g) raisins	pinch of salt
2 oz (50 g) sugar	

(Enough for five or six people)

Chop the suet finely, stone and cut the raisins across, put all the dry ingredients together, beat the egg with a little milk, stir well, put mixture into a greased mould sprinkled with brown sugar, cover with greased paper and steam for 1½ hours, and serve with a sweet sauce.

Sauce

1 oz (25 g) butter	1 gill (150 ml) water
¾ oz (20 g) flour	1 gill (150 ml) milk
1 dessertspoonful flour	

Cook the flour in the butter, add water and milk, boil, and add sugar.

477 FRENCH RAISIN PUDDING

some stale sponge cakes	2 oz (50 g) peel
milk to soak them	½ lb (225 g) raisins
4 eggs	wineglass of brandy
3 oz (75 g) fine sago	custard sauce (see No 658)
1 oz (25 g) sugar	

(Enough for six or seven people)

Soak the sponge cakes in milk, mix together all the ingredients, put into a well-greased mould and steam for 1½ hours. Serve with custard sauce flavoured with liquer.

478 SAGO SOUFFLÉ

2½ oz (65 g) small sago	½ pint (300 ml) milk
3 oz (75 g) butter	vanilla essence
3 oz (75 g) sugar	cherries and angelica
3 eggs	jam sauce (see No 650)

(Enough for five or six people)

Wash the sago and cook it till clear in the milk with the butter and sugar, allow to cool and beat in the egg yolks, add the vanilla and lastly the stiffly-beaten whites, mix very lightly, pour into a well-buttered soufflé tin, decorate with cherries and angelica cut in leaves, tie a band of buttered paper round the soufflé tin, steam very gently for forty-five to fifty minutes. Turn out carefully, serve immediately, with apricot sauce poured round.

479 VANILLA SOUFFLÉ

1½ oz (40 g) butter	4 yolks and 5 whites of eggs
1½ oz (40 g) flour	vanilla essence
1 gill (150 ml) milk	cherries and angelica
½ oz (15 g) sugar	jam sauce (see No 650)

(Enough for four or five people)

Cook the flour in the butter and add the milk, cook for a few minutes, allow the mixture to cool, add the sugar and beat in the yolks of eggs, flavour well with vanilla, whip the whites to a very stiff froth, stir in very lightly, pour the mixture into a well-buttered soufflé tin, decorated with cherries and angelica, tie a band of buttered paper round outside the tin, place a piece of paper on the top and steam gently for thirty-five to forty minutes. Serve at once with jam sauce poured round.

480 PINEAPPLE SOUFFLE

2 oz (50 g) butter	1 oz (25 g) sugar
3 oz (75 g) flour	yolks of 3 and white of 4 eggs
3 oz (75 g) pineapple	grated lemon rind
½ pint (300 ml) milk	pineapple sauce (see No 662)

(Enough for five or six people)

Make a panada with butter, flour and milk, stir till it boils, add the pineapple cut into tiny dice, sugar and grated lemon rind. When the mixture is cool beat in the yolks of eggs, whip the whites to a stiff froth and stir in lightly. Pour into a well-buttered soufflé tin decorated with pieces of pineapple, tie a band of buttered paper round the outside of the tin, cover with a piece of paper. Steam for an hour and serve at once.

Sauce

1 gill (150 ml) pine juice	1 wineglass sherry
1 oz (25 g) sugar	few pieces of pine

481 CHOCOLATE SOUFFLÉ

1 oz (25 g) butter	½ oz (15 g) sugar
1 oz (25 g) flour	yolks of 2 and whites of 3 eggs
1 gill (150 ml) milk	vanilla essence
3 oz (75 g) chocolate	chocolate sauce (see No 659)

(Enough for four or five people)

Make a panada with the butter, flour and milk in which the chocolate has been dissolved and mixed smoothly, cook for a few minutes, allow the mixture to cool and add the sugar, yolks of eggs and vanilla essence. Whip the whites stiffly and stir in lightly, pour into a buttered soufflé dish, tie round a band of buttered paper, bake in the oven for thirty-five minutes. Serve with chocolate sauce.

Note—This soufflé may be steamed as vanilla or sago soufflés. It will take forty-five to fifty minutes.

482 CUP PUDDINGS

2 eggs	flavouring
their weight in butter	pinch of salt
sugar	jam sauce
flour	

(Enough to fill eight darioles)

Cream the butter and sugar, add the sifted flour and eggs alternately, beating well between each, add the flavouring. Bake in well-greased dariole moulds in a quick oven for twenty minutes and serve with jam sauce poured round.

Note—This mixture can be steamed covered with greased paper if more convenient. Serve in the same way.

483 MOSS BASKETS

2 eggs	pistachio nuts
their weight in butter	cream
sugar	angelica
flour	liquer
apricot jam	

(Enough to make six baskets)

Cream the butter and sugar, add eggs and flour alternately, bake in well-buttered dariole moulds for fifteen to twenty minutes. Warm the jam (about two tablespoonfuls) and strain it, scoop out the centres of the cakes when cold, spread the top and sides with the jam and roll them in blanched and chopped pistachio nuts. Whip the cream, sweeten and flavour with a little liqueur, fill the centres, cut long thin strips of angelica and fix them across to form the handles.

484 MADELEINE

2 eggs	jam
their weight in butter	2 oz (50 g) desiccated cocoanut
sugar	glacé cherries
flour	carmine colouring

(Enough to fill eight darioles)

Make mixture as for cup puddings, bake for twenty minutes in a quick oven, make a tablespoonful of jam hot, add a drop or two of carmine to improve the colour, brush over the cakes and roll them in desiccated cocoanut, place a glacé cherry on the top. If served hot pour round some jam sauce, coloured nicely; if served cold, on a glass dish with a lace paper.

485 SPONGE PUDDING

2 eggs	2 tablespoonfuls water
2 oz (50 g) butter	2 teaspoonfuls baking powder
1 teacupful flour	pinch of salt
½ teacupful sugar	jam

(Enough for four or five people)

Mix the eggs, butter (melted) and sugar together and beat well, sift in the flour and baking powder and add the water, pour into a well-greased pie dish and bake in a moderate oven. When cooked turn out and spread a layer of jam on top. Serve hot or cold.

486 SWISS ROLL

2 eggs (3 if small)	½ teaspoonful baking powder
2 oz (50 g) flour	pinch of salt
3 oz (75 g) sugar	jam

(Enough for five or six people)

Whisk the eggs and sugar well in a warm place, sift the flour in gradually and stir lightly, add baking powder, turn quickly in a prepared baking tin, bake in a quick oven for about six minutes, turn on to a sheet of paper sprinkled with castor sugar, cut down the edges, spread with warm jam, roll up, sprinkle with sugar, serve with jam sauce if hot and on a glass dish with lace paper if cold.

Note—Apricot and raspberry are the most suitable jams to use for the Swiss roll.

487 PANCAKES

½ lb (225 g) flour	1½ oz (40 g) lard
1 pint (600 ml) milk	1 lemon
2 eggs	castor sugar
pinch of salt	

(Enough to make ten or twelve pancakes)

Make a batter with the milk, flour and eggs, beating well before all the milk is added, and allow it to stand for an hour or more if possible. Put the batter into a jug, melt the lard in a saucepan, pour a little into the frying pan—enough to cover the bottom of the pan. Pour in some batter, when brown on one side toss and brown the other side. Turn on to a piece of paper sprinkled with sugar, sift with castor sugar and squeeze over some lemon juice, roll up and put on a dish with a fancy paper. Serve very hot.

488 RICE CROQUETTES

4 oz (100 g) rice	flavouring
1 pint (600 ml) milk	egg and bread crumbs
1 oz (25 g) sugar	angelica

(Enough to make eight or ten croquettes)

Put the rice on in a saucepan to cook with the milk and flavouring. When tender and all the milk absorbed add the sugar, turn on to a wet plate, divide into equal portions and set aside to cool. When firm roll into balls, using a few crumbs, coat with egg and crumbs, fry a golden brown in hot fat, drain well, put a small strip of angelica into each to look like a stem, serve on a hot dish with lace paper with jam or jam sauce.

489 FRUIT FRITTERS

apples or bananas	2 tablespoonfuls tepid water
3 oz (75 g) flour	white of 1 egg
1 tablespoonful oil	pinch of salt

Put the flour and salt into a basin, make a well in the centre, pour in the oil, add the water gradually and mix smoothly, beat well. Let it stand for an hour if possible, then add the whipped white of egg lightly. Peel the apple, cut into slices, take out the core, leaving a ring, dip in the batter, fry in hot fat, drain well, dish on a lace paper, sprinkle with castor sugar. Serve at once.

Note—Bananas, oranges, apricots, pineapple may be used instead of apples.

490 RICE CREAM BEIGNETS

3 oz (75 g) butter	pinch of cinnamon
3 oz (75 g) castor sugar	¾ gill (110 ml) milk
3 eggs	½ teaspoonful baking powder
4 oz (100 g) sifted flour	vanilla essence
4 oz (100 g) crème de riz	

(Enough for five or six people)

Cream the butter, add the sugar, crème de riz and cinnamon, work together for about ten minutes, add by degrees the eggs and flour alternately, flavour with vanilla essence and lastly add the milk and baking powder. Put into a forcing bag with a plain pipe and force out portions about the size of a walnut, cutting it with a knife, fry in hot fat from eight to ten minutes. Pile on a lace paper on a hot dish and sprinkle with castor sugar.

491 SWEET OMELET

3 eggs	¾ oz (20 g) butter
little jam	1 teaspoonful castor sugar

Separate the whites and yolks of eggs, beat the whites to a stiff froth with the teaspoonful of sugar, mix lightly with the well-beaten yolks, melt the butter in an omelet pan, pour in the eggs, stir quickly till the mixture begins to set, put the omelet pan in the oven for a minute or two to brown slightly. Shape the omelet, put the warmed jam in the centre, fold over and turn on to a hot dish and serve immediately.

492 RUM OMELET

3 eggs	little jam
¾ oz (20 g) butter	rum
1 teaspoonful sugar	

Make like a sweet omelet, adding a few drops of rum to flavour, dish on a flat dish, pour over a little rum and set fire to it just as it is to be served.

Note—Good rum is necessary or it will not burn.

493 LEMON JELLY

6 lemons	stick of cinnamon
2 oz (50 g) gelatine	8 oz (225 g) loaf sugar
1½ pints (900 ml) water	2 tablespoonfuls sherry
3 or 4 cloves	white and shells of 2 eggs

(Enough to fill one and a half pint mould)

Peel the lemons very thinly, squeeze out the juice and add to the water with sugar, cloves, cinnamon and gelatine, making barely a quart (1.1 litres) liquid altogether. When the gelatine is dissolved add the slightly beaten whites and crushed shells, whisk well until boiling-point is reached, let it boil five or six minutes, move aside till the scum cracks, strain through a scalded cloth, add the sherry. If it does not run through clear at first pour it gently through the cloth a second time. When cool pour into a wet mould.

Note—A loosely woven teacloth is the best kind to use in preference to a jelly bag. Tie the four corners to the legs of an upturned chair, standing on another chair; place the bowl underneath.

French leaf gelatine is the best to use. It requires no previous soaking.

494 AMERICAN JELLY

1 pint (600 ml) milk	1 oz (25 g) castor sugar
2 eggs	vanilla essence
¾ oz (20 g) gelatine	

(Enough for four or five people)

Dissolve the gelatine in the milk, but do not boil it; add the yolks of eggs and sugar, beat the whites to a stiff froth and add with the vanilla essence to taste. Put into a wet mould. turn out when set.

495 CLARET JELLY

(Unclarified)

1 pint (600 ml) water	1 lemon
¾ pint (450 ml) claret	2 cloves
8 oz (225 g) loaf sugar	1 inch cinnamon
2 oz (50 g) gelatine	

(Enough for six or seven people)

Put the gelatine, sugar, lemon peel and juice, cloves and cinnamon into a saucepan with the water, which should be boiling, simmer for ten minutes, add the claret, strain into a wet mould, turn out when set.

Note—Claret jelly can be cleared as lemon jelly if preferred, adding whites and shells of two eggs.

496 MARASCHINO JELLY

1½ pints (900 ml) water	½ inch (1 cm) cinnamon
juice and rind of 3 lemons	2 oz (50 g) gelatine
½ lb (225 g) sugar	1 wineglass maraschino
2 cloves	1 teaspoonful vanilla essence
shells and whites of 2 eggs	

(Enough to fill one and a half pint mould)

Put all the ingredients in a large saucepan with the crushed shells and whipped whites of eggs, whisk until boiling-

point is reached, allow it to boil for five to six minutes. Stand aside partly covered till the scum cracks, strain through a teacloth through which boiling water has been poured. When quite clear pour into a wet mould.

497 APPLE JELLY

2 lb (900 g) apples	1 oz (25 g) gelatine
½ pint (300 ml) water	few pistachio nuts
8 oz (225 g) loaf sugar	carmine colouring
rind and juice of 2 lemons	½ pint (300 ml) cream

(Enough for six or seven people)

Peel, core and slice the apples, put them in a stewpan with water, sugar, lemon rind and juice, simmer gently until the apples are tender. Remove the lemon peel and rub the apples through a hair sieve, dissolve the gelatine in a little water, strain it into the apple purée, colour a nice pink with a few drops of carmine, pour into a wet border mould, turn out when set on to a glass dish. Whip, sweeten and flavour the cream, and fill the centre, sprinkle with chopped pistachio nuts.

498 WINE JELLY

1½ pints (900 ml) water	½ pint (300 ml) sherry
2 oz (50 g) leaf gelatine	2 cloves
1 gill (150 ml) lemon juice	½ inch (1 cm) cinnamon
rind of 2 lemons	whites and shells of 2 eggs

(Enough to fill one and a half pint mould)

Make as for lemon jelly (see No 493). A little brandy may be added if liked after clearing, but it must be allowed for in the quantity of water used.

499 FRUIT JELLY

1 quart (1.1 litres) lemon jelly	apples
bananas	glacé cherries
grapes	pistachio nuts
oranges	carmine colouring

(Enough for eight or ten people)

Prepare the fruit very carefully, cut the bananas into slices, the oranges into quarters, removing the pips, cut the apples into fancy shapes and take out the seeds from the grapes. Decorate the bottom of a quart mould with cherries and chopped pistachio nuts, set it on ice with a little lemon jelly, arrange the fruit in layers, setting them with jelly, adding a little colouring getting darker each time, and allowing each layer to get firm before adding the next. Fill the mould quite full.

Note—The lemon jelly for this must be made with more gelatine in proportion to support the fruit.

Fresh fruit such as strawberries, apricots, raspberries can also be used.

500 STRAWBERRY MOUSSE

2 lb (900 g) strawberries	juice of ½ lemon
1 gill (150 ml) water	3 whites of eggs
¾ oz (20 g) leaf gelatine	carmine colouring
2 oz (50 g) castor sugar	

(Enough for five or six people)

Rub the strawberries through a sieve and use half a pint (300 ml) of the purée. Dissolve the gelatine in the water, strain it to the purée and add the sugar and lemon juice and carmine colouring. Whip the whites of eggs very stiffly,

stir lightly into the mixture when it is cool, turn into a fancy mould, which should be decorated with some whole strawberries, turn out when set.

Note—Almost any ripe fruit can be used in this way, such as raspberries, apricots, etc.

501 COFFEE CREAM

½ pint (300 ml) milk	½ oz (15 g) gelatine
2 eggs (yolks)	1 gill (150 ml) strong coffee or
2 oz (50 g) sugar	coffee essence to taste
½ pint (300 ml) cream	little wine jelly

(Enough for five or six people)

Dissolve the gelatine in a little water or milk, make a custard with the yolks of eggs and milk, cook till it thickens, add sugar, strain in the gelatine, add the coffee or coffee essence. When cool add the whipped cream, mask the mould with a little wine jelly. Allow it to set before pouring in the cream. To unmould dip in warm water and turn on to a cold dish.

502 PINEAPPLE CREAM

¼ pint (150 ml) milk	½ pint (300 ml) cream
3 yolks of eggs	¾ oz (20 g) gelatine
2 oz (50 g) sugar	3 or 4 oz (75 or 100 g) pineapple
¾ pint (450 ml) pineapple syrup	1 wineglass noyeau
lemon jelly	

(Enough for five or six people)

Make a custard with the milk and yolks of eggs, stir till it thickens, add the sugar, dissolve the gelatine in the syrup, strain into the custard. When cool add the whipped cream and pulped pineapple, flavour with noyeau. Mask the mould with lemon jelly. Then pour in the cream.

503 CHOCOLATE CREAM

½ pint (300 ml) milk	½ pint (300 ml) cream
3 yolks of eggs	vanilla essence
2 bars chocolate	pistachio nuts
sugar to taste	lemon or wine jelly
½ oz (15 g) leaf gelatine	

(Enough for five or six people)

Dissolve the gelatine in a little water, make a custard with the milk (in which the chocolate has been dissolved) and eggs, stir till it thickens, strain in the gelatine, add the sugar and allow it to cool. Whip the cream, and add it to the custard with the vanilla essence. Pour the custard into a mould masked with wine or lemon jelly and decorated with pistachio nuts.

504 GINGER CREAM

½ pint (300 ml) milk	½ oz (15 g) gelatine
3 yolks of eggs	½ gill (75 ml) ginger syrup
2 oz (50 g) castor sugar	lemon or wine jelly
2 oz (50 g) preserved ginger	glacé fruits
½ pint (300 ml) cream	

(Enough for five or six people)

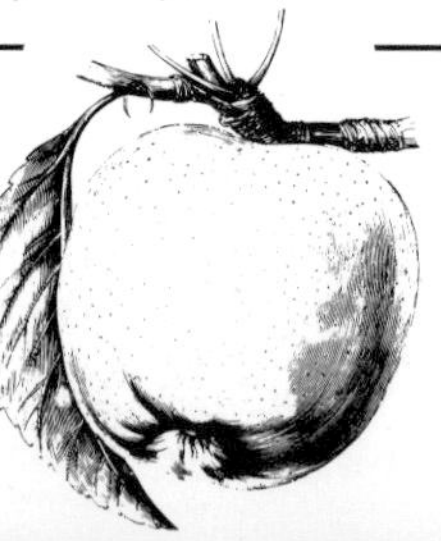

Rinse the mould with cold water, pour in a little jelly, place on ice to set, cut the glacé fruits and decorate the bottom of the mould, set it with a little more jelly, make a custard with the milk and eggs, stir till it thickens, add the sugar and the gelatine dissolved in the ginger syrup. When cool add the whipped cream and the ginger cut in small pieces. It must be nearly set before putting into the mould or the ginger will sink to the bottom.

505 RASPBERRY CREAM

raspberry jam	sugar
½ pint (300 ml) cream	noyeau
½ oz (15 g) gelatine	carmine colouring
lemon juice	lemon jelly

(Enough for five or six people)

Heat the jam, rub it through a hair sieve—enough to make half a pint (300 ml) of purée, dissolve the gelatine in a little water, strain into the purée, add lemon juice, and noyeau, colour with carmine. Whip the cream, stir to the purée, mask the mould with lemon jelly, pour in the cream. Turn out when set and garnish with chopped jelly.

Note—Fresh raspberries can be used. One lb (450 g) should make a half pint (300 ml) of purée.

506 STRAWBERRY CREAM

1 lb (450 g) strawberries	pistachio nuts
½ pint (300 ml) cream	carmine colouring
½ oz (15 g) leaf gelatine	lemon juice
2 or 3 oz (50 or 75 g) sugar	lemon or wine jelly

(Enough for five or six people)

Rinse a fancy mould with water, cover the bottom with jelly and set on ice, arrange some whole small strawberries with some chopped pistachio nuts and set with some more jelly. Pick the strawberries and rub them through a fine sieve, to the purée (about half a pint – 300 ml) add the lemon juice and gelatine dissolved in water and strained. Whip the cream and add to the other ingredients, sweeten and colour it, pour into the mould.

Note—A little brandy may be added if liked and strawberry jam can be used instead of the fresh fruit.

507 PISTACHIO CREAM

1 oz (25 g) pistachio nuts	2 oz (50 g) sugar
½ pint (300 ml) milk	little maraschino
½ pint (300 ml) cream	green colouring
½ oz (15 g) leaf gelatine	wine jelly

(Enough for five or six people)

Blanch and pound the pistachio nuts and boil them in the milk, dissolve the gelatine in a little water, strain it to the milk and add sugar and maraschino to flavour, mix some shredded pistachios with a little liquid wine jelly and pour it into the bottom of the mould and allow it to set on ice. Whip the cream, add lightly to the other ingredients, colour a pretty pale green and pour into the mould. Turn out when set and decorate with chopped jelly.

508 VANILLA CREAM

¾ pint (450 ml) cream	vanilla essence
½ oz (15 g) gelatine	preserved fruits to decorate
½ gill (75 ml) water	wine jelly
½ oz (15 g) sugar	

(Enough for five or six people)

Rinse the mould with cold water, pour in a little melted wine jelly, set on ice. When firm make a pretty decoration of preserved fruits, cover with jelly and allow to set. Dissolve the gelatine in a little water, whip the cream,

strain in the gelatine, add the sugar and vanilla to taste, stir all together carefully and pour in the mould.

509 GATEAU DE RIZ

½ pint (300 ml) milk	½ oz (15 g) gelatine
2 oz (50 g) rice	little lemon jelly
1 gill (150 ml) double cream	pistachio nuts
1½ oz (40 g) sugar	

(Enough for five or six people)

Cook the rice gently in the milk till tender, turn it into a basin and when nearly cold add the dissolved gelatine, sugar and the cream half whipped, and mix very lightly. Prepare a mould with a thin layer of lemon jelly and blanched and chopped pistachio nuts, allow it to set before putting in the rice, oil the sides of the mould slightly and allow the rice to set a little before putting it in. Turn out and serve with cream.

510 CHARLOTTE RUSSE

3 gills (450 ml) cream	savoy biscuits
¼ oz (10 ml) gelatine	vanilla essence
1 oz (25 g) sugar	sherry, ½ gill (75 ml)
1 white of egg	cherries and angelica

(Enough for five or six people)

Dissolve the gelatine in the sherry, choose a small cake tin with straight sides, decorate the bottom of the tin tastefully with cherries and angelica. Set the mixture by pouring in a little lemon jelly. When quite set split the biscuits, trim and line the sides of the tin, joining them with white of egg. Whip the cream slightly, add sugar, flavourings and dissolved gelatine, pour into the mould. Turn out when set and quite firm.

511 SHORT CRUST NO 1

½ lb (225 g) flour	pinch of salt
¼ lb (100 g) butter, lrd or dripping	water to mix

Sift the flour, add the salt, rub in the butter or lard finely with the tips of the fingers, mix to a stiff paste with cold water, turn on to a floured board, roll out lightly and it is ready for use.

Note—The flour for rolling out the pastry should be taken out of quantity weighed for use, or the proportions will be altered.

512 SHORT CRUST NO 2

½ lb (225 g) flour	1 teaspoonful baking powder
3½ oz (90 g) lard or dripping	water to mix
pinch of salt	

Make as for short crust No 1.

513 SUET CRUST

½ lb (225 g) flour	½ teaspoonful baking powder
4 oz (100 g) suet	wter to mix
pinch of salt	

Chop the suet finely, mix all the dry ingredients together, mix to a stiff paste with cold water, turn on to a floured board, roll out to size required and use.

Note—If a cheap crust is required use less suet and one teaspoonful baking powder.

514 FLAKY CRUST

½ lb (225 g) flour	pinch of salt
5 oz (150 g) butter or butter and lard	water to mix

Sift the flour, add the salt, divide the fat into four portions, rub one into the flour, mix to a paste with water, roll out on a floured board to an oblong shape, put one portion of fat on in flakes two-thirds of the way down, fold into three, press the edges together, roll out again, keeping the edges square, flake on another portion of fat and repeat until all the fat is rolled in, roll out to the shape required and use as required.

Note—This crust can be made some time before it is wanted if kept in a cool place.

515 ROUGH PUFF PASTRY

½ lb (225 g) flour	salt
6 oz (175 g) butter or butter and lard	lemon juice
	water to mix

Add the salt to the flour, cut the butter into large pieces and mix with the flour, make a well in the centre, moisten with the lemon juice and water and mix carefully until it is a stiff paste, roll out to an oblong shape, fold in three, roll out again, repeat the process, keeping the rough edges in the same direction till it has been rolled four times and does not look streaky. It is then ready to use for covering meat pies, patties or for sausage rolls, etc.

516 PUFF PASTRY

½ lb (225 g) flour	pinch of salt
½ lb (225 g) butter (fresh)	water to mix
1 teaspoonful lemon juice	

Rub one oz (25 g) of the butter into the flour, make a well in the centre, pour in the lemon juice and water gradually working the flour into a stiff paste. Press the butter in a clean cloth to squeeze out all the water, knead the pastry until quite smooth, roll out on a floured board to an oblong shape, keeping the corners square, place the butter on in a layer two-thirds of the way down the paste, fold in three, press the edges together, set aside for twenty minutes, roll out to the same shape, fold as before, press the edges, repeat this and set aside again in a cool place for twenty minutes, roll out the pastry again, repeating the process twice more, set aside for the third time for twenty minutes, roll out and use. The pastry has in all seven rolls and is set aside three times. Always after folding remember to keep the rough edges turned the same way each time.

Note—A marble slab is best to make puff pastry on, and a hot kitchen must be avoided to make it successfully. It can be made two or three days before use if kept in a cool place. Less butter can be used for a cheaper pastry.

517 BISCUIT CRUST

½ lb (225 g) flour	yolk of 1 egg
4½ oz (115 g) butter	pinch of salt
1 oz (25 g) sugar	little water

Rub the butter into the flour, add the sugar, mix with the beaten yolk and a little water, knead until smooth, roll out and use as required.

518 RAISED PIE CRUST

1 lb (450 g) flour	1 gill (150 ml) water
4 oz (100 g) lard	pinch of salt

Boil the water and lard together, make a well in the centre of the flour, pour in the liquid, mix to a stiff dough as quickly as possible, knead until smooth, keeping it warm.

Note—A yolk of egg may be added to make the crust richer and milk used instead of water.

519 CHOUX PASTE

6 oz (175 g) flour	½ pint (300 ml) water
2 oz (50 g) butter	4 eggs

Put the water and butter in a saucepan and bring to the boil, sift the flour and add to the water and butter, cook well until it leaves the sides of the saucepan, allow the mixture to cool slightly, then beat the eggs in one at a time very thoroughly, sweeten and flavour and use as required.

520 FRUIT TART

any fruit (apples, cherries, gooseberries, etc.)	water
	short crust No 1
sugar	

Prepare the fruit, half fill the pie dish, add sugar and water and fill up with fruit. Roll out the pastry, place the pie dish on it and cut out the top, brush the edges of the dish with water and line them with strips of pastry, moisten them and place on the top, press the edges together and cut round sharply, work the edges up with a knife and decorate them. Brush over the tart with water or whipped white of egg, sift with sugar and bake for about half an hour, serve hot or cold.

521 TARTLETS

jam	short crust No 1
	(see No 511 or 512)

Roll out the pastry, line some patty tins with it, put some jam in each, bake in a quick oven for about fifteen minutes.

Note—A crust of bread can be put in instead of the jam, and removed when the pastry is cooked, and warmed jam put in after.

Flaky, rough puff or puff pastry can be used for tartlets.

522 LEMON CHEESE CAKES

½ lb (225 g) loaf sugar	juice of 2 or 3 lemons
2 oz (50 g) butter	grated rind of 1 lemon
2 oz (50 g) grated biscuits	short, flaky or puff pastry (see No 512–516)
yolks of 3 eggs	
whites of 2 eggs	

Put the sugar, grated biscuit, butter, grated lemon rind and lemon juice into a saucepan and melt altogether, when a little cool stir in slowly the beaten eggs, cook slowly until it thickens, stirring occasionally. Line the patty tins with pastry, fill with the mixture and bake in a quick oven from fifteen to twenty minutes.

Note—A double saucepan is best for making the lemon curd mixture, and will keep well if tied down in a jar.

523 TREACLE PASTRY

golden syrup	pastry short crust (no 1 (see
bread crumbs	No 512)
lemon juice	

Roll the pastry out to a square shape, mix the bread crumbs into the syrup, add some lemon juice, spread the mixture on the pastry, not too near the edge, roll out the rest of the pastry to the same shape, place it on the top, fold over the edges, brush the pastry with white of egg, sprinkle with castor sugar, bake on a greased tin in a quick oven. When done cut across in neat sections, serve hot or cold.

Note—Flaky or rough puff pastry can be used.

524 MACAROON TARTS

¼ lb (100 g) ground almonds	white of 3 eggs
¼ lb (100 g) castor sugar	½ lb (225 g) puff or flaky
some raspberry jam	pastry (see No 514)

(Enough to make fourteen to sixteen tarts)

Line some patty tins with the pastry, cut some strips to go across the top, put a little jam in each, whip the whites to a stiff froth, stir in the sugar and ground almonds lightly, put a spoonful of this mixture in each tart and cross with two strips of pastry, bake in a quick oven from fifteen to twenty minutes.

525 CURD CHEESE CAKES

1 quart (1.1 litres) milk	little nutmeg
1 tablespoonful rennet	3 oz (75 g) ratafias
4 oz (100 g) butter	2 tablespoonfuls sherry
4 oz (100 g) sugar	currants
4 yolks and 1 white of egg	puff pastry (see No 516)
grated rind of 1 lemon	

Warm the milk, add the rennet and leave until cold and set, turn on to a hair sieve to separate the curds from the whey, cream the butter and the sugar together, add the well-beaten eggs, lemon rind, nutmeg, crushed ratafias and sherry and the curds. Line some patty tins with puff pastry, half fill with the mixture and bake in a quick oven from fifteen to twenty minutes.

526 MAIDS OF HONOUR

½ pint (300 ml) milk	2 yolks of eggs
½ pint (300 ml) warm water	2 tablespoonfuls clotted or
1 egg	whipped cream
juice of half a lemon	grated rind of half a lemon

For the Mixture

1 oz (25 g) ground almonds	cinnamon
1½ oz (40 g) currants	little brandy
½ oz (15 g) sugar	puff pastry (see No 516)
nutmeg	

Put the milk, warm water, egg and lemon juice into a lined pan, as the curd forms skim and put it on muslin to drain. Mix all the other ingredients together, then add the curds. Line some patty tins with puff pastry, put in the mixture and bake in a quick oven about fifteen to twenty minutes.

527 APPLE DUMPLINGS

6 or 8 apples	6 or 8 cloves
8 oz flour	sugar
4 oz lard and butter	water
pinch of salt	

(Enough for six or eight people)

Make the pastry with flour and butter and lard, add pinch of salt, mix stiffly with water, cut into as many pieces as apples, allowing roughly one oz. of pastry to each apple, peel and core the apples, keeping them whole, place each on a piece of pastry, fill the hole with sugar and a clove, work the pastry round the apple, brush over with water, sprinkle with sugar, bake till the apple is cooked – about twenty minutes.

528 DUTCH APPLE PUDDING

1 lb (450 g) apples	grated rind of ½ lemon or
2 oz (50 g) currants	orange
2 oz (50 g) peel	juice of ½ lemon
3 or 4 oz (75 or 100 g) sugar	flaky pastry, 10 oz (275 g)
½ teaspoonful mixed spice	(see No 514)

(Enough for eight or ten people)

Peel, core and chop or slice the apples, clean the currants and chop the peel, mix all the ingredients together, divide the pastry in half, roll out one portion to a square, put on a layer of the mixture, cover with other portion of pastry, fold over the edges, brush over with water, sprinkle with castor sugar, bake in a hot oven from half to three-quarters of an hour, cut into neat sections and serve hot or cold.

529 MINCE PIES

mincemeat (see No 553)	flaky or puff pastry (see No 514 or 516)

Roll the pastry out to about a quarter of an inch (0.5 cm) in thickness, cut into rounds, line some patty tins with some of the rounds, brush round the edges with water, put in some mincemeat, place on a cover, press the edges together, work them up with a knife, brush with white of egg, sprinkle with castor sugar, bake in a quick oven for about twenty minutes. Serve hot or cold.

530 SPANISH PUFFS

½ pint (300 ml) water	4 eggs
2 oz (50 g) butter	1 dessertspoonful castor sugar
6 oz (175 g) flour	vanilla essence

(Enough for five or six people)

Bring the water and the butter to the boil, add the sifted flour, cook well until it leaves the sides of the pan, allow it to cool, then beat the eggs in thoroughly one by one, add the sugar and vanilla essence, put the mixture into a forcing bag with a plain tube, force it through and cut off about an inch (2.5 cm) in length and drop it into hot fat about six or eight at a time. When they become twice the size, cut one in half to see if they are cooked. They usually take from eight to ten minutes. When cooked remove them from the fat, drain well on paper, sprinkle with castor sugar, serve piled up on a hot dish with a lace paper.

Note—Half this quantity makes a nice dish.

531 ECLAIRS

choux paste (see No 519)	vanilla essence
cream	chocolate icing
sugar	

(Enough to make twelve to fourteen eclairs)

Make the pastry as for "Spanish Puffs." Put the mixture into a forcing bag with a plain tube, force it through on to a greased baking tin in three-inch (7.5 cm) lengths, bake in a hot oven for half an hour, cover with another tin to keep them airtight. When done place on a pastry rack to cool, whip and flavour the cream, raise the pastry on one side of the eclair and fill it with cream, make the chocolate icing, dip the eclair in it and allow it to dry.

Note—Coffee icing can be used instead of chocolate.

532 ALMOND TARTLETS

2 oz (50 g) ground almonds	2 tablespoonfuls sherry
2 oz (50 g) cake crumbs	castor sugar
2 eggs	short crust No 1 (see No 511)
some strawberry jam	

(Enough to make ten or twelve tartlets)

Line some patty tins with the pastry, put a teaspoonful of strawberry jam in each, separate the yolks from the whites of eggs, mix the ground almonds, crumbs, sherry, yolks and sugar (to taste) together and put some in each tart, whip the whites stiffly, add some castor sugar and a few drops of almond essence, pile some of this meringue on top of the almond mixture, bake in a moderate oven about thirty minutes.

533 CUSTARD TARTLETS

½ pint (300 ml) milk	sugar to taste
2 eggs	nutmeg
½ oz (15 g) corn flour	short crust No 1 (see No 511)

(Enough to make ten or twelve tartlets)

Line some patty tins with the pastry, mix the cornflour smoothly with some of the milk, add it with the well-beaten eggs to the remainder of the milk, sweeten to taste, put some of the mixture into each tartlet, bake in a moderate oven about thirty minutes.

Note—Any flavouring, such as vanilla or almond, can be used. The nutmeg should be grated on the top.

534 BAKEWELL PUDDING

rough puff pastry (see No 515)	flour
egg	½ teaspoonful baking powder
its weight in butter	2 tablespoonfuls jam
sugar	1 white of egg

(Enough for seven or eight people)

Line a plate with the pastry, work up the edges and decorate them, put the jam in the middle, cream the butter and sugar together, add the egg and a little of the flour and beat well, stir in the rest of the flour and the baking powder, spread this over the jam. Bake in a quick oven for thirty minutes, whip the white of egg stiffly with some castor sugar, pile it roughly on the top and bake till crisp.

535 PINEAPPLE PUDDING

½ tin pineapple chunks	2 eggs
2 oz (50 g) butter	1½ oz (40 g) sugar
2 oz (50 g) flour	short or flaky pastry (see No
¾ pint (450 ml) milk	511 or 514)

(Enough for six or seven people)

Line the edges of a pie dish with pastry, making a double border, cut the pineapple into small pieces, put into the pie dish with a little of the syrup, make a sauce with the butter, flour and milk, stir till it boils, cook for five minutes, let it cool and add the beaten yolks, sugar and little syrup, pour over the pineapple. Bake in the oven till the pastry is cooked, whip the whites stiffly with castor sugar added, pile on the top, decorate with a few pieces of pineapple, bake till crisp.

536 LEMON PUDDING

2 oz (50 g) cake or bread crumbs	2 eggs
	rind and juice of 2 lemons
3 oz (75 g) butter	short or flaky pastry (see No
3 oz (75 g) sugar	511 or 514)

(Enough for five or six people)

Line the edges and decorate a pie dish with pastry, cream the butter and the sugar together, add the eggs and cake crumbs and beat well, pour the mixture into the pie dish, bake in a moderate oven for three-quarters of an hour, till the mixture feels firm.

537 APPLE AMBER PUDDING

2 lb (900 g) apples	3 eggs
1 lemon	short of flaky pastry (see No
1½ oz (40 g) butter	511 or 514)
3 oz (75 g) sugar	

(Enough for six or seven people)

Peel, core and slice the apples, put them in a stewpan with the grated lemon rind, juice and sugar, cook till quite tender, then pass it through a sieve, add the well-beaten yolks of eggs. Line the edges of a pie dish and decorate them with pastry, pour in the apple mixture and bake in a quick oven for about half an hour, whip the whites to a stiff froth with a little sugar, pile roughly on the top of the pudding, sift over some sugar and bake till crisp.

538 COBURG PUDDING

6 or 8 apples	strip of lemon rind
marmalade	3 eggs
2 oz (50 g) cornflour	sugar
1 pint (600 ml) milk	short or flaky crust (see No 511 or 514)

(Enough for six or seven people)

Stew the apples till tender, line and decorate the edges of a pie dish with pastry, put in a layer of stewed apples, cover this with a little marmalade, then put another layer of apples, mix the cornflour smoothly with some of the milk, put on the remainder to boil with the lemon rind, add the cornflour, stir till it thickens and cook thoroughly, add the beaten yolks of eggs, pour over the apples in the pie dish

and bake in a moderate oven till pastry is cooked. Whip the whites stiffly, pile on the top, sprinkle with sugar and crisp in the oven.

539 LEMON PIE

1 tablespoonful cornflour	2 eggs
1 gill (150 ml) cream or milk	sugar
2 lemons	short or flaky pastry
¼ teaspoonful cinnamon	

(Enough for six or seven people)

Line a plate or shallow pie dish with pastry, decorate it, mix the cornflour smoothly with the cream or milk, add the cinnamon, sugar, grated rind and juice of lemons and the beaten yolks of eggs, pour the mixture into the plate or dish, bake in a quick oven about half an hour, whip the whites stiffly and pile roughly on the top, sprinkle over a little castor sugar, bake till crisp and a pale brown colour.

540 MANCHESTER PUDDING

4 oz (100 g) bread crumbs	1 oz (25 g) sugar
1 pint (600 ml) milk	lemon rind
2 eggs	short or flaky crust
jam	

(Enough for five or six people)

Boil the milk with strips of lemon rind, strain on to the crumbs, add the sugar. When cool add the yolks of the eggs, grease a pie dish, line the edges with pastry, put a layer of jam on the bottom, pour in the mixture and bake for three-quarters of an hour. Whip the whites to a stiff froth, adding some sugar, pile roughly on the top of the pudding, sift over with castor sugar, bake till crisp.

541 CARAMEL CUSTARD

4 yolks of eggs	10 lumps of sugar
¾ pint (450 ml) milk	½ gill (75 ml) water
1 oz (25 g) sugar	1 teaspoonful lemon juice
vanilla essence	

(Enough for three or four people)

To make the caramel put the water, sugar and lemon juice in a saucepan and boil together until a rich brown. Pour into a warm mould and turn the tin round until it is coated all over. For the custard beat up the yolks of eggs, add the sugar and vanilla essence, add the milk, strain it into the mould, cover with greased paper and bake very slowly in a moderate oven, standing the mould in a flat tin with water in it. Turn out carefully and serve hot or cold.

542 SUMMER PUDDING

any suitable fruit	bread
sugar	custard sauce (see No 657)

Stew the fruit with sugar, line a pudding basin with thin slices of stale bread, fitting to a round at the bottom, pour in the stewed fruit gradually, allowing the bread to get well soaked with the syrup, place on a round of bread,

cover with a plate and allow to stand till quite cold and set, turn out and serve with thick custard sauce or cream.

Note—The best fruits to use for this pudding are raspberries, red currants and black currants.

543 PINEAPPLE SNOW

½ tin of pineapple	whites of 3 eggs
3 oz (75 g) loaf sugar	wineglass of sherry
1 oz (25 g) loaf gelatine	

(Enough for five or six people)

Dissolve the gelatine in some of the pineapple syrup and a little water, cut the pineapple into small pieces, add to the syrup with the sugar and simmer for ten minutes, add the sherry and allow the mixture to cool, whisk the whites of eggs to a stiff froth and add the mixture and whisk till nearly set. Pile roughly in a shallow glass dish, decorate with some pieces of pineapple and serve.

544 APPLE CHARLOTTE

apples	2 oz (50 g) butter
stale bread	sugar
3 or 4 cloves	custard sauce (see No 657)

(Enough for four or five people)

Stew the apples (peeled and cored) till tender with sugar and cloves. Line a cake tin with bread dipped in clarified butter, join the edges together with egg. Pour in the stewed apples, cover with a round of bread dipped in butter, cover with buttered paper and bake in a quick oven, turning round to brown all sides alike, turn out carefully and pour custard sauce round.

545 COLD LEMON PUDDING

4 sponge cakes	½ pint (300 ml) cold water
2 oz (50 g) sugar	some blanched almonds
juice of 2 oranges	custard sauce or whipped cream
juice of 2 lemons	

(Enough for five or six people)

Add the juice of oranges and lemons to the water with the sugar, put the sponge cakes in a glass dish and soak well with the liquid. When quite moist stick with blanched almonds cut in strips and pour over a thick custard or whipped cream.

546 GOOSEBERRY FOOL

2 lb (900 g) gooseberries	1 gill (150 ml) water
½ lb (225 g) sugar	½ pint (300 ml) custard or cream

(Enough for six or seven people)

Make a syrup by boiling water and sugar together, put in the gooseberries and cook till tender. Rub through a sieve, mix with the cream or custard, pour into a glass dish and serve cold.

547 STEWED PEARS

2 lb (900 g) pears	4 cloves
6 oz (175 g) sugar	1 inch (2.5 cm) cinnamon
1 pint (600 ml) water	strip of lemon peel
little claret	carmine colouring

(Enough for six or seven people)

Peel the pears, cut them in half, take out the core, put them in a stewing jar with the water, sugar, lemon rind and spices, add the claret and some drops of carmine, cover with the peelings and stew gently in the oven for three or four hours. When cool put into a glass dish and pour the syrup over.

548 TRIFLE

6 or 8 sponge cakes	¼ lb (100 g) ratafias
2 eggs and 2 yolks	1 gill (150 ml) sherry
1 oz (25 g) castor sugar	2 tablespoonfuls brandy
apricot jam	1 oz (25 g) almonds
½ pint (300 ml) milk	2 oz (50 g) preserved fruits
½ pint (300 ml) cream	essence of vanilla

(Enough for eight or ten people)

Cut the sponge cakes in slices and spread with jam, put them together again and arrange in a glass dish with the ratafias, soak well with the sherry and brandy, make a custard with two whole eggs and two yolks extra, stir till it thickens, sweeten and flavour with vanilla and let it become quite cold. Just before serving pour the custard over the cakes, whip the cream, add sugar and flavouring. Force it over the mould and decorate with the preserved fruits and blanched and shredded almonds.

549 "POACHED EGGS"

sponge cake mixture	½ pint (300 ml) cream
½ tin apricots	few pistachio nuts

(Enough for eight or ten people)

Cut the cake into rounds, put into a glass dish and soak with some apricot syrup. Whip the cream, put a spoonful neatly on each round of cake, press half an apricot in the middle of the cream and sprinkle over a little finely-chopped pistachio nuts.

550 FRUIT SALAD

For Summer—	*For Winter—*
¼ lb (100 g) strawberries	2 tangerines
2 oz (50 g) white grapes	3 bananas
2 oz (50 g) black grapes	2 apples
raspberries	few pineapple chunks
currants (red and white)	¼ tin apricots
1 orange	¼ lb (100 g) prunes
juice of 1 lemon	juice of 1 lemon
wine or liqueur	wine or liquer
½ pint (300 ml) water	½ pint (300 ml) water
½ lb (225 g) loaf sugar	½ lb (225 g) loaf sugar
almonds and pistachio nuts	

(Enough for ten or twelve people)

Prepare all the fruit very carefully, removing all stems, seeds, pips and skin, cut in convenient sized pieces, place in a bowl, pour over some syrup made by boiling the sugar and water together for ten to fifteen minutes, add the wine or liqueur flavouring, allow to steep for several hours. Place in a salad bowl, decorate with almonds blanched and shredded and chopped pistachios. Keep on ice if possible.

Note—The fruits used can be varied according to taste and season, but as many kinds as possible should be used.

In a salad made with fresh juicy fruits less syrup will be required. In both kinds it should be coloured with a few drops of carmine.

551 COMPÔTE OF FRUIT

fruits (all kinds in season)	lemon juice
½ lb (225 g) loaf sugar	noyeau or any liqueur
½ pint (300 ml) water	

Make a syrup with the sugar and water, boil for ten minutes, prepare the fruit carefully, cut into neat dice or fancy shapes and stew *very slightly*. Turn into a basin and allow to stand till cold, add noyeau or any other liqueur to taste, put in a salad bowl or glass dish, piling up fruit in centre, colour the syrup with a few drops of carmine, decorate with blanched and shredded almonds and pistachio nuts.

552 ICE PUDDING

¾ pint (450 ml) milk	2 oz (50 g) dried fruits
1 egg	½ oz (15 g) citron
yolks of 2 eggs	1 gill (150 ml) cream
2 oz (50 g) loaf sugar	1 tablespoonful brandy
½ oz (15 g) pistachio nuts	2 tablespoonfuls maraschino

(Enough for six or seven people)

Make a custard with the eggs and milk, when cold put it into a freezing machine. When half frozen add the dried fruits cut in pieces, candied peel, chopped pistachios, brandy and maraschino, etc., and lastly the whipped cream. When well frozen pack into a pudding mould and leave to freeze in an ice cave till required.

553 MINCEMEAT

1 lb (450 g) raisins	½ lb (225 g) Demerara sugar
1 lb (450 g) currants	1 teaspoonful cinnamon
1 lb (450 g) sultanas	¼ of a nutmeg
1 lb (450 g) apples	rind and juice of 2 lemons
½ lb (225 g) candied peel	2 tablespoonfuls orange
½ lb (225 g) suet	marmalade
pinch of salt	¼ pint (150 ml) rum

Stone the raisins, chop the suet, peel and core the apples, wash the currants, chop all finely except the currants. These should be added last with the spices, salt, marmalade and rum. Mix well together, put into jars, tie down and store in a dry place.

Note.—This quantity will make about 6 lb (2.75 kg) mincemeat. Brandy may be used instead of rum if liked.

554 MERINGUES

4 whites of eggs	cream
8 oz (225 g) castor sugar	flavouring

Cut some strips of stiff white paper, rub them well with white wax, place them on a baking sheet. Whip the whites

of eggs very stiffly, then stir in the sugar as lightly as possible, put the mixture in a forcing bag with a plain tube, force on to the prepared paper in egg shapes. Sift with icing sugar, bake in a slow oven till crisp, remove from the paper, scoop out carefully the soft part, place them the hollow side upwards and put back in the oven to dry. Fill with whipped and flavoured cream, joining two together.

555 BANANA TRIFLE

4 to 6 bananas	apricot jam
½ gill (75 ml) sherry	½ pint (300 ml) cream

Take off the skins of the bananas, cut them lengthways, spread with jam and lay them in a glass dish, pour over the sherry and allow them to soak. Just before serving pour over the cream, which should be half whipped, garnish with some banana on the top.

556 RICE SOUFFLÉ

2 oz (50 g) rice	3 eggs
3 oz (75 g) butter	½ pint (300 ml) milk
3 oz (75 g) sugar	vanilla essence

(Enough for four)

Wash the rice, boil it in the milk with butter and sugar, when cool stir in the yolks of eggs and add vanilla, whisk the whites very stiffly, fold them lightly into the rice, pour into a well buttered mould decorated with cherries and angelica, steam very gently for about forty-five minutes, serve with jam sauce (see No 650).

557 ALMOND PUDDING

3 oz (75 g) ground almonds	2 oz (50 g) sugar
1 pint (600 ml) milk	2½ oz (65 g) ground rice
2 eggs	2 oz (50 g) browned almonds

(Enough for three or four people)

Mix the ground rice with a little milk, boil the remainder, pour over the rice, return to the pan and stir till it thickens, add 1½ oz (40 g) ground almonds, beaten eggs, sugar and some of the browned almonds. Butter a pie dish, line it with the remainder of ground almonds, pour in the mixture, bake for fifteen minutes, sprinkle the top with a few browned almonds.

558 SNOWDEN PUDDING

½ pint (300 ml) bread crumbs	few raisins
2 oz (50 g) suet	3 oz (75 g) sugar
2 oz (50 g) flour	vanilla
2 oz (50 g) glacé cherries	jam sauce (see No 650)

(Enough for four or five people)

Butter the mould well, stone the raisins, decorate the sides of the mould with them, chop the suet finely, mix with the flour, bread crumbs, sugar, cherries, moisten with milk, add vanilla essence, pour into the prepared mould, cover with greased paper and steam for one and a half hours, serve with jam sauce.

559 APPLES AND RICE

3 or 4 apples	½ gill (75 ml) water
2 oz (50 g) rice	lemon essence
3 oz (75 g) sugar	liqueur
1 gill (150 ml) cream	4 or 5 sheets gelatine

(Enough for three or four people)

Bake the apples, rub through a sieve, boil the rice, drain, rinse with hot water and dry. Mix the rice with apple pulp, add sugar, lemon essence and liqueur if liked, dissolve the gelatine in the water, strain into the mixture, when on the point of setting pour into a mould, when set turn out and decorate with whipped cream and glacé cherries.

560 BARONESS PUDDING

1 gill (150 ml) cake crumbs	2 eggs
3 oz (75 g) suet	1 teaspoonful cinnamon
2 oz (50 g) flour	lemon juice
sugar	

(Enough for four or five people)

Mix all the dry ingredients together, moisten with the eggs, add the lemon juice, pour into a well buttered pie dish, bake for forty-five minutes, turn out and serve with jam sauce (see No 650).

561 BOMBE OF FRUITS

A 6d (20 cm) sponge cake	2 oz (50 g) sugar
macédoine of fruit	almonds
apricot jam	1 lemon

(Enough for four people)

Scoop out the centre of the sponge cake, fill with the macédoine of fruit, boil two tablespoonfuls apricot jam with water, lemon juice and sugar, strain over the cake and sprinkle with shredded almonds and serve.

562 CINNAMON PUDDING

1 lb (450 g) prunes	½ lb (225 g) bread crumbs
2 oz (50 g) sugar	2 eggs
2 teaspoonfuls cinnamon	

(Enough for three or four people)

Soak the prunes, stew till quite soft, remove stones and rub through a sieve, mix all the ingredients together, pour into a buttered basin or mould, steam for three-quarters of an hour, serve with a sweet sauce (see No 656).

563 BANANA PUDDING

6 sponge cakes	2 oz (50 g) ground almonds
½ pint (300 ml) custard	¼ pint (150 ml) sherry
6 bananas	1 tablespoonful jam

(Enough for five or six people)

Spread the cakes with the jam, cut the bananas in slices and lay them on the bottom of a glass dish, lay in the sponge cakes and ground almonds, soak well with sherry, pour over the custard, decorate with slices of banana and chopped pistachio nuts.

145

564 COCOANUT PUDDING

½ lb (225 g) desiccated cocoanut	2 oz (50 g) preserved ginger
3 oz (75 g) cake crumbs	1 oz (25 g) glacé cherries
2 oz (50 g) butter	3 eggs
	jam sauce (see No 650)

(Enough for five or six people)

Well butter a mould, decorate the bottom with cherries, boil the butter and cocoanut in the milk, let it reduce, add the sugar, when cool add the ginger, yolks of eggs beaten and the whites whipped stiffly, pour carefully into the prepared mould and steam for two hours, serve the cocoanut with jam sauce.

565 ICED PEACHES

1 tin of peaches	½ pint (300 ml) raspberry
½ pint (300 ml) vanilla ice	sauce (see No 469)

(Enough for four or five people)

Lay the peaches on ice, put the vanilla ice in the centre of a dish, place the peaches round and pour over the iced raspberry sauce and serve.

566 COFFEE PUDDING

1 gill (150 ml) black coffee	sugar to taste
3 sponge cakes	2 oz (50 g) almonds
2 eggs	1 gill (150 ml) milk

(Enough for three or four people)

Break the sponge cakes into small pieces, beat the eggs, add sugar to taste, coffee, milk and almonds, pour over the sponge cakes and allow to soak for a few minutes. Well butter a mould or cake tin, pour in the mixture, cover with paper, steam for three-quarters of an hour, serve with a sweet sauce (see No 656).

567 COLLEGE PUDDINGS

½ lb (225 g) flour	2 eggs
4 oz (100 g) suet	grated rind of lemon
4 oz (100 g) brown sugar	2 oz (50 g) bread crumbs
4 oz (100 g) currants	½ gill (75 ml) milk

(Enough for four or five people)

Mix all the dry ingredients, moisten with the eggs and milk, fill some small buttered dariole moulds with the mixture, place in a shallow stewpan, cover with buttered paper and steam for one hour, serve with wine sauce.

568 PRINCESS PUDDING

6 medium-sized apples	½ pint (300 ml) water
2 tablespoonfuls marmalade	¼ pint (150 ml) cream
2 oz (50 g) sugar	cherries and angelica

(Enough for four people)

Peel the apples and remove the core with a cutter without breaking them. Bake in a moderate oven with the sugar and water. When cold fill up the centres with marmalade. Arrange neatly on a dish. Whip the cream stiffly, sweeten and flavour it, pipe over the apples, decorate with cherries and angelica.

569 CHESTNUT CREAM

½ lb (225 g) chestnuts	½ oz (15 g) gelatine
½ pint (300 ml) cream	sugar to taste
¼ pint (150 ml) milk	

(Enough for four or five people)

Melt the butter in a stewpan, add flour and mix till smooth, add the milk and stir till it boils. Add the sugar, vanilla and eggs. Drop from a teaspoon into hot fat and fry four minutes. Serve hot on fancy paper sprinkled with castor sugar.

570 BEIGNETS SOUFFLE

1 oz butter	1 egg
1½ oz flour	1 teaspoonful sugar
1 gill milk	vanilla flavouring

(Enough for three or four people)

Melt the butter in a stewpan, add flour and mix till smooth, add the milk and stir till it boils. Add the sugar, vanilla and eggs. Drop from a teaspoon into hot fat and fry for four minutes. Serve hot on fancy paper sprinkled with castor sugar.

571 PRUNE PUDDING

½ lb (225 g) prunes	sugar
4 oz (100 g) bread crumbs	lemon juice
2 eggs	little port wine

(Enough for three or four people)

Stew the prunes in water with lemon juice and sugar, pass through a sieve and to every cupful of pulp add half teacupful of crumbs and one beaten egg, mix well together, sweeten if necessary and add a little port wine. Put the mixture into a greased mould and steam for 1½ hours. Serve with the following sauce.

Prune Sauce

Take some of the prune purée, add port wine and sugar, thicken with a teaspoonful of arrowroot.

572 BISHOP'S PUDDING

1 pint (600 ml) milk	1½ oz (40 g) sugar
2 oz (50 g) ground rice	2 eggs
2 oz (50 g) ground almonds	marmalade

(Enough for four or five people)

Mix ground rice smoothly with a little of the milk, boil the remainder and pour over the rice, add almonds, sugar and well-beaten eggs. Pour into a pie dish and bake for twenty minutes. Serve hot with a layer of marmalade on top.

573 CUSTARD PUDDING

½ pint (300 ml) milk	vanilla essence
2 eggs	1 tablespoonful jam
12 ratafias	sugar to taste

(Enough for three or four people)

Beat the eggs, add the milk, crushed ratafias, sugar and vanilla. Put jam in the bottom of a dish, pour over the custard, bake gently in a moderate oven for half an hour.

574 APPLES À LA CRÈME

6 apples	½ pint (300 ml) water
3 whites of eggs	cherries and angelica
2 tablespoonfuls sugar	cream

(Enough for three people)

Put the apples in a dish with the sugar and water, bake gently till soft. When cold cover with stiffly beaten white of egg, bake till set, decorate with cherries and angelica and serve with cream.

575 MARASCHINO PUDDING

½ pint (300 ml) cake crumbs	2 oz (50 g) ground almonds
½ pint (300 ml) milk	2 eggs
1 oz (25 g) sugar	1 tablespoonful maraschino

(Enough for four or five people)

Mix all ingredients together, place in a buttered mould, cover with greased paper, steam for three-quarters of an hour. Turn out and serve with jam sauce (see No 650).

576 PRALINE SOUFFLÉ

½ pint (300 ml) thick cream	½ oz (15 g) gelatine
2 oz (50 g) almond rock	sugar to taste
1 oz (25 g) grated chocolate	

(Enough for four or five people)

Crush the rock, whip the cream, sweeten and add melted chocolate and crushed rock, dissolve the gelatine in a little water, add carefully, pour the mixture into a wetted mould, turn out when set and decorate.

577 CORNETS À LA CRÈME

¼ lb (100 g) good short pastry	cocoanut
(No 511)	whipped cream
jam	

(Enough for three or four people)

Make the pastry, roll out thinly, cut into rounds and fold over round cornet tins, bake about fifteen minutes, when cold brush with jam, dip into cocoanut. Fill the centres with flavoured whipped cream.

578 APRICOT PATTIES

½ lb (225 g) puff pastry	whipped cream
½ pint (300 ml) apricot pulp	apricot jam

(Enough for three or four people)

Make puff pastry patties in the usual way. When cold fill the centres with jam, cover with apricot purée, decorate with whipped cream, piped on with a rose tube.

579 SWISS PUDDING

6 sponge cakes	custard
2 oz (50 g) whole almonds	jam
1 gill (150 ml) lemon syrup	½ pint (300 ml) cream

(Enough for three or four people)

Spread the sponge cakes with jam, lay in a glass dish, soak well with lemon syrup, pour over a good custard, decorate with whipped cream, sprinkle over shredded almonds.

580 CAMBRIDGE PUDDING

½ pint (300 ml) bread crumbs	4 oz (100 g) currants
3 oz (75 g) flour	3 oz (75 g) suet
2 eggs	1 gill (150 ml) sherry
¼ lb (100 g) sultanas	jam sauce (No 650)
2 oz (50 g) peel	

(Enough for five or six people)

Prepare all the ingredients and mix well together, moisten with beaten eggs and sherry, pour into a buttered mould, cover with paper, steam for two hours, serve the pudding with jam sauce.

581 NORMANDY PUDDING

3 eggs	½ tin pine chunks
½ oz (15 g) butter	little sugar

(Enough for two people)

Make a purée by passing the pine through a sieve. Make it hot. Whip the whites of the eggs stiffly with a pinch of sugar, stir in the beaten yolks, melt the butter in an omelet pan, pour in the mixture and allow to set. Put in a quick oven for a minute or so to set the top. Dish on a hot dish with the pine purée folded in the centre and serve at once.

582 MARQUISE PUDDING

4 eggs	½ gill (75 ml) milk
4 oz (100 g) butter	3 tablespoonfuls apricot jam
4 oz (100 g) macaroons	1 oz (25 g) pistachio nuts
4 oz (100 g) castor sugar	wine sauce
¼ oz (10 g) ground rice	

(Enough for five or six people)

Cream the butter and sugar together and beat in the yolks one at a time, mix the ground rice with the milk and stir into the mixture with the crushed macaroons and jam. Whip the whites to a stiff froth, stir in lightly with half the pistachio nuts blanched and chopped. Well butter a mould, sprinkle over the rest of the chopped pistachios, pour in the mixture and steam for 1½ hours. Serve with wine sauce.

583 SULTANA PUDDING

¼ lb (100 g) butter	6 oz (175 g) sultanas
¼ lb (100 g) sugar	2 eggs
6 oz (175 g) flour	little milk
	½ teaspoonful baking powder

(Enough for five or six people)

Cream the butter and sugar, add the eggs and flour alternately and beat well, clean the sultanas carefully and add also a little milk if necessary, and lastly the baking powder. Pour into a prepared basin or mould, cover with greased paper and steam for 1½ hours. Serve with a sweet sauce (see No 656).

584 MARBLE JELLY

2 pints (1.1 litres) lemon jelly	sherry
maraschino	colourings

(Enough for five or six people)

Take half the jelly and colour it green and flavour with maraschino, colour the other half pale pink and add a little sherry. Whisk both colours separately till quite frothy and almost set. Put a little plain lemon jelly in the bottom of the mould and let it set, put in a small piece of green jelly and a small piece of pink, set with plain jelly, repeat the process till all jelly is used. When set, turn out and decorate with chopped jelly.

585 LECHE CREAM

1½ pints (900 ml) milk	2 eggs
4 oz (100 g) flour	rind of ½ lemon
2 oz (50 g) castor sugar	cinnamon
1 oz (25 g) ratafias	little jam

(Enough for five or six people)

Mix the flour and sugar smoothly with some of the cold milk, put the remainder on to boil with the lemon rind. Spread the bottom of a dish with jam, sprinkle over half of the ratafias crushed. Strain the boiling milk over the flour, return to the saucepan and stir till it boils and thickens, add the eggs well beaten, pour over the jam, sprinkle the top with cinnamon and decorate with whole ratafias.

586 FRENCH PANCAKES

2 oz (50 g) flour	1 oz (25 g) butter
2 eggs	½ gill (75 ml) milk
2½ oz (65 g) castor sugar	½ gill (75 ml) brandy
2 oranges	orange sauce (see No 653)

(Enough for four or five people)

Sift the flour into a basin with ½ oz (15 g) castor sugar, mix smoothly with the eggs, oiled butter and milk, beat well. Stir in the brandy and the grated orange rind, set aside for an hour or more. When required fry in thin pancakes in clarified butter, dust with sugar, roll up and serve very hot with orange sauce.

587 PINEAPPLE SNOW

tin pine chunks	1 gill (150 ml) water
3 oz (75 g) loaf sugar	whites of 3 eggs
1 oz (25 g) gelatine	crushed macaroons
1 glass sherry	

(Enough for four or five people)

Cut up the pine, put it with the juice and the sugar in a stewpan and simmer for ten minutes. Dissolve the gelatine in a little water, add with one gill (150 ml) water and the sherry. Cook for a few minutes, pour into a basin and allow to cool. When beginning to set add the stiffly beaten whites of eggs. Whisk in a cool place till quite light and frothy. Pile up on a glass dish, sprinkle over some crushed macaroons and serve.

588 BANANA CHARLOTTE

sponge fingers	½ gill (75 ml) lemon or wine
4 bananas	jelly
1 oz (25 g) castor sugar	½ gill (75 ml) milk
½ oz (15 g) gelatine	½ pint (300 ml) cream

(Enough for four or five people)

Line a plain charlotte mould with sponge fingers, split and joined together with white of egg, decorate the bottom of the mould. Dissolve the gelatine in the milk, rub the peeled bananas through a sieve and warm the purée with the jelly, dissolved gelatine and sugar. Pour into a basin and allow it to cool. Whip the cream and stir in lightly, pour into the prepared mould, set on ice, unmould carefully and serve.

Note.—Gooseberry Charlotte can be prepared in much the same way.

589 SPANISH FRITTERS

4 sponge cakes	sugar
ground almonds	apricots
lemon juice	pancake batter (see No 487)

(Enough for four or five people)

Make one pint (600 ml) pancake batter and let it stand an hour. Cut the sponge cakes across, hollow out the centre, taking care not to break the shape, put in half an apricot, cover with a thin layer of almond paste made with ground almonds, sugar and lemon juice. Dip in pancake batter, drop into hot fat, fry a golden brown, drain and sprinkle with sugar and dish on a fancy paper.

Note.—Cooked apples, peaches, strawberries, or bananas can be used instead of apricots.

590 OMELETTE SOUFFLÉ

3 yolks and 5 whites of eggs	1 oz (25 g) cornflour
2 oz (50 g) castor sugar	flavouring

(Enough for four people)

Mix the yolks and sugar well together in a basin, add the flavouring and the cornflour, whisk the whites to a stiff froth and lightly add to the yolks, pile the mixture high on a buttered plated dish. Shape the sides with a knife, make a hole in the centre, bake in a moderate oven for about fifteen to twenty minutes, dust with sugar and serve.

591 MALTESE PUDDING

½ lb (225 g) Madeira cake	½ pint (300 ml) milk
½ pint (300 ml) orange juice	3 yolks of eggs
grated rind of 3 oranges	2 whites of eggs
1 oz (25 g) cornflour	custard sauce (see No 657)

(Enough for five or six people)

Mix the cornflour smoothly with the milk and stir till it boils. Rub the cake through a sieve, add to it the orange juice, grated rind, yolks of eggs and milk, and cornflour when cool. Whip the whites stiffly and stir lightly into the other ingredients. Pour the mixture into a well-buttered mould and steam for two hours. Turn out and serve with a good custard sauce, flavoured with orange.

592 DIPLOMATIC PUDDING

½ pint (300 ml) milk	2 oz (50 g) macaroons
3 yolks of eggs	2 oz (50 g) glacé cherries
1 oz (25 g) castor sugar	1 oz (25 g) angelica
½ gill (75 ml) cream	½ gill (75 ml) water
1 oz (25 g) gelatine	½ pint (300 ml) wine jelly

(Enough for five or six people)

Decorate the bottom of a plain mould with cherries and angelica, set with wine jelly on ice. Whip the remainder of the jelly and line the inside of the mould with it. Warm the milk and mix with the yolks of eggs, stir till it thickens but do not let it boil, add the sugar and pour over the crushed macaroons. Dissolve the gelatine in the water, strain into the mixture and add the cream. Put into the prepared mould to set. Turn out and pour a sauce round made with apricot jam, a little water, maraschino flavouring, boiled, strained and allowed to cool.

593 OSTEND PUDDING

6 oz (175 g) bread or cake crumbs	1 oz (25 g) almonds
3 oz (75 g) butter	3 oz (75 g) preserved ginger
4 oz (100 g) castor sugar	4 eggs
3 oz (75 g) suet	½ gill (75 ml) sherry
	ginger sauce (see No 468)

(Enough for four or five people)

Cream the butter and sugar together, add the cake crumbs, suet, almonds and ginger finely chopped, beat up four yolks and two whites with the sherry and stir altogether. Whip the remaining two whites to a stiff froth and add lightly. Decorate a well-buttered mould with pieces of ginger and almonds, pour in the mixture and steam for two hours. Serve with ginger sauce.

594 COMPÔTE OF STRAWBERRIES

4 oz (100 g) rice	strawberries
1 pint (600 ml) milk	syrup
½ pint (300 ml) cream	colouring
sugar	

(Enough for three or four people)

Boil the rice in the milk till quite tender, add sugar to taste and flavouring. When cold add a little cream and place in a mound on a glass dish. Arrange ripe picked strawberries on the mound. Whip the cream stiffly, decorate the dish with it, using a rose forcing pipe, pour a little coloured syrup round the dish.

Note.—Any suitable fruit, such as peaches, pears and bananas, can be served in the same way.

595 RAINBOW CREAMS

½ pint (300 ml) cream	little lemon jelly
½ pint (300 ml) custard	flavourings
1 oz (25 g) gelatine	colouring

(Enough for seven or eight people)

Dissolve the gelatine in a little water and add to the custard. Whip the cream and stir in lightly, divide the mixture into three portions, leave one white, one a pretty green and one pink. Add different flavourings to each. When set put a portion of each coloured cream in a small paper soufflé case and decorate with a little finely chopped lemon jelly. This quantity should fill eight to ten cases.

596 DANTZIC JELLY

1½ pints (900 ml) wine jelly (see No 498)	1 sheet of silver leaf
	3 sheets of gold leaf

(Enough for five or six people)

Rinse out a fancy mould with water and pour in some good, well-flavoured, wine jelly. When on the point of setting shake in the gold and silver leaf, mixing it in well and evenly with a fork. This must be done carefully so as not to cloud the jelly.

597 ST CLOUD PUDDINGS

3 oz (75 g) cake crumbs	1 oz (25 g) almonds
3 oz (75 g) chopped cherries	½ oz gelatine
½ pint (300 ml) milk	coffee essence and sugar to
2 eggs	taste
	coffee butter icing

(Enough for five or six people)

Make a custard with the milk and eggs. When thickened pour over the cake crumbs, add sugar and coffee essence to taste and allow to cool. Dissolve the gelatine in a little water and strain into the other ingredients, pour into small dariole moulds. When set turn out, pipe over with coffee butter icing, sprinkle with pistachio nuts and browned chopped almonds.

598 ITALIAN CREAMS

½ pint (300 ml) milk	1 tablespoonful maraschino
4 yolks and 2 whites of eggs	1 oz (25 g) gelatine
1 oz (25 g) castor sugar	few pistachio nuts
1 gill (150 ml) cream	vanilla
½ gill apricot pulp	wine jelly

(Enough for five or six people)

Make a custard with the milk and yolks of eggs. Strain into a basin, dissolve the gelatine, strain into the custard with the apricot pulp, flavour with vanilla, whip the whites of eggs and cream and stir in lightly to the mixture, flavour with maraschino, decorate some small moulds with pistachio nuts cut in slices and set with a layer of wine jelly. When firm fill the moulds with the mixture. When set turn out and decorate the dish with chopped jelly.

599 PEACH MOULDS À LA REINE

1 gill (150 ml) claret or port jelly	¾ oz (20 g) gelatine
7 or 8 preserved peaches	maraschino
½ lemon	pistachio nuts
½ pint (300 ml) cream	syrup

(Enough for six or seven people)

Line some small moulds with the jelly and decorate with chopped pistachio nuts. Set them on ice. Rub the peaches through a sieve, add enough syrup to make a pint, stir in the lemon juice. Heat the purée and strain in the dissolved gelatine, whip the cream, stir in lightly, add the maraschino. Pour into the dariole moulds, turn out when set and decorate with chopped jelly.

600 CONSERVATIVE PUDDING

12 sponge fingers	¾ pint (450 ml) milk
3 oz (75 g) ratafias	¼ gill (40 ml) brandy
2 oz (50 g) glacé cherries	vanilla essence
1 oz (25 g) sweet almonds	custard or wine sauce (see
1 white and 3 yolks of eggs	No 657)

(Enough for six or seven people)

Butter a plain charlotte mould and line the bottom with paper, arrange round a ring of cherries cut in halves. Line the sides of the mould with cut and trimmed sponge fingers. Fill the centre of the tin with the ratafias, broken trimmings of biscuits, the almonds blanched and shredded. Beat the yolks and whites of eggs together, add the milk, brandy, vanilla and sugar. Strain into the mould. Let it stand a little, then cover with greased paper and steam for 1½ hours. Turn out and serve with custard or wine sauce.

601 RASPBERRY CREAM TART

1 pint (600 ml) milk	sugar to taste
2 eggs	raspberry jam
1 oz (25 g) flour	short crust (see No 511)
1 oz (25 g) butter	

(Enough for four or five people)

Mix the cream smoothly with a little of the milk, add the remainder, sweeten and boil till the flour is cooked. When nearly cold add the yolks of two eggs and 1 oz (25 g) melted butter. Line a pie dish with short crust, put a layer of raspberry jam at the bottom of it and slowly pour in the mixture and bake until the pastry is cooked. Make a meringue with the whipped whites, pile on the top and place in the oven to lightly brown.

602 NELSON PUDDING

2 oz (50 g) bread crumbs	rind of ½ lemon
2 oz (50 g) ratafias	4 eggs
1½ oz (40 g) cornflour	glass of sherry
1 oz (25 g) ground almonds	½ pint (300 ml) milk
1½ oz (40 g) suet	cherries and angelica
2 oz (50 g) castor sugar	

(Enough for five or six people)

Decorate a plain buttered mould with cherries and angelica, mix the cornflour with the milk and boil, stir in the beaten eggs, crushed ratafias, bread crumbs, almonds, suet, sugar, lemon rind and sherry. Pour into the prepared mould and steam from 1½ to 2 hours. Serve with custard sauce (see No 658).

SAUCES

603 WHITE SAUCE

2 oz (50 g) flour	1 pint (600 ml) milk
2 oz (50 g) butter	salt and pepper

Melt the butter, stir in the flour, allow it to cook without taking any colour, add the milk gradually, mixing smoothly, stir till it boils, boil for five minutes, add the seasoning.

Note.—This is the foundation white sauce. By adding various ingredients to this a great variety of sauces can be easily made.

604 BÉCHAMEL SAUCE

2 oz (50 g) butter	small bunch of herbs
2 oz (50 g) flour	½ pint (300 ml) white stock
1 small shallot	½ pint (300 ml) milk
6 peppercorns	little cream
blade of mace	salt and pepper
strip of lemon rind	

Put the milk or stock into a saucepan with the shallot and the peppercorns, mace, lemon peel and herbs tied in muslin, simmer for fifteen minutes and strain. melt the butter in a saucepan, cook the flour in it, add the flavoured stock and milk gradually and allow it to cook well, add salt and pepper and a little cream last. Strain if not smooth.

605 ANCHOVY SAUCE

½ pint (300 ml) white sauce	lemon juice
essence of anchovy	cayenne

Make the white sauce as directed, add enough essence of anchovy to colour the sauce a pale pink, add a squeeze of lemon juice and a little cayenne pepper. Served with fish.

606 CAPER SAUCE

½ pint (300 ml) white sauce	salt and pepper
(using half milk and half stock)	lemon juice

Add the capers chopped to the white sauce and season. Served with boiled mutton.

607 EGG SAUCE

½ pint (300 ml) white sauce	salt and pepper
2 hard-boiled eggs	lemon juice

Chop the hard-boiled eggs roughly, add to the sauce and season with salt and pepper and add a little lemon juice. Served with boiled salt cod and other kinds of boiled fish and boiled fowl.

608 PARSLEY SAUCE

½ pint (300 ml) white sauce	½ tablespoonful chopped
pepper and salt	parsley

Chop and blanch the parsley, add to the sauce and season. Served with boiled fish, boiled mutton, rabbit, fowl, and calf's head, etc.

609 ONION SAUCE

½ pint (300 ml) white sauce	salt and pepper
3 or 4 onions	

Boil the onions till tender, chop and add them to the white sauce and season. Served with roast shoulder of mutton and boiled rabbit.

610 SHRIMP SAUCE

½ pint (300 ml) white sauce   lemon juice
1 oz (25 g) shelled shrimps   salt and pepper
cayenne   colouring

Add the shrimps to the sauce and season with salt and pepper and lemon juice. Colour with a drop of carmine. Served with turbot and other fish.

611 CELERY SAUCE

½ pint (300 ml) white sauce   lemon juice
1 head of celery   salt and pepper
pinch of mace

Cook the celery till tender, chop and add to the white sauce, season with a squeeze of lemon juice, pinch of mace, salt and pepper. Serve with boiled turkey and fowl.

612 FENNEL SAUCE

½ pint (300 ml) white sauce   salt and pepper
½ tablespoonful fennel

Chop the fennel and add to the white sauce and season. Serve with boiled mackerel.

613 LOBSTER SAUCE

½ pint (300 ml) white sauce   lemon juice
½ a lobster or a small tin   salt and cayenne
carmine

Before making the white sauce simmer the shells of the lobster in the milk and use it. If a tin is used make the sauce in the ordinary way. Cut the lobster into small pieces and add to the sauce, season with lemon juice, salt and cayenne, colour with a drop or two of carmine. A little cream added is an improvement. Suitable to serve with boiled turbot, salmon or sole.

614 OYSTER SAUCE

½ pint (300 ml) white sauce   lemon juice
(using fish stock)   salt and cayenne
6 to 8 oysters   cream

Scald the oysters and remove the beards, add to the white sauce with their liquor, season with salt, cayenne and lemon juice and add the cream. Served with boiled fish, boiled poultry and grilled steak.

615 MUSTARD SAUCE

½ pint (300 ml) white sauce   salt and pepper
1 dessertspoonful made
mustard

Add the made mustard to the sauce and season. Served with grilled herrings.

616 MAÎTRE D'HÔTEL SAUCE

½ pint (300 ml) white sauce   juice of ½ lemon
½ tablespoonful chopped   salt and cayenne
parsley

Chop and blanch the parsley, add to the sauce with the strained lemon juice, season with salt and cayenne. Served with fish, boiled meat and with vegetables.

617 MELTED BUTTER

1½ oz (40 g) butter   ½ pint (300 ml) water
1 oz (25 g) flour   salt and pepper

Make as white sauce, season with salt and pepper. Can be served as a plain savoury sauce for fish, boiled meats and vegetables.

618 HOLLANDAISE SAUCE NO 1

4 oz (100 g) butter   sprig of thyme
4 yolks of eggs   1 tablespoonful vinegar
1 shallot   salt and pepper
1 bay leaf

Simmer the flavouring in the vinegar, melt the butter in a saucepan and mix in the yolks, stir till the sauce thickens, strain the vinegar and add to the yolks and butter, season with salt and pepper.
This sauce is best made in a double saucepan. It must not boil or the eggs will curdle.

619 HOLLANDAISE SAUCE NO 2

½ pint (300 ml) white sauce   lemon juice
2 yolks of eggs   salt and cayenne

Add the yolks to the white sauce, cook but do not allow the sauce to boil, add lemon juice, salt and cayenne. Served with boiled fish and dressed vegetables.

620 WHITE CHAUDFROID SAUCE

1 pint (600 ml) béchamel sauce   ½ oz (15 g) gelatine

Soak the gelatine and add to the sauce, stir till dissolved but do not boil the sauce. Used to coat cold poultry and game, for making entrées, etc.

621 TOMATO SAUCE

2 oz (50 g) butter   1 gill (150 ml) milk
1 oz (25 g) flour   salt and pepper
3 or 4 tomatoes

Slice the tomatoes and cook them in the butter, pass through a sieve, make a white sauce, using one gill (150 ml) of milk and one gill (150 ml) of the tomato purée, boil the sauce and season with salt and pepper. The sauce is suitable to serve with fish.

622 BROWN SAUCE (PLAIN)

2 oz (50 g) butter or dripping   1 pint (600 ml) stock
2 oz (50 g) flour   salt and pepper

Melt the butter or dripping in a saucepan, add the flour and brown it carefully, taking care it does not burn, add the stock gradually, stirring it till it boils, boil for five to ten minutes and add the salt and pepper.

Note.—This is the foundation brown sauce. A great variety of brown sauces can be made by adding various ingredients to this foundation.

623 ESPAGNOLE SAUCE

2 oz (50 g) butter	1 oz (25 g) ham
2 oz (50 g) flour	2 or three mushrooms
1 shallot	1 pint (600 ml) brown stock
1 carrot	salt and pepper
1 or 2 tomatoes	

Melt the butter, fry the chopped shallot, carrot and mushrooms until a golden brown. Add the flour and brown it. Add the stock gradually, stirring all the time. Bring to the boiling-point, add the tomatoes, let it boil gently from half to three-quarters of an hour, skimming and stirring occasionally, season and strain and it is then ready to use.

624 PIQUANTE SAUCE

½ pint (300 ml) Espagnole sauce	1 gherkin
	2 tablespoonfuls vinegar
1 dessertspoonful capers	1 teaspoonful chopped parsley
1 shallot	salt and pepper

Chop the shallot, capers, gherkin and parsley finely, put with the vinegar into a saucepan and cook for a few minutes, add to the Espagnole sauce, boil up and it is then ready to use.

Suitable to serve with cutlets, dressed vegetables or fish.

625 ORANGE SAUCE

½ pint (300 ml) brown sauce	2 tablespoonfuls sherry
juice of 1 lemon	rind of 2 oranges
juice of 1 orange	salt and pepper
pinch of castor sugar	

Put the orange and lemon juice, sherry and sugar into a stewpan with the brown sauce, simmer till reduced to two-thirds, skimming occasionally, pass through a tammy cloth, add the shredded orange peel (which should be put into cold water and brought to the boil), boil up the sauce and season. Served with wild duck.

626 ITALIENNE SAUCE

½ pint (300 ml) brown sauce (Espagnole)	2 tablespoonfuls sherry
bunch of herbs	salt and pepper

Tie the herbs in muslin, add to the brown sauce with the sherry, simmer from fifteen to twenty minutes, strain and it is ready to use. Suitable to serve with cutlets, fish or dressed vegetables.

627 REFORM SAUCE

½ pint (300 ml) brown sauce	2 teaspoonfuls red-currant jelly
juice of ½ lemon	
1 wineglass of port	salt and cayenne
bouquet garni	

Add the herbs, lemon juice, port and jelly to the brown sauce, simmer and skim till reduced to two-thirds, season and pass through a tammy cloth. Suitable to serve with cutlets and any meat.

628 TOMATO SAUCE

2 oz (50 g) butter	1 small carrot
2 oz (50 g) flour	1 oz (25 g) ham
1 lb (450 g) tomatoes	½ pint (300 ml) stock
1 onion or shallot	salt and pepper
pinch castor sugar	

Melt the butter in a saucepan, fry the chopped shallot, ham and carrot, cut up, for a few minutes, add the flour and cook, allowing it to brown slightly, stir in the stock smoothly, bring to the boil, add the tomatoes cut in slices, simmer from half to three-quarters of an hour, stirring occasionally, strain or sieve, add sugar, salt and pepper. This sauce can be served with any meat, fish or dressed vegetables.

629 APPLE SAUCE

1 lb (450 g) cooking apples	little water
1 oz (25 g) butter	sugar

Peel, core and slice the apples, put them into a saucepan with a little water and cook to a pulp, beat smooth, add the butter and sugar to taste. Can be served with roast pork, duck and goose.

630 RAVIGOTE SAUCE

½ pint (300 ml) white sauce	chervil
parsley	lemon juice
tarragon	seasoning
garden cress	

Add to the white sauce equal quantities of the finely chopped herbs with a squeeze of lemon juice. Suitable to serve with fish, cutlets, and dressed vegetables.

631 CARDINAL SAUCE

2 oz (50 g) butter	½ oz lobster coral
¾ oz (20 g) flour	½ gill (75 ml) cream
½ pint (300 ml) fish stock	nutmeg
lemon juice	salt and pepper

Pound the lobster coral with one oz (25 g) of butter in a mortar and rub through a sieve, melt the butter in a stewpan, add the flour, cook together for three or four minutes without browning, stir in the stock, and stir until it boils, then add the lemon juice, coral butter, nutmeg, salt and pepper, and lastly the cream. Do not boil after the cream is added.

632 MINT SAUCE

2 tablespoonfuls mint	1 gill (150 ml) vinegar
1 oz (25 g) castor sugar	salt
½ gill (75 ml) boiling water	

Wash the mint and chop very finely, dissolve the sugar in the boiling water, add the vinegar and mint, stir before serving. Served with roast lamb.

633 HORSERADISH SAUCE NO 1

1 root of horseradish	½ gill (75 ml) cream
½ teaspoonful mustard (mixed)	½ gill (75 ml) milk
	½ gill (75 ml) vinegar
1 teaspoonful castor sugar	salt and pepper

Grate the horseradish finely, mix with mustard, sugar, salt and pepper, add the milk, cream and vinegar, then mix all together.

634 HORSERADISH SAUCE NO 2

1 root of horseradish	1 tablespoonful vinegar
1 gill (150 ml) cream	salt and pepper
½ teaspoonful sugar	

Grate the horseradish finely, whip the cream, stir in lightly the horseradish, sugar, vinegar, salt and pepper. Served with roast beef, steak, etc.

635 CURRY SAUCE

1 oz (25 g) butter	½ pint (300 ml) stock
1 sour apple	1 dessertspoonful chutney
1 or 2 shallots	lemon juice
½ oz (15 g) flour	pinch of sugar and salt
½ oz (15 g) curry powder	

Chop the apple and shallot finely, melt the butter and fry them a pale brown, add the flour and curry powder and cook well, stirring occasionally, stir in the stock smoothly and simmer for twenty-five to thirty minutes, skimming off the fat as it rises, strain and add the chutney, lemon juice and seasonings. Served with meat and fish.

636 MAYONNAISE SAUCE

2 yolks of eggs	1 tablespoonful vinegar
1½ gill (225 ml) salad oil	1 tablespoonful tarragon
1 teaspoonful castor sugar	vinegar
salt and pepper	1 tablespoonful cream

Stir the oil into the yolks drop by drop, mixing well all the time, add the vinegar slowly, then the sugar and salt, cayenne and cream. This is served as a salad dressing and as a sauce for salmon and cold fish, etc.

637 TARTARE SAUCE

mayonnaise sauce	chopped parsley
chopped capers	chopped gherkin

Add the capers, gherkin and parsley to the mayonnaise, with a little lemon juice.

638 BREAD SAUCE

1 pint (600 ml) milk	1 onion
4 oz (100 g) bread crumbs	2 cloves
2 oz (50 g) butter	2 tablespoonfuls cream
blade of mace	salt and pepper

Boil the milk with the onion stuck with cloves and the mace, rub the bread crumbs through a wire sieve, pour the seasoned milk over them, return to the saucepan and cook well, add the butter, salt and pepper and the cream just before serving. Served with roast game and poultry.

639 GRAVY FOR ROAST JOINT

When the joint is roasted place it on a hot dish in the oven, pour off all the fat, leaving the sediment, which is the gravy from the meat, sprinkle a little salt in the pan, add some water or if preferred well-flavoured stock, a little bovril or colouring if necessary, boil up, stirring well all round the pan, dissolving all the brown particles, strain round the meat.

640 GRAVY FOR ROAST VEAL

Pour off the fat, leaving the gravy, pour into the dripping pan of a pint (600 ml) of white sauce with the gravy, boil up and pour over the joint.

641 PANADA OR THICK SAUCE

2 oz (50 g) flour	½ pint (300 ml) pint liquid
2 oz (50 g) butter	

Melt the butter, add the flour, mix smoothly and cook for a few minutes, add the liquid and cook well until the mixture leaves the sides of the saucepan. Can be used for binding ingredients in cutlets, croquettes, rissoles. etc.

642 ROUX

2 oz (50 g) butter	2 oz (50 g) flour

Melt the butter in a saucepan, stir in the flour and cook well. A *white* roux should not colour; a *brown* roux should cook till a good dark brown.

643 VEAL FORCEMEAT

4 oz (100 g) bread crumbs	½ teaspoonful mixed herbs
2 oz (50 g) suet	little grated lemond rind
1 teaspoonful chopped parsley	1 egg
	salt and pepper

Chop the suet, add bread crumbs, parsley, herbs and lemon rind, mix with beaten egg, season and then use as directed.

644 CHESTNUT FORCEMEAT

½ lb (225 g) chestnuts	stock
½ lb (225 g) bread crumbs	nutmeg
½ lb (225 g) butter	salt and pepper
1 egg	

Peel and boil the chestnuts until the skin can be removed, stew them in some stock, when cold pound them with the bread crumbs, add butter, nutmeg, salt and pepper, bind with egg and use as directed.

645 SAGE AND ONION STUFFING

6 or 8 onions	1 oz (25 g) butter or dripping
½ lb (225 g) bread crumbs	little milk
1 tablespoonful sage	salt and pepper

Peel the onions, put them in a saucepan with cold water and a little salt and boil them until half done, chop them and add to the other ingredients, moisten with a little milk, season well and use as directed.

646 DEVIL PASTE

1 teaspoonful French mustard	2 oz (50 g) butter
1 teaspoonful English-made mustard	1 teaspoonful chutney
	black pepper

Work all the ingredients into the butter with a knife and rub well into meat before grilling.

647 ASPIC JELLY

1½ pints (900 ml) stock or water	½ gill (75 ml) sherry
1 onion	2 tablespoonfuls vinegar
1 small carrot	2 tablespoonfuls tarragon vinegar
1 small turnip	10 peppercorns
stick of celery	salt
2 cloves	2½ oz (65 g) gelatine
bunch of herbs	whites and shells of 2 eggs
rind and juice of ½ lemon	

If stock is used remove the fat, put stock into a saucepan with all the ingredients except the whites and shells and the sherry, stir over the fire till the gelatine is dissolved. Whisk the whites slightly and add with the crushed shells. Whisk well until it comes to the boil, then stop whisking and let it boil gently for ten minutes. Then set aside for a few minutes with the lid partly on. Strain through a hot tea cloth, put the sherry through the cloth last.

Note.—More gelatine must be used in hot weather.

648 BOUQUET GARNI

sprig of parsley	strip of lemon rind
sprig of marjoram	blade of mace
sprig of thyme	2 cloves
1 bay leaf	6 peppercorns

Tie all together in a small piece of muslin. Used in making stock, soups, gravies, etc. If the fresh herbs are unobtainable a pinch of dried mixed herbs will answer the purpose.

649 FRYING BATTER

3 oz (75 g) flour	2 tablespoonfuls tepid water
pinch of salt	whipped white of 1 egg
1 tablespoonful oil or melted butter	

Put the flour into a basin, add the salt, make a hole in the centre, pour in the oil or melted butter, add the tepid water gradually and stir till smooth, beat for ten minutes. Let it stand from half an hour to an hour. Then add the whipped white lightly and it is ready to use.

Note.—This batter is suitable for coating fish, meat, fruit fritters, etc., for frying.

SWEET SAUCES

650 JAM SAUCE

2 tablespoonfuls jam	carmine
1 teaspoonful lemon juice	1 gill (150 ml) water

Put all the ingredients into a saucepan, boil for ten minutes, strain and colour.

651 LEMON SAUCE

1 gill (150 ml) water	½ teaspoonful cornflour
2 oz (50 g) sugar	rind and juice of 1 lemon

Boil the sugar, water and lemon rind together, add the lemon juice and thicken with the cornflour.

652 TREACLE SAUCE

2 tablespoonfuls treacle or golden syrup	1 gill (150 ml) water
	lemon juice

Put all together in a saucepan and boil for five minutes.

653 ORANGE SAUCE

½ pint (300 ml) water	2 oz (50 g) sugar
rind and juice of 2 oranges	1 teaspoonful cornflour
juice of 1 lemon	

Boil the water, sugar and orange rind together for ten minutes, strain and thicken with the cornflour.

654 MARMALADE SAUCE

2 tablespoonfuls marmalade	lemon juice
1 gill (150 ml) water	1 dessertspoonful sugar

Boil together for five minutes and strain.

655 APRICOT SAUCE

2 tablespoonfuls apricot jam	a squeeze of lemon juice
1 gill (150 ml) water	carmine

Boil together for five minutes, strain and colour with a drop or two of carmine.

656 SWEET PUDDING SAUCE

1 oz (25 g) butter	½ oz (15 g) castor sugar
½ oz (15 g) flour	any flavouring
½ pint (300 ml) milk	

Melt the butter, add the flour and cook it for a minute, stir in the milk and boil gently for five minutes. Any flavouring can then be added, such as vanilla, lemon or almond essence, brandy or sherry.

657 CUSTARD SAUCE NO 1

½ pint (300 ml) milk	½ oz (15 g) cornflour
1 egg	½ oz (15 g) sugar

Mix the cornflour with a little of the milk, put the rest on to boil. When boiling stir in the cornflour and cook for three minutes, add the sugar. When a little cool add the beaten egg, stir till it thickens—but it must not boil again, add flavouring if required.

658 CUSTARD SAUCE NO 2

3 or 4 yolks of eggs	½ oz (15 g) sugar
½ pint (300 ml) milk	flavouring

Cook in a double saucepan until the custard thickens—it must not boil, add sugar and flavouring.

659 CHOCOLATE SAUCE

2 oz (50 g) chocolate	sugar
½ pint (300 ml) water	vanilla
½ oz (15 g) crème de riz	brandy

Melt the chocolate in the water, thicken with the crème de riz, add sugar, vanilla and brandy to taste.

660 GERMAN SAUCE

2 yolks of eggs	1 oz (25 g) sugar
1 gill (150 ml) sherry	

Put the ingredients into a double saucepan, whisk until the sauce becomes thick and frothy. The sauce must not boil else it will curdle.

661 GUARDS' SAUCE

2 oz (50 g) good fresh butter	brandy
4 oz (100 g) icing sugar	

Cream the butter and sugar together until quite smooth, beat in slowly the brandy to flavour—about a tablespoonful or a little more.

662 PINEAPPLE SAUCE

1 gill (150 ml) water	1 oz (25 g) sugar
1 gill (150 ml) pineapple syrup	few pieces pineapple

Boil all together for five minutes, serve with pieces of pineapple in the sauce.

EXTRA RECIPES

663 SCALLOPED TOMATOES

5 or 6 tomatoes	butter
bread crumbs	salt and pepper

Cut the tomatoes in slices, place in a well-buttered pie dish with some bread crumbs sprinkled between, season well, put a layer of bread crumbs on top and some small pieces of butter and bake about twenty minutes till a nice brown.

664 EGG KROMESKIES

2 hard-boiled eggs	salt and pepper
½ gill (75 ml) white sauce	frying batter
thin slices bacon	

Chop the hard-boiled eggs finely, moisten with the white sauce and season well, roll some of the mixture in thin slices of bacon, dip into frying batter and fry a golden brown in hot fat, drain well, dish on a fancy paper, garnish with fried parsley.

665 ANCHOVY TOASTS

8 anchovies	6 or 7 croûtons of bread
2 tablespoonfuls tomato sauce	

Skin, fillet and pass the anchovies through a sieve, mix with tomato sauce, spread thickly on rounds of toast or croûtons of fried bread and serve very hot.

666 ASPARAGUS SOUP

1 bundle of asparagus or sprue	1 oz (25 g) flour
1 quart (1.1 litres) white stock	1 gill (150 ml) cream
1 pint (600 ml) milk	1 gill (150 ml) green peas
1 oz (25 g) butter	pinch of sugar
	salt and pepper

Cut off the asparagus tips, clean and cut the rest into short pieces, boil them in water for fifteen minutes, melt the butter in a stewpan, mix the flour in smoothly, add the stock and milk, stir until it boils, remove the scum, put in the pieces of asparagus and sugar, boil till the former is tender, then pass the soup through a sieve, return it to the pan, season and add the cream, warm it up, boil the peas and asparagus tips separately until tender, drain and put them in the soup tureen and pour the hot soup over, serve with small croûtons of fried bread.

667 PURÉE OF SPINACH

2 or 3 lb (900 g – 1.4 kg) spinach	1 oz (25 g) butter
	1½ oz (40 g) flour
1 pint (600 ml) white stock	salt and pepper
1 pint (600 ml) milk	

Wash and vein the spinach, cook till tender with just sufficient water to keep it from burning, drain it well and rub through a hair sieve, melt the butter in a stewpan, mix in the flour smoothly, stir in the stock and the spinach and allow it to boil, add the milk and seasoning and simmer for a few minutes and serve with small croûtons of fried bread.

668 PEA PURÉE

1 pint (600 ml) green peas	2 tablespoonfuls cream
1 pint (600 ml) stock	salt and pepper

Boil the peas with a lump of sugar, when tender rub through a sieve, return to the pan, add the seasoning and reheat; just before serving add the cream.

669 SPINACH OMELET

some cooked spinach	little cream
3 eggs	salt and pepper
1 oz (25 g) butter	

Warm the spinach, season and add a little cream, beat the eggs thoroughly, add the seasoning, heat the butter in an omelet pan, pour in the eggs, stir lightly, and then allow it to set. When cooked sufficiently place the omelet pan in a quick oven or under the gas to set the top, shake to the side of the pan, lay on the spinach, fold over and serve immediately.

670 SAVOURY BISCUITS

6 or 8 water biscuits	3 oz (75 g) Parmesan cheese
1 oz (25 g) butter	salt and cayenne
mustard	

Mix the grated cheese with the butter, made mustard, salt and cayenne, spread on one side of the biscuit, place on a baking-tin in a hot oven for five minutes, sprinkle well with grated cheese and serve at once.

671 SWISS APPLE PUDDING

some apples	lemon rind
water	bread crumbs
sugar	butter

Peel and core the apples, stew them with water, sugar, and lemon rind till tender. Remove the lemon rind, place in a buttered pie dish with some bread crumbs, put a layer of bread crumbs on the top and some small pieces of butter, sprinkle over some castor sugar and bake in a quick oven till nicely browned.

672 JUNKET

1 pint (600 ml) milk	sugar
1 teaspoonful rennet	nutmeg
brandy	cream

Warm the milk to blood heat, add the sugar and brandy, pour into a deep glass dish, stir in the rennet and set aside to set, grate over some nutmeg and pour over the cream and serve.

INDEX

The number in italics, appearing just after each entry, refers to the recipe number.

POULTRY AND GAME

VEGETABLES AND SALADS

SAVOURY AND BREAKFAST DISHES

The number in italics, appearing just after each entry, refers to the recipe number.

SWEET DISHES

The number in italics, appearing just after each entry, refers to the recipe number.

SAUCES

SWEET SAUCES

EXTRA RECIPES

The number in italics, appearing just after each entry, refers to the recipe number.